CW01668775

THE PHILOSOPHY OF CHARL

Charles W. Mills (1951–2021) was considered by many to be the most well-known philosopher specializing in political philosophy and critical philosophy of race. This is the first collection of essays to critically examine the key themes of Mills's philosophy across his major works.

The chapters in this volume engage with major themes such as the racial contract, non-ideal theory, metaphysics of race, epistemology of ignorance, and corrective justice. They also explore Mills's engagement with philosophical figures including Frederick Douglass, W. E. B. Du Bois, Maria Lugones, Immanuel Kant, Karl Marx, and John Rawls. Furthermore, the contributors seek to uncover unexplored terrain which may be illuminated by applying many of Mills's key insights.

The Philosophy of Charles W. Mills will be of interest to scholars and advanced students working in political philosophy, philosophy of race, Africana philosophy, and Black political thought.

Mark William Westmoreland, PhD, teaches philosophy at Ocean County College. He is the co-editor (with Andrea J. Pitts) of *Beyond Bergson: Examining Race and Colonialism through the Writings of Henri Bergson* (SUNY) and author of "Bergson, Colonialism, and Race" in *Interpreting Bergson* (Cambridge) and other essays on race and pedagogy.

"This volume offers an original collection of essays that showcase new, exciting, and much-needed philosophical work, carrying on the legacy of the remarkable late Africana philosopher Charles Mills. It invokes the promise of the future of political philosophy at the intersection of philosophy of race and Africana philosophy."

Elvira Basevich, *University of California, Davis, USA*

THE PHILOSOPHY OF CHARLES W. MILLS

Race and the Relations of Power

Edited by Mark William Westmoreland
With a Foreword by George Yancy

Routledge
Taylor & Francis Group
NEW YORK AND LONDON

Cover image via Getty: Reshavskyi

First published 2025
by Routledge
605 Third Avenue, New York, NY 10158

and by Routledge
4 Park Square, Milton Park, Abingdon, Oxon, OX14 4RN

Routledge is an imprint of the Taylor & Francis Group, an informa business

ISBN: 978-1-032-39494-7 (hbk)
ISBN: 978-1-032-39495-4 (pbk)
ISBN: 978-1-003-34998-3 (ebk)

DOI: 10.4324/9781003349983

Typeset in Sabon
by KnowledgeWorks Global Ltd.

CONTENTS

FOREWORD

George Yancy

It is with honor that I write the foreword to this long overdue book on the deeply engaging and extraordinary philosophical corpus of philosopher Charles W. Mills. While there have been several journal issues dedicated to examining Mills's work in terms of its complexity, meta-philosophical importance, critical interventions and expansions within Anglo-American political philosophy, its profound ethical, social, and epistemological implications, and its unique contribution to Africana philosophical thought, this is the first book. Hence, I salute philosopher Mark Westmoreland for his sustained passion and determination to bring this text into existence and for his deep admiration for Mills's philosophical work and the latter's unflagging mentorship. In this regard, Mills, in my experience, was a rare scholar-mentor. Not only did Mills profoundly and undeniably impact the field of philosophy through his clarity and rigor of argumentation, but he also cared for students and colleagues. In a field like philosophy, and academia more generally, where philosophers often try to "outperform" other philosophers for the sake of appearing "superior," Mills demonstrated kindness, collegial generosity, and stellar mentorship.

Years ago, philosopher Adrian M. S. Piper warned me of just how disillusioning the field of philosophy can be. Piper spoke of power plays, backstabbing, and how the field is saturated with relationships predicated on power, status, and one-upmanship. I would add forms of egomania, pomposity, and childish jealousies. All of these can be witnessed across race and gender lines within the field of philosophy. Mills, however, as many will attest, made himself available and cultivated and nurtured so many scholars trying to find their way within the field. I recall very specifically the concern that Mills demonstrated as I continued to publish high-profile public articles that generated white racist backlash for me. Mills wrote to me with deep concern, taking seriously the racial epithets and death threats that I received. He was also aware that my name had been placed on the Professor Watchlist, which is designed to expose professors who allegedly discriminate against conservative students and who propound "leftist" propaganda in the classroom. I have never discriminated against conservative students and have no desire to "propagate" or "spread" (the etymological root meaning of the word propaganda) "leftists" views.

Mills was keenly aware of political processes and efforts designed to silence critique. It's important to note that Mills's concern, his form of mentorship, was given freely. It was only after his death that I learned from Linda Alcoff that Mills had been subjected to FBI surveillance in the US. This revelation reinforced my philosophical respect for Mills but also deepened my appreciation for his *lived* understanding of the very real dangers of present-day forms of McCarthyism. In this vein, I am certain that Mills would be appalled by the current military policing and brutal handling of students who have continued to practice civil disobedience on their college campuses. When it came to speaking with *parrhesia* outside of the classroom, Mills was there to help me think carefully about the political gravitas and consequences involved in writing high-profile public articles. His concern was invaluable; it was a manifestation of mentorship that communicated: you are not alone.

I regret the fact that it took me so long to meet Mills; it was around 1998. This was the year that my first book, *African-American Philosophers, 17 Conversations*, was published. The book was the first of its kind to engage with Black philosophers about their points of entry into the field of philosophy and how the field's whiteness impacted them personally and metaphilosophically. Had I known Mills, I am certain that the book would have been called "18 Conversations." In fact, Mills's authored book, *Blackness Visible: Essays on Philosophy and Race*, was published the same year, 1998. It was only around this time that I vaguely recall the existence of his philosophical bestseller, *The Racial Contract* (1997). Having left Yale in 1990 with my MA in philosophy, I had moved outside of philosophical communities where I would have been informed about the latest work in the field, especially work produced by Black philosophers. So, my regret is twofold.

I regret only coming to meet Mills *the person* as late as 1998. I also regret the fact that I was not aware of the meta-philosophical overlap in our work sooner. Had I known, I would have drawn from Mills's work and thereby significantly improved my own. For example, in one of my favorite essays by Mills, "Non-Cartesian *Sums*: Philosophy and the African-American Experience," which served as the first chapter of *Blackness Visible*, though first published in 1994, he begins the essay explaining how he, teaching an introductory course in African-American philosophy, was forced to think more systematically about race and philosophy. I too was forced to think at the intersections of race and philosophy while preparing for *African-American Philosophers, 17 Conversations*. Although I did not have the language then, my aim was to map, through critical and exploratory dialogue, what it meant to be Black under non-ideal conditions and yet to do philosophy, to be drawn to philosophy, where ideal theory was praised. These days, I would call what I was doing the "density project," which I see as a process of exploring the deep existential phenomenological and messy reality of race and how it is lived, how it constitutes the fundamental horizon within which embodied Black people exist. What I discovered in the dialogues for my book was a unique species of (non-Marxist) alienation that Black philosophers felt as their individual and collective experiences were incongruous with or belied many of the issues and themes studied within traditional mainstream philosophy, a site of the proverbial "Dead White Guys." I had put my finger on a mode of racial *unheimlichkeit*, a distinct sense of not being philosophically *at home*. What emerged from those deeply engaging dialogues was what Mills calls "different kinds of silences and invisibility" (1998, 3). I was overwhelmingly aware of the monochromatic whiteness of the field of philosophy (having studied philosophy at the University of Pittsburgh and then

Yale), but not explicitly aware of what Mills called "the *conceptual* or *theoretical* whiteness of the discipline," (2) though I had already begun to take seriously the importance of *moving the center* of philosophical conversation away from whiteness and emphasizing what I then termed the "embodied cogito" vis-à-vis Cartesian selves/substances that were deemed ahistorical. What I had done, in effect, is described what Mills calls "Non-Cartesian *Sums*" and "Cartesian *Sums*," respectively. For me, the former were racialized as Black selves through a racial matrix that presupposed a dynamically relational mode of existence. Black people were existentially haunted by a racist social ontology that violently *othered* them. For Mills, non-Cartesian *sums* (that is, Black people who are deemed "sub-persons") were "relational, not monadic; dialogic, not monologic" (9). My reference to Cartesian selves as ahistorical implied deep metaphysical assumptions, reflecting Mills's understanding of (white) Cartesian *sums* (selves) that are metaphysically "the consequent of a proof," not the (Black) *sums* who fight insistently against forms of anti-Black racism, those *sums* who affirm their dignity in a world that refuses to recognize their humanity/personhood. Like Mills, the world of Ralph Ellison's invisible man spoke to me about what it means to be Black in a world of anti-Blackness. The Cartesian conceptual world, where one doubts the existence of others and by extension the existence of one's oppressor, is a world of fantasy. The comfort of doubting the existence of others is, as Mills says, "a perk of social privilege" (8).

Given the above, it is clear why I found especially important Mills's philosophical treatment of whiteness and his sustained effort to tarry within the non-ideal social ontological space of Black people. Mills's sustained philosophical analysis and critique of the whiteness of Anglo-American political philosophy is monumental, especially within the context of radically rethinking the mythology that underwrites traditional social contract theory. As Mills argues, "In the social contract, the crucial human metamorphosis is from 'natural' man to 'civil/political' man, from the resident of the state of nature to the citizen of the created society" (1997, 12). Demythologizing the whitewashed conceptualization of traditional social contract theory, Mills brings to our attention that "the crucial metamorphosis is the preliminary conceptual partitioning and corresponding transformation of human populations into 'white' and 'non-white' men" (12–13). Through the articulation of the Racial Contract, which, when taken seriously, ought to function as a conceptual *Gestalt* switch for all philosophers working in Anglo-American political philosophy, Mills fundamentally unsettles white political philosophy (despite its continued evasion), and provocatively reveals that, generally speaking, "a lot of philosophy is just white guys jerking off" (1998, 4). This humorous and yet powerful image is meant to convey the serious philosophical insularity and abstraction (that is, in terms of *abstracting away from* the real world) of European or Anglo-American philosophers. What is recycled as "philosophically relevant" *simpliciter* turns out to be relevant to white people only, and then only relevant to a certain gender. On this score, "rights," "personhood," "equality," and "dignity" were never ideals meant to apply to those who are racially Black. As Mills writes, "A lot of [European and Anglo-American] moral philosophy will then seem to be based on pretense, the claim that these were principles that people strove to uphold, when in fact the real principles were the racially exclusivist ones" (4). In this case, European and Anglo-American liberalism was always already racist. Racism was not an external virus, as it were, that attacked the otherwise political health of liberalism. Rather, liberalism was malignant *ab initio*, involving, as Mills writes, "a universe of white right, white

Recht, a white moral and legal equality that is reciprocally linked to a non-white inequality" (134). Liberalism embodies, for Mills, a *Herrenvolk* ethics.

As one of only a handful of Black philosophers who have published prolifically on whiteness, I admire Mills's clarity and courage *to name* the whiteness of philosophy. After all, whiteness, as the transcendental norm, functions as the background in terms of which the process of *specific* racialized naming is installed. In short, to be Black is to be named and marked vis-à-vis the unnamed and unmarked reality of whiteness. In short, whiteness is the condition that generates "racial differences" while remaining the same. Mills understands what is at stake in the first sentence of *The Racial Contract*, where he writes, "White supremacy is the unnamed political system that has made the modern world what it is today" (1997, 1). This is Mills's decisive argument, and it is intended to unmoor white political philosophy and its white practitioners from "illusory idealizing abstraction, the never-never land of pure theory" (130). Defying unequivocally Lyotardean incredulity toward metanarratives, Mills argues that the Racial Contract "is explicitly predicated on the *truth* of a particular metanarrative, the historical account of the European conquest of the world, which has made the world what it is today" (129). It's important to note Mills's emphasis on the hegemony of white supremacy and its impact on making the *modern world* and making the world what it is *today*. There is no evasive tactic or milquetoast discourse in Mills's work that construes white supremacy as something in the past or as only marginal vis-à-vis our everyday lives. Understanding the relationship of racialization to modernity, Mills is keenly aware of how the metaphor of light is linked to the axiology and ontology of Euro-identity. As Mills writes, "Whiteness becomes the identity of both enlightenment and of the human bearers of enlightenment" (2021, 17). He continues, "Whiteness is light; whiteness is all-encompassing; whiteness is the universal; whiteness is Euro-illumination" (17).

To fully appreciate the radical implications of the Racial Contract and its description "of the world as it actually is" (1997, 129), just think about the impending dystopic authoritarian proclivities of the far right and its attempt to whitewash history, distort the truth, fabricate reality, ban books, and control the political imaginations of the demos. Mills's contribution is not just a significant correction confined to the esoteric field of philosophy; it embodies a dangerous truth about our shared world, where truth feels as if it has been forced into exile. To speak the truth under such conditions, to describe the world as it is, reminds me of the courage of James Baldwin, where he writes a letter to his nephew about the *sine qua non* of forcing "our [white] brothers to see themselves as they are, to cease fleeing from reality and begin to change it" (1995, 9). For Baldwin, there is no white "innocence." Indeed, as he writes, "It is the innocence which constitutes the crime" (5). I would argue that central to Mills's work is the uncovering of the feigned racist "innocence" of European and Anglo-American political philosophy, along with its normative assumptions. Mills, like Baldwin, is aware that white people deploy all sorts of maneuvers to avoid the truth about themselves and the racist world that they have created, to maintain their innocence. Indeed, for Mills, the Racial Contract "*produces the ironic outcome that whites will in general be unable to understand the world they themselves have made*" (1997, 18). Through an epistemology of ignorance, a term coined by Mills, white ignorance resists; it fights back. It is "an ignorance [...] not to be intimidated, an ignorance that is active, dynamic, that refuses to go quietly—not at all confined to the illiterate and uneducated but propagated at the highest levels of the land, indeed presenting itself unblushingly as knowledge" (2017, 49). In such a world, we may all find ourselves policed and threatened by the Orwellian nightmarish "Ministry of Love," which operated for Big Brother in *1984*, where each of us, like the protagonist Winston Smith, will unconsciously trace: 2+2=5. In such a world, *The Racial Contract* will be one of those *seditious* books consumed by flames created and sustained by the tyranny of whiteness.

It is precisely such a world that Mills politically and philosophically abhors. Mills's project is informed by a counter-epistemic framing of a fictional white world, a world in which racially Black sub-persons or "niggers" are believed to be teleologically "inferior." Mills tarries with anti-Black historicity and exposes the lie of white philosophical ideals that were believed universal. Hence, Mills begins with "the reality of a partitioned social ontology as the starting point rather than the ideal abstraction of universal equality, qualified with an embarrassed marginal asterisk or an endnote to say that there were some exceptions" (1998, 7). To think critically and correctly about European and Anglo-American philosophy, its actual aims, and the racist morphology of its philosophical claims, one *must* begin within the context of a partitioned social ontology, a partition that lays bare the millions of Black bodies reduced to sub-humanity through white anti-Black murderous barbarity. What I find absolutely fascinating is that the earlier Mills who was faced with creating connections between philosophy and race when teaching his first course in African-American philosophy, became the Mills who later precisely theorized Black philosophy as a better positioned framework for "illuminating modernity more thoroughly and relentlessly, more free from illusions, than its (typically) white protagonist" (2021, 25). It is here that Mills links the insights of W. E. B. Du Bois's understanding of "second sight" and standpoint theory, which he does not limit to the United States but applies to the Black diaspora. Mills is aware that the epistemic implications of both views in no way entail absolute veridicality vis-à-vis the social structure of reality. He is, however, aware of the historically terrorized existence of Black people and what that means in terms of installing a cognitive advantage that they possess about their oppression and their oppressors. Mills writes, "Blackness really indicates not a particular band of wavelengths but a particular societal position, and not just any subordinated non-white position but a peculiar location within the nexus of multiple oppressions created by white supremacy" (25). Troubling the semiotics of whiteness, Mills conceptualizes and articulates Blackness as a site of illumination. After all, as Mills argues, "For no other non-white group has race been so enduringly constitutive of their identity, so fundamental for racial capitalism, and so lastingly central to white racial consciousness and global racial consciousness in general" (35).

Black philosophy has a special role to play in terms of exposing the hypocrisy and structure of whiteness both in philosophy and within the world that we inhabit today. White social and political philosophy has, (consciously and unconsciously), failed to interrogate, in a sustained and robust fashion, questions of racial justice. Mills indicts both white philosophers from the right and the left for this failure and hypocrisy. For Mills, white social and political philosophy "whitewash, they white-out, crucial aspects of social reality, above all the fact of white racial domination and its holistic impact over the past few hundred years" (36). Yet, Mills's project is by no means limited to describing the non-ideal existence of Black life or the non-ideal conditions of people of color under white supremacy. He offers an alternative to racial liberalism/racial capitalism in the form of what he calls Black radical liberalism, which "seeks to transform liberalism to make it responsive to the realities of the Black diasporic experience in modernity and the correspondingly necessary reordering of liberal normative priorities" (2017, 203).

The powerful book that you have before you will engage many of the particulars of the political merits or faults of such an ambitious political reconfiguration of the US and other places where racial liberalism continues to exist and continues to function according to the logics of "an invented delusional world" (1997, 18). I am neither as visionary nor as socially and politically astute as Mills. My hope, though, which Mills shares, is that a world of social justice for all people will prevail. However, my sense of hope continues to be haunted by the structural systemic embeddedness of whiteness and its psychic opacity, a form of opacity that is virtually impervious to full cognitive transparency, that waits to erupt (to ambush) in a form that might cost Black life. Mills knew what was at stake. At the end of *The Racial Contract*, he understood that there would be those who would pretend not to see or claim not to recognize the work that he had accomplished in that text. He saw that structured denial as resulting from those who continue to be complicit with an "epistemology of ignorance required by the original Racial Contract" (133). In this sense, white people remain ignorant of themselves and the world that they have helped to make. For me, it is the ontological *investment* in *this world* of whiteness by white people that gives me great pause as I think about the possibility of the manifestation of anything like the insights of a Black radical liberalism that Mills powerfully proposes. When it comes to whiteness, the language of rehabilitation, reconstruction, compensatory justice, corrective justice, and restorative repair fail to capture the requisite *eradication* of the insidious structure of whiteness and the *metaphysical comfort* that it provides for embodied white people.[1] In this world, the structure of whiteness ontologically needs Blackness to negate, even as it ontologically needs Blackness to consume in caricatured and monstrous form. Perhaps what I am naming here has to do with the recursive production and consumption of Blackness that supports the structural homeostasis of whiteness. Hence, Blackness/anti-Blackness is whiteness' ontological lifeline. So, for whiteness to permanently un-suture, to break the material institutional and discursive sutures that hold it together, and to undergo psychic *kenosis*, it must imperil its ties (its sutured safety) to Blackness/anti-Blackness. Mills also wondered if what is required of white people (from material costs to psychic costs) "might just be too great for whites to bear" (2021, 35). While I realize that history is not ontologically foreclosed, history does not promise a damn thing when it comes to the death of whiteness (not of white people). Whiteness consumes what we critically and defiantly throw at it. That is what it does, that is its structural elasticity. Whiteness has room for us all, as long as it remains hegemonically and normatively in place—if only surreptitiously. Hence, if I am correct about whiteness, its history, its binary structure, and its various psychic needs, I am unhopeful that whiteness will yield; it will only self-destruct and, in its wake, we will all perish.

Note

1 For a powerful discussion of whiteness as metaphysical comfort and the need for white people to fall apart, see my conversation with philosopher Alison Bailey in Yancy 2017, 61–64.

Bibliography

Baldwin, James. 1995. *The Fire Next Time*. New York: Modern Library.

Mills, Charles W. 1997. *The Racial Contract*. Ithaca: Cornell University Press.

Mills, Charles W. 1998. *Blackness Visible: Essays on Philosophy and Race*. Ithaca: Cornell University Press.

Mills, Charles W. 2017. *Black Rights/White Wrongs: The Critique of Racial Liberalism*. New York: Oxford University Press.

Mills, Charles W. 2021. "The Illumination of Blackness." In *Antiblackness*. Edited by Moon-Kie Jung and João H. Costa Vargas. Durham: Duke University Press.

Yancy, George. 2017. *On Race: 34 Conversations in a Time of Crisis*. Edited by George Yancy. New York: Oxford University Press.

INTRODUCTION

Mark William Westmoreland

Charles W. Mills (1951–2021) was one of the most influential philosophers in the Anglophone world throughout the last quarter century. His early work, beginning with a 1985 essay on ideology, focused primarily on Marxism. But by the mid-1990s, Mills was establishing a trajectory that would place him among the "who's who" in critical philosophy of race. His seminal work, *The Racial Contract* (1997), dramatically altered the way philosophers and political theorists understood the social contract tradition and the work of John Rawls. This book has become something of a best-seller among academic titles, leading to a 25th anniversary edition with a foreword by Tommie Shelby, a leading expert in Black political thought and Africana philosophy. In *The Racial Contract*, Mills shifted the way we out to think about the contract from being one of egalitarianism to one of racial exclusion. After the book's initial release, Mills published essays at a tremendous pace and regularly gave his entertaining and illuminating talks at conferences—talks often accompanied by a handout with creative diagrams, something that became famous in its own right.

Equally important, his philosophical work did not occur only in his writing. Dozens and dozens of philosophers consider him a mentor. Some of those were his colleagues. Others, like me, were graduate students when we met him. He transformed our generation's perspective on the role of philosophy within a racial polity. Despite his popularity—one that did not emerge until later, as his earlier work was dismissed by the gatekeepers of the time—Mills routinely took the time to talk with us at conferences, to exchange emails, and even to chat over the phone. In short, he revolutionized a generation with his keen insights and his honorable generosity. It is fair to say that, by the 2020s, anyone who begins a career in philosophy knows of Mills; that is, knows his work in political philosophy and philosophy of race even if those are not a person's primary areas of interest. Very few people have touched the intellectual and personal lives of their fellow scholars in the way that Mills did.

As of my writing this introduction (August 2023), no one has written a monograph nor has there been an edited collection primarily focused on Mills. As soon as I began studying Mills in 2005, I thought, "where is the secondary literature on this trailblazing thinker?

DOI: 10.4324/9781003349983-1

This guy is showing us what philosophy can and ought to do." When I personally met Mills in 2012, I mentioned the lack of a book about his philosophical corpus, to which he jokingly responded, "Well, there have been two journal collections about my work, and that's two more than I expected. I don't think there will be another." He was referring to an issue in *Small Axe* (1998) and a symposium entry in the *Journal of Political Ideologies* (2008). Time proved Mills wrong. Three more journals followed suit: *Politics, Groups, and Identities* (2015), *Critical Philosophy of Race* (2017), and *Ethnic and Racial Studies* (2018). The downside of each of these is twofold. First, aside from *Critical Philosophy of Race*, they have focused specifically on only one of Mills's texts, leaving aside most of Mills's other works. Second, the themes and topics are limited in scope and fail to highlight the breadth of Mills' philosophical contributions. Since his death, more have been published and are still being counted. Yet, there remains no book-length treatment of his work. The current volume seeks to remedy this absence.

To be honest, I thought of a project like this in 2008, when I first interacted with George Yancy—another towering figure in critical philosophy of race—who is well-known for his remarkable work as an editor. I was drawn to the appeal of editing, of collaborating with scholars to produce something greater than any one individual could have done. Yancy has graciously agreed to write our foreword, a task I know he counts as an honor—not because of me but because of Mills, whose work exemplifies the power of Black philosophy. In 2015, I shared an idea with Mills for an edited volume about his work that I would edit and that would include a lengthy response essay from him. We piddled with the idea for a few months and then hit pause. He had left Northwestern for a position at CUNY, and I was in the throes of writing my dissertation on racial profiling. The time simply was not right. In 2019, we were both at a conference and he mentioned the idea, adding, "If you really think there's a market for it, then let's do it." I remember that comment well, given that Mills often seemed so unassuming about his popularity among younger scholars. I mentioned this to Yancy at a conference later that year, and he encouraged me to do it and that there would be an audience. In the winter of 2020, the work began. Then, Covid happened—disrupting people's personal and professional lives. Mills continued his support of the volume and reaffirmed his commitment to write a response chapter. This was how my proposal was first crafted: a collection of critical engagements with his work, both highlighting strengths and weaknesses and identifying possible implications and extensions, followed by his reply. Then the tragedy occurred. In the spring of 2021, Mill's health was declining. Before the end of September, he would leave us forever. His death made me more determined to see the project through to its end. But this would require some changes; for example, there would no longer be a "response to critics" essay by Mills.

This volume is not a *festschrift* in the sense that it is meant simply to praise or honor the deceased. The contributors here seek to explain the main themes in Mills's work, highlight the reception of that work, and put forward their own critical yet charitable interpretation that identifies both the strengths and weaknesses, the benefits and shortcomings, of it. The authors represent a diverse group of scholars in terms of career stage, philosophical tradition and methodology, and social identity.

So much of an edited volume is outside of one's control. Contributors agree and then decline. Others promptly submit chapters. Occasionally, one receives a chapter or two that, while outstanding in their own right, simply do not fit with the other chapters. The themes and arguments within chapters shift. Life happens. Considering the vicissitudes of being an editor, I am grateful to all of the current authors, whether they be ones who have been on board since the beginning or ones who stepped up in the final months.

There are several ways of approaching the chapters in this volume. Imagine something like a large museum with corridors. The curator might have a purposeful order for engaging with the artifacts, but the visitors may wander according to their unique interests. Likewise, while I have arranged the chapters by their major themes, one could take an alternative path and read the chapters in any order.

In Chapter One, "Diagnosing White Aphasia: Mills and Domination Contract," Mark William Westmoreland touches on major themes that appear throughout this volume and introduces readers to Mills's description of the social contract as truly being a domination contract and, to be more precise, a racial contract. Having a domination contract at the heart of liberalism leads to a failure in securing justice for everyone. Instead, it protects whiteness and ensures the exclusion of Black life. Westmoreland argues that, given the racialization of liberalism, a racial polity is buttressed by a domination contract that excludes Black folks from full participation. Non-ideal theory, as described by Westmoreland, suggests that we diagnose the actual polity in which we live in order to bypass the obfuscation set by ideal theory and retrieve an understanding of the polity's exclusionary nature.

Chapters Two and Three continue the theme of contract. In "Curdled Contracts: Reading Mills through a Lugonesian Spirit," Taylor Rogers puts Mills's work in conversation with that of María Lugones. With the help of decolonial feminism, Rogers creatively explores what might be called "curdled contracts" and offers a critique of Mills's failure to adequately address the status of embodiment in relation to contractual processes. Although offering new insights about the way Mills's commitment to social contract theory can be read as successfully resistant, Rogers also takes a more critical orientation by arguing that Mills's modified contract theory maintains a problematic commitment to rational abstraction as a normative methodology for generating principles of (corrective) justice.

Corey Reed, in "Corresponding Contracts: The Intersectional Mills," explains that Mills's work often illustrates that the racial contract is one of many contracts integrated into our social landscape through oppressive and dominating hierarchies, and he welcomes the idea of "intersecting contracts." Reed's focus is not just on Mills's relationship with intersectionality, but on how he thinks race corresponds with other forms of oppression. Reed argues that his analysis of implicit and explicit contracts, the contractor/noncontractor and signatory/beneficiary dichotomies, have important contributions to intersectional literature. However, Reed also adds that there may be limitations to Mills's framework because he works within both liberalism and contract theory. Like Rogers, Reed identifies the limitations of Mills's theory of the social contract, particularly when discussing how race and gender intersect.

In Chapters Four and Five, the authors take up concerns about the intersection of race and class. Rafael Vizcaíno, in "Toward the Bourgeois Revolution: Situating Mills's Liberal Turn," argues that Mills's turn away from Marxism and toward liberalism is not so much an abandonment as critics would suggest. Rather, according to Vizcaíno, understanding Mills's early and middle periods (particularly Mills's ration to Marx) is crucial for interpreting Mill's suggestion that we ought to "occupy liberalism." Mills's later liberal turn, when read in relation to his earlier work on Marxism, can be seen as an attempt to advance a revised theory of radical social transformation not only for the twenty-first century but for the entire third millennium.

In "Mills on Class in Relation to Race," Lawrence Blum argues that Mills's claim of race being a relatively autonomous system of domination is inaccurate and that Mills's project of theorizing white supremacy will not be successful if that theorizing does not seriously attend to the significance of class. Blum argues that Mills fails to relate race to class in ways that highlight how entrenched or pervasive class is within a system of domination. Put differently, Blum argues that white supremacy cannot be understood without serious consideration of class concepts and processes. The two agree that race cannot be fully grasped using only class terms, and that class reductionism ought to be avoided. But the two part ways with regard to understanding the extent to which race can be viewed as having relative autonomy separate from concerns about economic exploitation.

The limitations of liberalism are taken up by Clevis Headley in the sixth chapter, "Mills, Contracts, and the Limits of Liberalism." Headley claims that Mills's reliance on the tools of liberalism, particularly those of John Rawls, works against his attempt to offer a non-ideal theory of racial justice that will allow for racial subordination to adequately be addressed. While Mills sought to reclaim liberalism from its racialization, and despite his project to read social contract theory as indeed an actual historical contract among Europeans to exclude non-Europeans from the original terms of the contract that established modern society, Headley contends that many serious philosophical deficiencies afflict Mills's thesis. Contra Mills, Headley probes whether it is indeed possible to rearrange the basic resources of liberalism in order to make it palatable with the realities of race and racial subordination.

In Chapter Seven, "A Page of History: Mills's Black Radical Kantianism and American Legal (Racial) Realism," Timothy Golden synthesizes Mills's Black Radical Kantianism (BRK) with key themes in Critical Race Theory in order to show how the ideal starting point of mainstream liberalism ignores racial oppression, and this will be reflected in legal matters. Golden discusses the salient features of Mills's BRK, particularly the differences between BRK and ideal theory: the differences between American legal realism and legal formalism. There is arguably a continuity between ideal theory, legal formalism, and the *Rechtsstaat* on one hand, and non-ideal theory, American legal realism, and the *Rassenstaat* on the other hand. To show this continuity, Golden discusses Justice Ketanji Brown Jackson's dissenting opinion in *Students for Fair Admissions, Inc. v. President and Fellows of Harvard College* as an example of what BRK looks like in American jurisprudence as an instance of American legal realism. Golden argues that theorizing injustice prior to the application of principles, and later legal judgments, is a necessary component to the pursuit of a just polity.

In the final chapter, "Building (Conceptual) Bridges: Mills's Non-Ideal Theory and Disciplinary Whitopias," Emmalon Davis takes up meta-philosophical concerns and the unique position Black philosophy has in addressing the injustices among us and returns us to the theme of ideal versus non-ideal theory and employs Mills's "racial contract" as a conceptual bridge, that is, as a methodological tool that challenges the "whitopia" of mainstream political philosophy. Taking the discipline of philosophy as the primary subject of analysis, Davis advances an alternative conception of *The Racial Contract* by arguing that in constructing a bridge, Mills offers a critical cartography of the discipline itself. These observations are contextualized in light of Mills's meta-philosophical views as they shifted over time, and Davis concludes with an invitation to explore new possibilities for non-ideal theory as a methodology of continued necessity.

I want to briefly note how sources are utilized. Mills often repurposed his journal articles as book chapters. Sometimes, he made substantial revisions. Rather than using only the book versions, I have kept the entries separate. There are cases when keeping the chronology of his work in mind is important; so one might find, for example, a reference to the original version of "European Specters" (1999) or one might encounter it as a chapter in *From Class to Race* (2003). In other words, I have intentionally chosen not to treat both versions simply as the one from 2003 but rather as distinct entries. This leads to a second point, namely, that I have used in-text parenthetical citations. This style was chosen in order to make it immediately clear to readers if/when Mills modifies his ideas.

By way of conclusion, I also want to acknowledge Laura, Brynne, and Adeline Westmoreland, "Team Westmo," for being so very patient with me. Of course, if I could thank Charles once more, I would do so without hesitation. I am sure he would have some witty remarks to make about why this all took so long. Two of the volume's contributors, Taylor Rogers and Lawrence Blum, regularly gave suggestions about ways to improve the volume and helped connect me with some of the contributors. I am pleased to have chapters from them. At Ocean County College, Christopher Ruth and Marilyn Kralik have always encouraged and supported my research. I appreciate their understanding of why work like this is important. Lastly, I want to thank the staff at Routledge, particularly Andew Weckenmann, who first supported the project, and Rosaleah Stammler, who judiciously nudged me along despite numerous setbacks.

1

DIAGNOSING WHITE APHASIA

Mills and Domination Contract

Mark William Westmoreland

The Waters of Domination

In this chapter, I explain the ways in which liberalism has always been racialized, both in theory and practice. A racial polity, particularly that of the United States, relies on what Charles W. Mills calls a "domination contract" in which there are persons with full rights and responsibilities, namely, whites, and sub-persons who continue to experience exclusion from the practices of radical egalitarianism. The US racial polity is set up in a way that utilizes controlling images of Blackness—negative images of projection and interpellation, that is, the process by which the white gaze creates sub-persons. I contrast domination contract theory with mainstream contract theory in order to show that the liberatory efforts of contract theory obfuscate, by way of ideal theory, the extent to which the contract is one of racial exclusion. Non-ideal theory, by contrast, allows us to establish principles of justice, to build our ships at sea, by first diagnosing the actual social matrix in which we find ourselves. As with all those with great insight, Mills is not without his critics. In the second section, I explain Mills's understanding of white supremacy through a debate between Christopher Lebron, a rising star in the discipline, and the eminent Mills, who is no longer with us. In the third section, I describe white aphasia, the willful erasure of racial domination, as one tool used within white supremacist liberal polities.

Political liberalism in all its variants (contractarian, utilitarian, [post-]Rawlsian) prides itself on being emancipatory, capable of liberating individuals from serfdom, theocratic hierarchies of divine right, economic exploitation, discrimination, tyranny, and so on. Liberalism has as its goal—the security of justice for individuals. Liberal countries share commitments to the rule of law, transparency, and consistency of procedural norms. In liberalism, the autonomous, free individual is the fundamental political unit who, by consent, grounds political authority. Both the rights and the responsibilities of individuals are said to be diffused equally and evenly among the citizenry. The authority of the government is understood to be the expression of the will of those who are governed. To varying degrees, such polities affirm pluralism across a field of values (cultural, religious, etc.), rely on market economies, demarcate spheres of the public and the private, and set limits on the government's ability to intrude into the lives of individuals.

DOI: 10.4324/9781003349983-2

However, the history of liberalism has repeatedly been one in which oppression remains central in so far as the proper political subject is always defined by the exclusion of others. Put differently, exclusion has been a historical constant throughout liberalism's life, so to speak. One hazard of liberalism is that it deceptively masks abuses of power and maldistribution of rights and responsibilities under the cloak of equality when such equality is actualized as equality for some but not all. For instance, were the enslaved Africans in eighteenth-century US society liberated from serfdom and exploitation? Are women free from experiencing discrimination based on gender? Are those who are Latiné able to navigate social space without criticism of poisoning the blood of the nation? Of course, the answers to these questions are obvious. But what about the progress that has been made in terms of who counts as a political subject? Have not liberal societies made improvements? On the one hand, if the bar is set this low (slavery, sexual violence, exploitation), then giving liberalism credit for improvement seems underwhelming. On the other hand, progress has indeed been made in that the list of political subjects continues to be expanded. However, imagine if a poll were taken of all those who lived in liberal societies throughout the last few centuries. How would those occupying social positions less than the most privileged in society evaluate liberalism? Here is my guess: the tally marks of oppression would reach a sum far greater than the marks of emancipation. My concern here is not whether we should keep liberalism or abandon it. Rather, I am concerned with our understanding of liberalism as an exclusionary political theory that needs to be re-evaluated in terms of how it fails to deal with its own tendencies toward domination.

Liberalism has been the mainstream approach to politics in Euro-modernity and contract theory has been the most influential explanation for liberalism. The two are not synonymous but do share similar conceptual spaces. To be sure, not all liberals employ contract theory and not all contract theorists support liberalism. Although there are many liberalisms and many contract theories, including divergent strands of contractarianism and contractualism, for our present purpose, we can identify some major themes that, while not shared by all contract theorists, provide a general sense of the inner workings of liberalism and social contract theory. In other words, I admit that I am painting with broad strokes.

There are at least three main facets of contract theory: the contract as political, moral, and epistemological. The social contract as political contract provides an explanation of why and how governments are created and how the government and individuals relate to one another in terms of rights, responsibilities, and obligations. The political contract might be used either to explain why and how the natural rights of the individual are waived or transferred to the state or to explain why and how individuals might restrict their natural rights in order to establish social harmony or civil society. This facet is central in the writings of classical social contract theorists, but it drops out of the picture in the works of contemporary contract theorists such as John Rawls. In both traditions, what we get is a justificatory claim of governmental power based on common consent. The political contract explains why, how, and (arguably) when individuals collectively determined that establishing a government is worthwhile in order to improve the conditions that exist in their pre-civil society arrangement. The moral contract is the second facet and speaks to norms regulating an individual's actions. It explores disagreement and consensus about the rights, the status of persons and their fundamental rights, and, more generally, the just arrangement of the basic structure of society. According to Mills, the third facet, the epistemology contract, is not made explicit in classical and Rawlsian contract theories. There are epistemic modes or conditions for thought implicit in the contract to which all parties to the contract must assent. This particular facet is foregrounded in what Mills describes as a racial contract, which is "the truth of the *social* contract" (1997, 64).

Mills gives two reasons for offering a theory of racial contract. First, he claims that such a theory can bring into conversation (a) mainstream moral, political, and social philosophy, which deals with idealized abstract notions of justice, rights, equality, and freedom, and (b) political theorists (Black American, Third-World, etc.) who focus their attention on tangible, historically embedded phenomena such as colonialism and racism. Although discussions of land rights, reparations, and forced assimilation are largely absent in (a) (granted, this is improving), these are precisely addressed in the works of (b). Second, a theory of racial contract is both descriptive and prescriptive, attuned to both history and suggestive of normative pursuits. "The notion of a Racial Contract," according to Mills, "might be more revealing of the *real* character of the world we are living in, and the corresponding historical deficiencies of its normative theories and practices, than the raceless notions [popular] in political theory" (1997, 7, emphasis mine). Whereas mainstream theory attempts to remove itself from the real world—from the contingencies of history—only later to apply theory to particular concretized problems, a racial contract theory takes the real world to be the very condition for theorizing. In other words, a racial contract theory emerges from within the contingencies themselves, provides critical interpretations of historical facts, and positions itself as immanently responsive to concrete problems of racial injustice.

The racial contract is also political, moral, and epistemological. The contract is not simply a thought experiment or heuristic tool; it is a historical reality. Mills argues that any polity theorized to be "predicated on the (past or present) universal inclusion of colorless atomic individuals will therefore get things fundamentally wrong from the start. Races in relations of domination and subordination centrally constitute the social ontology" (2017, 40). And although the racial contract cannot be assigned any one specific date on which the contract was created, it can be understood as having been written and ratified through a series of events that make up a substantial part of Euro-modern history. Mills identifies several such events: papal bulls, treatises, arguments about discovery and the essence of non-whites, and the "routinization of informal illegal or quasi-legal practices effectively sanctioned by the complicity of silence and government failure to intervene and punish perpetrators" (1997, 20–21). If classical contract theory holds that government is established by the consent of the people and if all people are afforded equal standing and social value, then Mills's theory of the racial contract reveals the inequality of those affected by the creation of government and the extent to which non-white people were kept away from both being involved in the contract's creation and from equally reaping its benefits. What justified separating those who had the opportunity to consent from those who did not? The aforementioned historical events shed light on this.

The historical events that comprise the formation of the contract all involve a distinction between one group of human beings characterized as having personhood (i.e., whites) and another group characterized as sub-persons (i.e., non-whites). In "White Right: The Idea of a *Herrenvolk* Ethics," Mills describes persons, those who "are rational self-directing entities who must be given equal respect and not treated merely as a means to an end," in contrast to sub-persons, those who "are not capable of becoming moral agents in the full sense, directing and legislating for themselves" (1998, 153). The latter were given a moral status that was inferior to the first group. This should not be surprising in so far as the participants and authors involved were Europeans and the objects of their inquiry were those outside of Europe whose lands, resources, and labor would become useful to European expansion. As historian Patrick Wolfe explains,

> Private property accrued from the admixture of labour and land. As this formula was colour-coded on the colonial ground, Blacks provided the former and Indians the latter, the application of Black people's labour to Red people's land producing the White man's property—a primitive accumulation if ever there was one. The two societies, Native and enslaved, were of antithetical but complementary value to White society. Whereas Black people were valuable commodities, Indians obstructed the expansion of settlement. Though juridically excluded, therefore, enslaved people were demographically fostered, to the extent that their numbers continued to grow. [...] In the Indian case, by contrast, no effort was spared to eliminate them, in ways that have varied according to context.
> *(2016, 3–4)*

While mainstream contract theory assumes that equal individuals equally consent to be governed for equally mutual benefit, a theory of racial contract highlights how human beings were intentionally divided racially and how that division was used as scaffolding to prop up a racial polity of white domination.

Because these divisions served various forms of exploitation, it can rightly be said that the racial contract has its own set of sub-species: expropriation contracts, slavery contracts, and colonial contracts. All these various modifiers—sexual, racial, colonial, etc.—of the social contract highlight the concrete instantiations of what is more appropriately called "the domination contract." The artificial contract that binds individuals together in a liberal society is one of domination. Yes, although we might know the history and/or theoretical elements of contract theory, there is a tendency to read that tradition in a race-neutral manner. By emphasizing race, Mills is not adding something to the tradition that has not been present; rather, he is shining light on a feature of the tradition that remains hidden, particularly to whites.

Mainstream contract theory refers to how theorists tend to think about contracts abstracted from any specific, existing society, but Mills's domination contract records closer to what an actualized contract theory looks like. He writes, "The point of analyzing [the domination contract] is not to ratify it but to use it to explain and expose the inequities of the actual nonideal polity and to help us to see through the theories and moral justifications offered in defense of them" (1997, 5). Mills is not a proponent of the domination contract in the sense that he wants its actualization to continue. Rather, Mills finds it helpful to name what the social contact *is*—a domination contract. White domination is a systemic arrangement that attempts to limit both the self-determination and self-development of people of color.

A brief biographical note might be helpful. Mills began his career working within the Black Marxist tradition. Shortly afterward, his writings shifted to focus more on issues of race and racism both within philosophy as a discipline and throughout society more broadly. To be clear, by "the whiteness of philosophy," Mills refers to "the conceptual or theoretical whiteness of the discipline" rather than the skin color of its practitioners

(1998, 2). "Western philosophy," Mills writes, "abstracts away from what has been the central feature of the lives of Africans transported against their will to the Americas: the denial of Black humanity and the reactive, defiant assertion of it" (9). His reading of Carole Pateman's *The Sexual Contract* (1988), which examines the social contract tradition in light of sexism and patriarchy, profoundly influenced him to take up an investigation into how the social contract tradition had been a tradition about white supremacy (see Westmoreland 2021). In a similar way to how Jean-Jacques Rousseau identifies a class contract and Pateman identifies a sexual contract within the social contract tradition, Mills identifies a racial contract at work. What unites these three radical critics of the tradition is their unwavering recognition of a domination contract. The social contract tradition ignores or obfuscates particular forms of oppression that have roots within the tradition. Mainstream contract presents itself as one of inclusion, freedom, consent, and egalitarianism. Mills, like Rousseau and Pateman, challenges this presentation and replaces it with a domination contract, one that is marked by exclusion, exploitation, and coercion. Mills draws his attention toward the racial domination contract and its expression in a racial polity of white supremacy. He is aware that this system of domination intersects with other systems such as patriarchy and capitalism. And although he attends to the salience of a racial contract, he admits that ideally a class contract, sexual contract, and racial contract ought to be synthesized. Domination is a kind of unfreedom involving unequal power relations that results in the maldistribution of resources.

In *Politics Against Domination* (2016), a book that, to be clear, makes no mention of Mills, Ian Shapiro identifies five features of domination. The first feature is that "domination always compromises someone's freedom" because of human action (20). Some kinds of unfreedom can result from non-human or non-agential causes. But what makes unfreedom in the mold of domination is that it results from human interventions into one another's lives when one illegitimately exerts power over another. Second, those who exert dominative power over others bear responsibility. Because domination is due to human action, human action also can lead to the reduction or removal of domination. Shapiro rightly points out a third feature, namely that "some kinds of domination matter more than others" (2016, 21). When a person or group has the ability to control who has access to necessary instrumental goods, goods needed to satisfy a person's most basic interests, the possibility of domination exists, particularly when access to those goods is restricted to such an extent that parity of participation in society is non-existent or close to it. Of course, there are relationships that contain unequal power dynamics, e.g., parent and child, teacher and student, employer and employee, police and citizen. Shapiro's fourth feature is that domination involves illicitness. Having power over another is not inherently problematic—as the aforementioned examples illustrate—but it becomes dominative power when it is exerted in abusive, manipulative, or coercive ways. The fifth feature refers to "domination's particularism [that] flows from its rootedness in human collective arrangements" (2016, 21). Domination occurs within specific contexts, contexts that involve particular individuals, groups, or institutions. This is why decisions about how best to reduce or eliminate domination must be handled case by case.

For Mills, white supremacy is a dominative political system in which whites exert illegitimate power over people of color generally and Black folks specifically. Because the racial polity is taken for granted, not seen for what it is, the majority of white people ignore their complicity with the system and avoid taking any responsibility for changing it.

Mills offers us a non-ideal theory. But what is meant by "ideal" and "non-ideal" theory? A concise way of distinguishing between the two is to identify ideal theory as an attempt at plotting a perfectly just society and the principles of justice that regulate it and to identify non-ideal theory as an attempt to ascertain specific injustices, detect what corrective measures can be taken to alleviate those injustices, and promote policies that would minimize any future harms. Ideal theorists aim for justice as such, a theory of justice that is ahistorical and decontextualized, that is universalizable, and not tied to any particular or set of particular socio-political phenomena. Their hope would be for an ideal theory of justice to later be applied within various contexts. Mills explains that "what distinguishes ideal theory is not merely the *use* of ideals, since obviously non-ideal theory can and will use ideals too. [...] What distinguishes ideal theory is the reliance on idealization to the exclusion, or at least marginalization, of the actual" (2017, 75). Non-ideal theorists begin with naming, diagnosing, and confronting practical problems as they arise in particular contexts. They shed light on the present moment, along with its historical underpinnings and future implications, and inquire as to why and how the contemporary is that which it is. Non-ideal theorists assess the risks and benefits of maintaining the contemporary as it is and the risks and benefits of altering the contemporary. Their goal is to justify practical solutions to practical problems.

In *Dark Ghettos: Injustice, Dissent, and Reform* (2016), Tommie Shelby describes four types of principles belonging to non-ideal theory. The first type, which is forward-focused, is concerned with changing institutions through reforms or revolution in order to eliminate injustice. The second is backward-focused, addressing reparations and making amends for prior and/or present harms. Both of these types operate within what is known as corrective justice. The third type of principle is part of a theory of punishment, whether it be retributive or restorative. Political ethics make up the fourth type and are the values, principles, and norms that ground any criticism of failures to advance justice and/or complicity with injustice. Political ethics is not only critical; it also provides a positive rubric or guide for how to determine one's duties within the context of advancing human flourishing.

So far, so good. But one clarification is in order. Shelby claims that a complete understanding of justice requires both non-ideal and ideal theory working in tandem. What is the relation between these two? Non-ideal theory, for Shelby, works to establish principles that can guide our responses to particular injustices. Ideal theory operates on a higher level, providing a common conception of justice and directing us about how to create the principles of non-ideal theory. Furthermore, ideal theory, Shelby claims, "provides evaluative standards for judging when a social order is seriously unjust and an objective to strive for in our resistance to oppression. Injustices are conceptualized as deviations from the ideal principles of justice, in much the same way that fallacious reasoning is conceived as a deviation from the rules of logical inference" (2016, 12). However, the ways in which injustice (and ideal theory) and fallacious reasoning (and logical inference) are not the same are fundamentally important.

First, our theorizing about justice is always done from our unique socio-historical context. Mills argues that, by definition, "racial justice is [...] a matter of non-ideal theory, since it presupposes the need for corrective measures to remedy the legacy and ongoing practices of racial oppression. [...] In ideal theory, certain problems do not even arise in the first place" (2007, 113). Iris Marion Young, defending a brand of critical or non-ideal theory, writes, "Social description and explanation must be critical, that is, aim to evaluate the given in normative terms. Without such a critical stance, many questions about what occurs in a society and why, who benefits and who is harmed, will not be asked, and social theory is liable to reaffirm and reify the given social reality" (1990, 5). Young identifies the problem of ignoring the reality of the ways in which society is actually structured to benefit some and harm others. To ignore the socio-historical realities that make societies and their political arrangements what they are is to snub the very problems theory seeks to address. What we take to be of importance and what we ignore, what we think belongs to a conception of justice, and what we choose to leave out, are affected by our context. For instance, if we were to live in a social world in which everyone agreed that we are essentially born to be carpenters, soldiers, priests, etc., then we might think one aspect of justice would be for us to actually take on those roles. If nature made one of us fit to be a carpenter, then to take up the role of priest would be unjust. We might even think that everyone is of equal worth without accepting equality of opportunity as a principle of justice. If we were to live in a society in which we all agree that some people are naturally suited to be slaves, then we would not see slavery as an unjust institution. We might even think that all full persons should be free while also thinking not all human beings are full persons. Today, both situations would strike us as unjust. The point I am trying to make is simply that ideal theory is not beyond being susceptible to flaws. Of course, non-ideal theory can have its share of problems as well, but its focus on pragmatics is helpful on the ground in ways that ideal theory's claim to universality is not.

Second, abstraction and idealization are not equivocal. Abstraction, as a kind of theorizing, steps back from phenomena in order to arrive at general concepts regarding the similarities among phenomena. As Mills frequently explains, a problem with ideal theory is that it idealizes abstractions too far away from particular phenomena. Mills provides a useful example that highlights how abstractions can be either ideal or non-ideal. He writes,

> *Liberal democracy* and *white supremacy* are both abstractions, but the former excludes racial domination while the latter highlights it. If, as mainstream scholars have traditionally done, one simply characterizes the United States as historically being a liberal democracy, while ignoring its long history of racial subordination of people of color, one will be employing an idealizing abstraction that serves apologist and obfuscatory ends. If, on the other hand, one characterizes the United States as historically being a white-supremacist polity (if liberal-democratic in pretensions), one will be employing a non-idealizing abstraction that, at least for race, makes salient its most important feature. So both terms are abstractions, but one is accurate in characterizing the objective reality under examination while the other is not.
>
> *(2019, 16)*

Both ideal and non-ideal make use of both abstractions and moral ideals. So where do the two part ways? On the one hand, ideal theory entails principles of justice that apply to a completely just society, a society of strict compliance (Rawls 1999a, 8, 15). It presupposes natural, social, and political conditions that are propitious to human flourishing. For example, ideal theory takes for granted the lack of flooding and famine, protests and riots, and corruption and abuse. It also presupposes that individuals and institutions strictly comply with principles of justice so that society is one in which crimes are not committed and wars are not fought. On the other hand, non-ideal theory presupposes a society of partial compliance to which we can apply corrective justice. The abstractions of non-ideal theory are approximately true to the extent that any kind of generalization is going to lack important nuances about the specific details of this or that phenomenon. This is in contrast to the abstractions of ideal theory, for which the particular phenomena are altogether irrelevant.

Whereas mainstream contract utilizes the framework of ideal theory, domination contract employs non-ideal theory. "The contrast [between these two]," Mills explains, "is that ideal theory asks what justice demands in a perfectly just society while non-ideal theory asks what justice demands in a society with a history of injustice" (2017, 34). Rawlsian ideal theory, which is representative of mainstream contract theory in its contemporary idiom, proceeds with the assumption that, if we were to remove any knowledge of our social identities and material circumstances, then we would all select a political configuration that protects basic rights and distributes resources to the benefit of those with the least advantage in society.

Rawls conceives of society as a cooperative undertaking. This venture, Rawls claims, is "for mutual advantage" (1999a, 4). Rawls is writing here about neither an ideal society nor potentially just societies in the future. He is describing society as he thinks it actually exists. Is he correct? On the one hand, Rawls admits that there are problems of scarcity and lack of consistent values. On the other hand, he does not take these problems seriously enough, which allows him to envision individuals striving together for a shared purpose (i.e., a just society). In contrast, a more accurate account of political progress would identify the role of struggle, of confrontation between values, of forms of resistance, and of the particular histories of domination and biases that contaminate the procedural steps of the veil of ignorance.

Non-ideal theory names specific problems and prescribes remedies to those problems. In more ways than one, all political action is about refashioning and creatively implementing tactics to deal with problems. Non-ideal theory is less about drawing a blueprint for the just society and more about, *in medias res*, how best to alleviate social ills. John Dewey, although writing about liberal democratic action and not non-ideal theory, argues that real people in real societies attempt to solve their problems in a step-by-step fashion "without foreknowledge of any ultimate result, and, for the most part, under the immediate influence of a number of differing impulses and slogans" (1993, 174). We build and rebuild our ships of justice at sea, as it were.

Mills on White Supremacy

The Color of Our Shame: Race and Justice in Our Time (2013) is Christopher Lebron's attempt, among other things, to rectify problems in the philosophical projects of both John Rawls and Mills. Lebron's book is excellent, but I use it here as a foil to further explain Mills's understanding of the white supremacist version of the domination contract. Because Mills (2019) has already responded in detail to Lebron's criticisms, I will only consider a few points of disagreement—those I take to be most related to the focus on "white supremacy" and the domination contract of the United States.

For Lebron, the problem with Mills's account of racial inequality is that he pins this inequality to white supremacy or white power. This attribution is, in Lebron's words, "overly simplistic and analytically empty" (2013, 10). Racial inequality and white supremacy are not equivalent. But he does find the term "white supremacy" helpful in so far as it calls us to think about how our past shapes our present, how *de jure* racial inequality bleeds into society even after the inequality is no longer explicitly codified in law. Furthermore, regardless of any racial progress that has been made in the United States, it remains the case that Black folks are underserved and often harmed by the basic structure of society. At the same time, "white supremacy" is unhelpful, Lebron claims, in so far as it lacks the explanatory force needed to provide a nuanced account of how the basic structure actually builds racial inequality into a society with formal equality.

Lebron speaks, in place of white power, of bad national character. The problem of racial inequality is one of social value. "Blacks," Lebron explains, "do not hold an equal place as whites in America's scheme of normative valuation and this scheme in the first instance motivates and justifies the distribution of goods, opportunities, and respect" (2013, 155). In Lebron's view, the failure of the United States to fulfill its commitment to freedom and equality for all is not only due to how the "rules of the game" (i.e., policies, procedures, and practices) are maintained but also to how the moral character of institutions and persons falls short (8). The national character of the United States, the ethical nature of our collective institutions and individuals, warrants normative judgments based on the polity's actions—racially unequal policies, procedures, and practices—and their underlying beliefs—that Black people lack the same moral value as white people.

Lebron claims that Mills "relies on overly blunt analytic devices such as 'white supremacy'" (2013, 19). Mills's insistence on employing "white supremacy," Lebron suggests, is simplistic and does not do the work that is needed for corrective justice. Furthermore, he claims that Mills's focus on outcomes discounts the causal aspect of racial inequality. Racial inequality, according to Lebron, should be addressed by attending to the problem of social value, that is, the problem that generates racial inequalities such as racialized poverty, incarceration, health, and the like. The problem of social value is why Michael Brown's body lay partially uncovered, blood exposed, for four hours after being murdered by police officer Darren Wilson. The problem of social value is also why George Floyd was not believed when he told police officers that he could not breathe. The problem of social value is why, despite all racial progress, racial inequality persists. The problem of social value is causal of the first order: "the fact that Blacks do not occupy an equal place in the scheme of normative attention and concern upon which our society depends in the first place to justify the distribution of benefits and burdens, as well as to identify those who are deserving or appropriate recipients" (46). By focusing here on recognition, Lebron describes his project as normative rather than social-scientific. His concern is about the motivations and beliefs in which Blackness is not allotted value equally within the social matrix.

Lebron states that the emphasis on social value can teach three lessons that compensate for what he identifies as shortcomings in Mills's work. The first lesson is that we should take earnestly the political nature and history of racial inequality. Second, the emphasis on social value encourages us to think seriously about the moral character of people within a polity and the extent to which they are conditioned by the racial power dynamics of that polity. The third lesson synthesizes the first two and is paramount for any positive project favoring racial justice. "Racial justice," Lebron writes, "must have something to say about the character of persons and institutions as developed within current patterns of racial power and against the full backdrop of our racial history" so that efforts toward equal recognition and, subsequently, (re-)distributive justice are better implemented (2013, 53).

Mills's most famous line is no doubt the following: "White supremacy is the unnamed political system that has made the modern world what it is today" (1997, 1). He later fleshes this out in "White Supremacy as Sociopolitical System," published in *From Class to Race: Essays in White Marxism and Black Radicalism*: "*White Supremacy* as a concept thus registers a commitment to a radically *different* understanding of the political order, pointing us theoretically toward the centrality of racial domination and subordination" (2003, 184). Hardly anyone would deny that political liberalism has been the dominant political system of Euro-modernity. But behind that system—hidden from view and unnamed—is white supremacy. Although liberalism appears as anti-feudal, egalitarian, and liberating, behind the veneer of freedom and equality, we find an exclusionary system of racial domination. The United States is paradigmatic of the tension between inclusion and exclusion, liberation and domination, freedom and slavery.

White supremacy, with all its tensions, should be understood as a political system in itself. While white supremacy is not so much about individual attitudes, it is structural. As Mills explains in numerous essays, including "The Racial Polity," "White Right," (both in 2003), and his recent "White Supremacy" entry in *The Routledge Companion to Philosophy of Race* (2018), white supremacy is not necessarily dependent on racist intentions or racist feelings. The most succinct way of summarizing white supremacy is that it is a system of domination that unjustly benefits whites.

Lebron misunderstands Mills's notion of white supremacy on a few accounts. First, Lebron misses the point about white supremacy being a system run by whites in the interests of whites. He is correct that Mills does not hold the hyperbolic view that a specific group of "whites widely coordinate activities to co-opt and subordinate Blacks" (2013, 37). The more palatable view is that white people occupy positions of power disproportionately to their population and that Black people are systematically disadvantaged in contrast with their white counterparts. For Lebron, this view is weak because it treats white advantage as epiphenomenal, because it lacks an account of intentional causality. How would Mills respond?

First, Mills accounts for a variety of causes involving both white group motivations as well as structural constraints, whose "cumulative outcome is the reproduction of illicit white advantage [and] differential power" (2019, 8). Coordination is not required. Second, whites tacitly consent to a system of white domination. This consent is not a matter of consciously reflective decision-making about whether or not they want a *de jure* white supremacist polity. Few would affirm such an explicitly racist social matrix. Instead, it is a matter of clinging to the status quo, of aversion to attempts that would make the polity more egalitarian. As the saying goes, equality feels like oppression to those with privilege. It is about the choices white folks make daily that maintain their racialized advantage. The intentional causality is located in white group motivations that maintain white differential power and structural inequalities that advantage whites. And these two sources are mutually reinforcing.

This is not to say that white supremacy remains stable or that it appears the same in all instances. White supremacy has metastasized, and its causal efficacy is now diffused, meaning that there is not some illuminati-like counsel of white power brokers who set a final, unified theory of how to dominate people of color. Put differently, the machinations of white supremacy are found in its multifarious permutations that are not reducible to any one person or specific group of powerful people—permutations sustained by myths of white exceptionalism and practices of Black exclusion. White supremacy shifts or modulates over time in response to various socio-political vicissitudes, and it does so without any need for permission by a literal counsel of white masterminds. What then explains racialized disparities if there is no mass-scale, coordinated effort to disadvantage and harm Black folks?

Lebron counters the direction taken by Mills and claims that white interests play a genealogical role in racial inequality but white interests do not play a causal role, or at least "the causal link between distinct white interests and distinct cases of Black disadvantage becomes less clear-cut" (2013, 39). In his response to Lebron, Mills writes, "[Lebron] seizes upon what might admittedly be one of my less felicitously phrased characterizations of white supremacy—'a *system* run by, and in the interests of, whites'" (2019, 8). But Mills means by this more than white racism and includes what he dubs *Herrenvolk* ethics (master-race ethics). *Herrenvolk* ethics refers to a differential set of moral codes according to which rights and responsibilities are unequally distributed based on race. Lebron wants to push more responsibility onto how institutions develop bad character, given that some moral failures arise from structural dynamics of the social matrix. But Lebron's second and third lessons are not contrary to what Mills argues. Mills's *Herrenvolk* ethics is not coextensive with white supremacy, which is another error made by Lebron. It is only one feature of white supremacy. *Herrenvolk ethics* is not just political but is also moral; it is what allows for there to be implied categories of person and sub-person.

It matters little if anti-Black oppression is due to the action or inaction, the committing of acts (explicit or implicit, intentional or unintentional) that harm Black people, or the failing to act in ways that alleviate those harms. Whether racial oppression is for white group interest or personal interest matters little with regard to the negative consequences experienced by Black folks. One of the goals of describing *Herrenvolk* ethics is to highlight how white moral psychology often fails to realize bad character because the system masks bad character as good character, mistaking vice for virtue. At play in this reversal is the role of white epistemology, which is a form of racial ignorance and racialized moral rationalization whereby the realities of racial domination are obscured.

Racial ignorance and racialized moralizing impact the form and substance of institutions in the United States. One thing that is involved in the myriad of institutions within the social matrix of the United States is the optical/perceptual/vision/meaning-making nature of the white gaze. The white gaze is the filter through which full humanity of Black folks is unseen and forgotten. Although Lebron does not use this phrasing, he is familiar with the substance of the concept: "The actions of whites are assumed to be reasonable, while the actions of Blacks are prima facie deviant and criminal" (2013, 7). Law enforcement officers look upon Black bodies with suspicion as if the latter were inherently criminal. In hospitals, Black folks are thought to not feel pain like white folks. In schools, Black students are assumed to lack the capacity to excel beyond their white peers. In various levels of government, the few Black people that occupy political positions are viewed as angry, seeking payback, or "out to destroy America." In the workplace, Black employees are assumed to be lazy or capricious, or they are thought to be an unearned diversity hire that stole a job from a more qualified, white candidate. Advertising agencies evaluate Black models as lacking in the prerequisite beauty. And the list continues.

By coding the Black body as abnormal or deviant, the functioning of the white gaze allows what was once *de jure* white supremacy to remain intact as *de facto* white supremacy. But we should be cautious to not be misled into thinking that white supremacy takes the same shape in every locale and every moment. White supremacy is not rigid but rather exists with a high degree of plasticity. "White supremacy," Mills argues, "is [neither] synchronically uniform [n]or diachronically static" (1998, 101). Even after an explicitly white supremacist polity sheds its overtly racist structure, the polity takes up new modes of racial domination. Or, more poetically stated, even though a snake sheds its skin, it still lives as a snake, often more menacing and cunning. Although its old skin is pushed aside to whither in the brush, the snake continues to hunt the same prey as before and does so with enhanced strategies. In short, white supremacy evolves—sometimes to adapt alongside other systems of domination and sometimes in response to Black resistance and other acts of defiance by people of color.

Lebron asks, "What sustains the systemic nature of racial inequality at the level of institutional procedure and outcomes? Additionally, given that persons populate institutions, how is it that explicit racism can mostly be a thing of the past but that persons nonetheless seem to reason in racial ways" (2013, 4)? Of course, and I doubt Lebron would disagree, these questions are asked by all of us working in critical philosophy of race. What Lebron thinks is unique is his answer, that is, "that the problem of racial inequality is *the problem of social value*" (4). Social value speaks of the standing one has within a social matrix—in this particular instance, the standing Black folks have in an anti-Black racist society, the presumed lack of being worthy of equal recognition. He writes, "Thus, social value serves as an analytic lynchpin for constructing explanation, giving content to description, and systematically justifying a distinct set of prescriptive moves" (4). On the prescriptive side of things, Lebron argues that shame serves as a vehicle for accountability, for holding accountable our society and coming to terms with our morally deficient national character. Although his way of articulating the details of the problem and a potential solution is unique, Lebron's emphasis on differential normative standing is not entirely new.

Recognition, and not only redistribution, has been a major component of Mills's philosophical project despite what Lebron says to the contrary. For instance, the fact that Black people have not been fully recognized as equal persons is a theme throughout Mills' work. In his 1994 article "Under Class Under Standings," which was reprinted in *From Class to Race* (2003), Mills describes a *Herrenvolk* Kantianism in which there is a rift between the categories of person and sub-person, the former being attributable only to white people. The conventional Kant, or idealized Kant, defines a person as an autonomous agent, as an end in oneself, and as one who ought to be given equal respect based on equal standing. But this belies the problem of Kant's racism. It is clear from Kant's writings on race that Kant did not view all humans as equal persons. The problem faced by commentators is how to juggle Kant's moral egalitarianism with his racist views on human difference.

Mills resolves this tension by developing the category of sub-person, a category not explicitly stated in Kant's writing but is implicitly operative. Kant thought that all persons are ends in themselves, that is, autonomous agents who ought not be used as mere means. At the same time, Kant, Mills argues, did not hold that all humans were full persons. Given his writings on race, it is clear that Kant considered various non-white racial groups as inferior and lacking the full gamut of prerequisites necessary for personhood. These racial groups have the implied designation of sub-person. Mills's conclusion is that we should understand the Kantian themes of egalitarianism and universalism as applicable to white folks (persons) but not to non-white people (sub-persons).

Let us consider how personhood functions politically in the contract tradition, a tradition that claims to count all individuals as equal. According to Mills, the social contract is actually a racial contract, one that undergirds white supremacy. The racial contract has been an agreement among one subset of human beings, namely whites, and exclusionary toward non-whites, i.e., those "of a different and inferior moral status, sub-persons, so that they have a subordinate civil standing in the [racial polity]" (1997, 11). Put differently, the contract is really an agreement among "the people who count," that is, the people who have social value of equal worth (3). Personhood and the possession of rights are taken for granted for white people (at least white men). By assuming that rationality and autonomy are the only factors for personhood, those party to the contract accomplish at least two things. First, race is thought to play no role in the affordance of rights. Second, those racialized as non-white become invisible and, consequently, lack parity of participation within the social matrix.

Lebron is correct to identify the problem of social value as fundamental to racial inequality. But again, this aspect of racial inequality is not lost on Mills. Rather, it has been a key feature of his work for three decades. Perhaps more peculiar is that, despite his insight into how institutions can manifest and produce bad character, Lebron thinks that "we, as a nation, have fallen away from our ideals" (2013, 61). Lebron's conception of social value presumes that the Founders did, but that the extension of social value to Black people has failed. But those ideals were not originally meant to apply to people of color in the first place. Rather than the polity slipping away from its commitment to egalitarianism, the polity today, as it was in the late eighteenth century, remains committed to equality of *white* persons. For Mills, the concern is that not all people are considered as having full personhood. Put differently, the Founders and Framers never meant, nor did their ideas imply, that Black people were to be equal participants in the grand experiment of the United States.

Next, I want to explore Lebron's criticism of Mills's modification of Rawls. Lebron suggests that Mills downplays the significance of institutions within the polity. It is true that Mills does not write full essays on particular institutions on a micro level. Nevertheless, he does frequently point his readers to the works of social scientists and historians to flesh out what he is doing philosophically. Lebron's further claim that Mills fails to offer insight into particular institutions, such as welfare policy or crime policy, may be countered by noting that Mills has, throughout his career, written about racial exploitation, property, and economics more broadly. If Lebron is urging Mills (and all political philosophers) to spend more time developing interdisciplinary scholarship that works on a micro level, then I tend to agree. But I am not convinced that Lebron himself does this, so I am skeptical that this is his point. Is Mills's error, according to Lebron, that Mills stays too tied to the ideal theory of Rawls?

If Lebron is challenging Mills for focusing so much on Rawls and the basic structure of society, then we should recall that Mills's emphasis on Rawls has been due in large part to the well-recognized position of Rawls in political philosophy. Why pay so much attention to Rawls given the fact that he says close to nothing about racial (in)justice? For one, Rawlsian liberalism has been the dominant trend in mainstream political philosophy. A majority of political philosophers engage with Rawls in one way or another. Second, Rawls is largely responsible for moving the discipline in a different direction, that is, from a focus on obligation to a focus on social justice. Political philosophy, post-Rawls, has taken seriously the (in)justice of society's basic structure. But Rawls and his intellectual descendants have not taken the injustice of racial domination seriously enough. His emphasis on distributive justice within well-ordered societies closes off the possibility of dealing with compensatory justice within societies that are ill-ordered—societies like the United States.

Friend and foe alike will readily admit that Rawls is a fixture in discussions of distributive justice. Mills, as well as I, gives attention to Rawls not because he is an obvious target due to name recognition but because he is wrong about his underlying assumptions about society. And when I claim that he is wrong, I am not only referring to the famous veil of ignorance thought experiment but to something fundamental to his entire philosophical enterprise—his description of the basic structure and its role in society's striving toward mutual advantage. The notion of the basic structure of society populates Rawls's writings from some of his earliest to some of his most recent (1999b, 161; 1999b, 6; 2005, 11).

For Rawls, the basic structure forms a system, a network, a constellation of institutions constituting an underdetermined whole. "The basic structure of society," Rawls explains, "is the way in which the main political and social institutions of society fit together into one system of social cooperation, and the way they assign basic rights and duties and regulate the division of advantages that arises from social cooperation over time" (2001, 10). This structure includes the politico-juridical, the economic, the family, and, more broadly, civil society. It is within this network that people associate with one another and with particular institutions. Furthermore, the basic structure is the vehicle through which individuals and groups pursue their interests. For Rawls, the institutions of the basic structure are part of a "cooperative venture for mutual advantage" (1999a, 4), that is, of a society that, although there may be disagreement and some conflicts of interests within it, is primarily one in which everyone equally participates in pursuing what is good or mutually advantageous for them.

Here lies the problem: society is clearly not working toward mutual advantage. It was not doing so in the late eighteenth century, and it does not do so today. But another problem is the assumption that society, albeit one that is not fully well-ordered, is actually a cooperative venture. According to Mills, and this is where he undermines Rawls's notion of cooperative venture, the United States was never intended to be this way. Mills writes,

> Eurocentrism is not the (relatively) innocent one of genealogy [...] but a systematic ignoring of the experiences of the nonwhite political subject, ubiquitously manifest in the "whiteness" of Rawls's perspective on time and space, his tacit conceptions of the populations he is speaking about and to, and his assumptions about how best to frame their narrative. [...] he also focuses on Europeans and the problems and issues that affect the white population, and not—in his native United States—the problems of Blacks and Native Americans. [...] He does so within a (sanitized) European conceptual apparatus, ethnically cleansed of its actual discursive history of ethnic cleansing.
>
> *(2017, 150–51)*

The idea of actual societies, like the United States, being cooperative ventures is intellectually dishonest. The United States began as a white settler state, utilizing the white advantages gained through the loss of life and land, through slavery and genocide, and through exploitation and conquest. To say otherwise would be a result of "white amnesia" (Mills 1997, 69).

White Aphasia

According to Mills, "white amnesia" is the willful forgetting of past injustices. Because amnesia, to be without memory (*a-mnesis*), is understood to be caused by brain damage rather than an act of will, the term, even as a metaphor, may not be best suited for what Mills attempts to highlight. For Mills, amnesia, in the context of contemporary white supremacy, is the suppressing, or to a lesser degree, the downplaying of inescapable historical facts. Perhaps a better term would be "white aphasia," which is not so much a matter of forgetting racialized history but of mutilating history in the sense of turning off our attunement to the significance of certain historical facts. In "Global White Ignorance," Mills identifies this as "racial erasure: the retrospective whitningout, the whitewashing, of the racial past" (2015, 220).

The concept of white aphasia is something I borrow from Ann Laura Stoler. According to Stoler, "Colonial aphasia [...] emphasize[s] both loss of access and active dissociation. [It] is a disremembering, a difficulty speaking, a difficulty generating a vocabulary that associates appropriate words and concepts with appropriate things" (2011, 125). Although writing of France and its colonial legacy, Stoler's use of "aphasia" is a helpful modification to what Mills's attempts to describe in terms of white supremacy within the context of the United States. Presently, there is an aversion to the vocabulary of white supremacy: mischaracterizing instantiations of racial domination, misrecognizing the implications or effects of racial domination, and misidentifying intentionality within a racial polity. These difficulties arise in part because of the blurry line between presence and absence. Without the presence of an overt, explicit racial polity, the white population of the United States struggles with a kind of psychical damage, an occlusion of knowledge, that expresses itself in multifarious forms such as white denial, white fragility, and white rage.

White folks routinely try to distance themselves from colonial and white supremacist histories. This sometimes involves minimizing racial discrimination, terror, and violence as if these things belong solely to the past or are anomalous in our present moment. Other times, the distancing involves choosing to not "know" of white supremacy. The issue is not one of trying to separate the good ones ("us") from the racists ("them") but one of acknowledging how all whites are entangled in the web of white supremacy regardless of their intentions.

Too often, conversations centered around racial justice consider only one of these spheres or only one specific phenomenon within a given sphere. Consider the good-intentioned advocate for racial justice who claims that "if we can end mass incarceration, the rest will follow" or "by ending economic injustice, we will indirectly alleviate racial injustice." While these goals ought to be lauded, they are nevertheless insufficient for addressing white supremacy largely understood as a synergistic system of racial domination.

The aforementioned claims of the advocate most likely come from the belief in the adequacy of mainstream contract theory or the paradigm of liberalism or liberal democracy that treats racism (in all its various idioms) as exceptions rather than the rule. The problem, Mills explains, is one of framing—the big-picture paradigm of liberal society along with its racialized facts, descriptions, and interpretations. Debates involving racial justice are not only "axiological clashes but rival pictures of the factual" (2004, 26). Since the mainstream narrative about the United States assumes a racial egalitarianism, it can be difficult to identify the ways in which liberalism is already set up to benefit white folks. To imagine the

United States as a racially egalitarian polity with only a few unfortunate manifestations of racism is to miss the fact that the polity is meant to maintain a racial hierarchy. The actual polity was never meant to be racially egalitarian; instead, its mode of existence is precisely how the "white racial frame" is supposed to work (Feagin 2013).

Now, I want to turn to the lasting effects of the colonializing aspect of the domination contract. In the era of Euro-modernity, race has been the organizing rubric for colonial endeavors. Wolfe suggests that

> what sets race apart from other ideological constructs—and definitely embeds it in the late eighteenth century—is its merger of two central but otherwise distinct elements of Enlightenment discourse. Race reconciled the great taxonomies of natural science with the political rhetoric of the rights of man. The political optimism infusing the belief in improvement sat awkwardly with the immutable categories of philosophical realism, opposing the hierarchical structuring of natural-scientific classifications to the formal equality that constituted citizenship in liberal-democratic theory. As a taxonomy par excellence, however, race provided categorical boundaries within genus *homo* that ensured the exclusiveness of the bearers of the rights of man.
>
> *(2016, 8–9)*

In the wake of the colonization of North America, indigenous populations decreased by disastrous proportions. Historian David Stannard refers to this phenomenon as the American Holocaust—the vicious flame that killed 95 percent of the Native Americans (see Stannard 1992 and Frank 1978). In the seventeenth through nineteenth centuries, large portions of indigenous populations were wiped out by disease and colonial brutality (see Crosby 1972 and Wallerstein 1974). Likewise, the wretched conditions of slavery, including the torturous Middle Passage, killed millions of Africans—committing a sort of genocide that would not be paralleled until the Nazi regime. Such horrors were buttressed by the political imaginary of modernity—one that understood the Other, that is, the Native, the African, and so on, as the functional limit of reason, as the body in opposition to thought. The decolonial psychiatrist Frantz Fanon summarizes this as follows: "In the white world, the [person] of color encounters difficulties in elaborating [one's] body schema. The image of one's body is solely negating" (2008, 90). Bodies of people of color were understood to be external markers of a threat to rationality. In order to defend civilized society by the governing of bodies, colonizing nations exercised their cynegetic power, that is, the hunting of human beings for the purpose of exclusion.

Because of the racial polity, whites have an interest in seeing the social matrix wrongly. The domination contract, Mills claims, "prescribes for its signatories an inverted epistemology, an epistemology of ignorance, a particular pattern of localized and global cognitive dysfunctions (which are psychologically and socially functional), producing the ironic outcome that whites will in general be unable to understand the world they themselves have made" (1997, 18). The white racial frame allows whites to see the good in or defend as necessary things like colonization, slavery, Jim Crow, etc. Or, it allows whites to condemn these phenomena but deny any ongoing consequences that these might have produced. At the same time, it allows whites to see the world as, for example, a meritocracy. Framing the polity as egalitarian allows for whites who acknowledge the racial horrors of the past to blame non-white problems on the culture or pathology of the racialized Other.

The ways in which the mainstream framework of liberal egalitarianism operates allow for whiteness, with its accumulation of wealth predicated on land theft, slavery, genocide, and supremacist ideology, to go unnamed. Even when the racial exploitation of Black labor and Red land is acknowledged, scholars working within the mainstream framework have a tendency to badly conceptualize the ongoing effects of the racial polity or what historian Roxanne Dunbar-Ortiz rightly describes as the colonialist settler-state.

In *An Indigenous Peoples' History of the United States*, Dunbar-Ortiz provides a counter-history to the conventional narrative of the United States being fundamentally about liberty and equality. I identify two versions of the popular narrative. In the first version, non-whites are antagonistic to the forward march of liberalism. In the second, people of color are erased from the story.

The first version presents white people as the triumphant protagonists against the Calibans of "the dark continent" and the savages of the so-called New World. In this narrative, people of color serve as foils—darker races that, because they impede the development of civilization, ought to be executed, expelled, or exploited in order to achieve a *Herrenvolk* polity, that is, a polity created in the interests of a master race. "Settler colonialism," Dunbar-Ortiz correctly explains, "requires violence or the threat of violence to attain its goals. People do not hand over their land, resources, children, and futures without a fight, and that fight is met with violence" (2014, 8). The historical context for Dunbar-Ortiz's claim is the genocide or ethnic cleansing of Native Americans committed by the US government and settlers acting with governmental approval. But this is also true for the Black lives stolen from Africa and brought into the Western Hemisphere.

The second version of the US narrative, the one that erases non-white people, plays on the notion that North America was vacant during European conquest, that the land was *terra nullius*. Engaging racial aphasia, white supremacy employs an erasure, a misremembering, that is based on the idea that colonized lands were vacant. The vacancy could be based on the (false) assumption that no human beings lived in a given area. Or it could be based on the (ethnocentric) belief that, while human beings did live in a given area, there were no signs of civilization. If the land belongs to no one, then whoever discovers it may lay claim to it. And surely European settlers continued to pour into the Americas for centuries—"discovering" lands from the Atlantic Ocean to the Pacific Ocean, from the Great Lakes to the Gulf of Mexico. One example of this occurs when people claim that Native Americans did not farm; therefore, the land did not belong to the indigenous. The first clause is a lie, given the evidence for indigenous farming. The second clause is ethnocentric in that it is built on the beliefs that (a) human beings were meant to mix their labor with the land and (b) if a people group left the land uncultivated, then other groups had an ordained right to expropriate the land.

The Doctrine of Discovery, related to the Treaty of Tordesillas (1494) and subsequently developed into international law, upheld the idea that any lands not inhabited by Christians (and its associations with whiteness) were justifiably the objects of colonial control. The Doctrine was upheld by Founding Fathers like Thomas Jefferson. Later, in 1823, the Supreme Court confirmed the legitimacy of this doctrine in *Johnson v. M'Intosh* when Chief Justice John Marshall opined that discovery trumps the right of occupancy and that Native Americans could remain on the land but could not hold sovereignty or title of the land, which belonged to the discoverer or those to whom the discoverer transferred the title. Chief Justice Marshall's opinion, which was unanimous, pretended as if pre-Columbian Americans had not already discovered the land.

Johnson v. M'Intosh illustrates a kind of willful ignorance—one that is systemic and conditions the white gaze to perceive and create a reality in which no other fully human persons are present. Not only that, the willful ignorance is so strong under a white supremacist polity that any corrective maneuvers, that is, any attempts to right the epistemological error, are met with resistance. Due to its framing, the US narrative is not falsifiable so to speak. Dunbar-Ortiz writes,

> The main challenge for scholars in revising US history in the context of colonialism is not lack of information, nor is it one of methodology. Certainly, difficulties with documentation are no more problematic than they are in any area of research. Rather, the source of the problems has been the refusal or inability of US historians to comprehend the nature of their own history, US history. The fundamental problem is the absence of the colonial framework.
>
> *(2014, 7)*

The lack of comprehension is found in popular culture as well. For example, President Obama said in an interview that "America was not born as a colonial power" (2009). He was attempting to convince Arab nations that the United States wanted to establish lasting partnerships, that the United States was not seeking to nation-build but rather to cultivate better diplomatic relations. To make his point, President Obama claimed that the United States could be trusted because the United States had not, in the past nor in recent times, engaged in colonialism.

When the United States declared independence, there were two to four million people living in the thirteen colonies. The majority of these people lived within a two-day journey of the coast. One has to wonder how the country expanded if it was not by settler colonialism. But this wonder is easily resolved once we look at the actual historical record of the newly-formed republic. For example, consider the eighth piece of legislation passed in the first session of the First Congress of the United States. The *Northwest Ordinance* was passed on August 7, 1789, and gave the federal government, not individual states, the authority to expand westward. These lands were not barren wastelands; they were not vacant. Rather, these were lands already containing vibrant nations of various sizes, societies with politicians and priests, farmers and artists, scientists and philosophers. Native Americans had already established infrastructure as well as international political and economic agreements. What the settlers found was not *terra nullius* but a land populated and civilized.

There is a popular tendency, of which President Obama was exemplary, of disassociating the United States from its own holocausts, to put it as Stannard or Aimé Césaire would. Before European settlers came to North America, there were tens of millions of people already living across the entire continent. Today, there are only a few million making up a small percentage of the overall population. And, although this measure is problematic, what the federal government labels Native American Reservations make up less than two percent of the land area within the borders of the United States. Not only was President Obama denying that colonization is part of US history; he demonstrated the power of framing. The ideological framing of (the myths of) exceptionalism, Manifest Destiny, and the Doctrine of Discovery obscures the contradictions of liberalism, democracy, and political freedom. The myth becomes the reality. In reality, the narrative is so very entrenched in the US mental landscape that, sadly, the overwhelming majority of people tacitly condone settler colonialism, genocide, and imperialism. To challenge the myth of whiteness or, specifically, the national narrative of the United States, which President Obama failed to do, is to challenge the origin story of the nation and, more fundamentally, its essence.

White aphasia, active forgetting, is not limited to the general public but shows up among philosophers as well. We could ask of Rawls, "Why are European imperialism, African slavery, Native American expropriation, Jim Crow, and so on not part of the 'general facts' about society and history, knowledge of which you are supposed to take with you behind [Rawls's veil of ignorance]" (Mills 2004, 29)? This question expresses Stoler's notion of aphasia—the willful choosing to bracket and delete a set of facts and vocabulary necessary for adequately giving an account of the present condition. Regimes of race change shape regularly in response to the needs of the dominant group and in reaction to antiracist and anticolonial resistances. But in each regiminal idiom of race, whiteness is crucial, and this is no less the case in the United States in the twenty-first century than it was in previous eras. The source of the difficulty for many to register this is the problem of framing.

Consider the lack of cognitive dissonance in a figure like Thomas Jefferson (1743–1826). With Jefferson, we find an intentional exclusion. In the Declaration of Independence, he writes of the "merciless Indian Savage" shortly after reference to the idea of all men being equal. To speak of the Indian as equal would have been the source of dissonance for Jefferson. The social position of "Indian" excluded equality. Mills highlights how Thomas Jefferson could speak of the equality among "men" and, at the same time, deny that all human beings are "men." He writes,

> When Thomas Jefferson excoriates the "merciless Indian Savages" in the Declaration of Independence, the, neither he nor his readers will experience any cognitive dissonance with the earlier claims about the equality of all "men," since savages are not "men" in the full sense of the word. Locked in a different temporality, incapable of self-regulation by morality and law, they are humanoid but not human. To speak of the "equality" of the savage would then be oxymoronic, since one's very location in these categories is an indication of one's inequality.
>
> *(2017, 62)*

In his treatment of Frederick Douglass' speech about the Fourth of July, Mills writes, "My claim is [that the ideals of the Founders and Framers] were never racially inclusive in the first place" (2019, 10). Furthermore, "even a cognizer with no personal antipathy or prejudice toward Native Americans," Mills argues, "will be cognitively disabled in trying to establish truths about them insofar as such a category and its associated presuppositions will tend to force his conclusions in a certain direction, will limit what he can objectively see" (2017, 62). Earlier, in *Blackness Visible*, Mills writes,

> Douglass saw, correctly, that July Fourth belonged to white Americans rather than to all Americans, and his anger at this appropriation continues to resound with us. What he did not see was how old and foundational this exclusionary ownership was, the white property of differential rights at the heart of the white property-owning polity that justifies its racial architecture and shapes the moral consciousness and sense of entitlement of its white citizens.
>
> *(1998, 200)*

The associated presuppositions are part and parcel of the content projected by the white gaze. Our situatedness affects our perception and understanding of our social world, and we develop habits or patterns of thought and practices in conjunction with expectations or prejudices that have been conditioned by our experiences in life. The perceptions, ideas, habits, and expectations of members of the dominant group will be radically different than those of the subordinate group. We not only receive the world but make it—creating our social world based on mutually reinforcing thoughts and practices, both of which are limited by our group experience. But all should guard against group solipsism, particularly those of the dominant group whose ignorance is not impotent but can perpetuate epistemic and behavioral injustice. While on the one hand, all groups encounter ignorance and irresponsibility, on the other, these failings are not experienced equally across groups, nor are their effects of equal intensity.

Today, most whites do not show intentional exclusion. Instead, they tend to misrecognize the racialized social matrix, which excludes people of color from the moral community. For example, white resistance to Latiné immigrants is rooted in purity myths: "they're all murderers and rapists," one might say. Or, "They don't assimilate." "They take all our jobs." We heard calls of "law and order" and "entitlements are killing us" in the 1990s that said Black people had a natural proclivity toward criminality ("Beware of super-predators") and "they're a bunch of welfare queens." In each case, America is really "white America." Through a series of events or conventions in which the contract is ratified, signatories have been those positioned as white in the matrix. They are those with full personhood, for whom the state is meant to serve. Other racial groups, straddling the fence between civil society and the state of nature, are said to bring a host of problems that threaten whiteness as property. This kind of ignorance is powerful. By denying the social conditions that give rise to poverty and criminality, whites can wash their hands clean as if they bear no responsibility for the unjust conditions within the racial polity.

The novelist James Baldwin, criticizing the ignorance of white America, writes, "This is the crime of which I accuse my country and my countrymen, and for which neither I nor time nor history will ever forgive them, that they have destroyed and are destroying hundreds of thousands of lives and do not know it and do not want to know it" (1993, 5). Whites tend to lack the motivation to catch epistemic error in this regard. Furthermore, whites have a diminished capacity to catch such errors and/or alleviate them. Baldwin explains this lack of motivation and capacity by claiming that whites "cannot face what this fact says about themselves and their country" (2000, 165). "No one colonizes innocently," as the Négritude and decolonial philosopher, poet, and politician Aimé Césaire would say (2000, 30). White mythologies must remain intact for the domination contract. Put differently, white ignorance does not entail a lack of knowledge but a willful covering of that knowledge with the band-aid of false belief. Because white false beliefs about people of color are thought to be systemically justified, white people can ignore the claims about racial injustice made by people of color. Not only are their claims ignored, but they also appear as false so that the true claims of subordinate racial groups are made false and the false claims of whites are made true. The polity, with its racial and colonial contracts, is set up in a way that makes this ignorance powerful in so far as it maintains white dominance.

Conclusion

For mainstream contract theory, the social contract serves as a means for establishing and stabilizing a just society. Contract theorists argue that equality and freedom are fundamental to establishing a just society. The goal of contract theory is to justify a society in which all parties to the contract are afforded equal rights and access to participation. It attempts to root this egalitarian principle in the rationality and autonomy of the individual.

Mainstream contract theory overemphasizes individuality and ignores the extent to which individuals belong to particular groups. Unlike mainstream contract, which obfuscates the role of structures and institutions, domination contract places the onus on institutions and their corrupting influences on people. So, yes, Mills devotes much attention to Rawls and the basic structure of society. But this does not mean he ignores the roles that other, derivative or tertiary, institutions play in racial inequality. Mills takes seriously the fact that institutions both "form and corrupt us" (2007, 100).

The goal of domination contract is to justify and maintain unjust institutions. If it can be said to promote freedom and equality, it does so only for the dominant group. Rather than establish a cooperative venture, domination contract sets up a hierarchical polity in which some receive benefits and privileges while others are disadvantaged and oppressed. In place of egalitarianism, rationality, and consent, we find inequality, ignorance, and exploitation.

The purpose of mainstream contract is for someone to approve and advocate for the contract in so far as one believes that it generates an ideally just polity. However, mainstream contract lacks the explanatory force of domination contract. Mainstream theory, which treats racial injustices as a bug and not a feature, struggles to account for how liberalism, steadily receiving more global appeal through the course of Euro-modernity, develops and expands through racism and colonialization. Domination contract, however, emphasizes the dominative aspects of liberalism, that is, the actual historical, structural manifestations of liberalism. The purpose of the domination contract is to have the reader condemn the social (racial, sexual, or otherwise dominative) contract. This condemnation involves both realizing the prevalence of, for example, racial injustice and seeking the curative channels needed for creating a more just society.

To be clear, Mills is not articulating the domination contract in order to promote and maintain its existence but to show that the mainstream tradition has always been a dominative one. Put differently, the domination contract undergirds the unjust polity in which we find ourselves rather than any ideally just polity. Its heuristic purpose is to help us ascertain the various dimensions of the racial polity in order to adjudicate which proposals for corrective justice would best serve the liberal impulses toward universal freedom and equality.

Using the device of domination contract allows us to better grasp the facts—the historical realities of white supremacy—in terms of both their causes and effects. It has the advantage over mainstream contract theory of offering a solid origin of the racial polity instead of dealing in hypothetical or rhetorical metaphors of a state of nature. Inequality is woven into the fabric of the polity in large part because the supposed contract is really one that serves the interests of the few. The domination contract highlights the point that the contract actually excludes the overwhelming majority of people. In short, the mainstream contract, far from being theoretically or practically egalitarian, lacks the potency to address the historical facts of racial inequality. For Mills, the domination contract, however, provides "the emancipatory reach of the egalitarianism of the prescriptive contract [to] gain its full leveling scope rather than being, as at present, effectively confined to achieving the freedom and equality of a few" (2007, 105). One might ask, "Why not jettison contract theory altogether?" On the one hand, this is understandable given how fraught the tradition has been with racial injustices. On the other hand, as Mills's recent work has highlighted, contract theory remains useful if it undergoes radical modifications beginning with its emphasis on ideal theory. The alternative or modified contract theory must utilize the framework of non-ideal theory instead. What would result is no longer a conversation about different conceptions of an ideal polity but a discussion about which corrective policies and practices would remedy racial injustice.[1]

Note

1 I am grateful to Joe Betz, John Carvalho, Charles Mills, Sally Scholz, and George Yancy for commenting on sections of earlier drafts of this chapter. Any misunderstandings or errors are my own.

Bibliography

Baldwin, James. 1993. *The Fire Next Time*. New York: Vintage Books.

Baldwin, James. 2000. *No Name in the Street*. New York: Vintage Books.

Césaire, Aimé. 2000. *Discourse on Colonialism*. Translated by Joan Pinkham. New York: Monthly Review Press.

Crosby, Alfred W., Jr.1972. *The Columbian Exchange: Biological and Cultural Consequences of 1492*. Westport: Greenwood Press.

Dewey, John. 1993. "The Public and Its Problems." In *The Political Writings*. Edited by Debra Morris and Ian Shapiro. Indianapolis: Hackett Publishing Company.

Dunbar-Ortiz, Roxanne. 2014. *An Indigenous Peoples' History of the United States*. Boston: Beacon Press.

Fanon, Frantz. 2008. *Black Skin, White Masks*. Translated by Richard Philcox. New York: Grove Press.

Feagin, Joe R. 2013. *The White Racial Frame: Centuries of Racial Framing and Counter-Framing*. 2nd ed. New York: Routledge.

Frank, Andre Gunder. 1978. *World Accumulation, 1492–1789*. New York: Monthly Review Press.

Lebron, Christopher J. 2013. *The Color of Our Shame: Race and Justice in Our Time*. New York: Oxford University Press.

Mills, Charles W. 1997. *The Racial Contract*. Ithaca: Cornell University Press.

Mills, Charles W. 1998. *Blackness Visible: Essays on Philosophy and Race*. Ithaca: Cornell University Press.

Mills, Charles W. 2003. *From Class to Race: Essays in White Marxism and Black Radicalism*. Lanham: Rowman & Littlefield.

Mills, Charles W. 2004. "Racial Exploitation and the Wages of Whiteness." In *What White Looks Like: African American Philosophers on the Whiteness Question*. Edited by George Yancy. New York: Routledge.

Mills, Charles W. 2007. "With Carole Pateman." In *Contract and Domination*. Malden: Polity.

Mills, Charles W. 2015. "Global White Ignorance." In *The Routledge International Handbook of Ignorance Studies*. Edited by Matthias Gross and Linsey McGoey. London: Routledge Press.

Mills, Charles W. 2017. *Black Rights/White Wrongs: The Critique of Racial Liberalism*. New York: Oxford University Press.

Mills, Charles W. 2018. "White Supremacy." In *The Routledge Companion to the Philosophy of Race*. Edited by Paul Taylor, Linda Martín Alcoff, and Luvell Anderson. New York: Routledge.

Mills, Charles W. 2019. "Theorizing White Racial Domination and Racial Justice: A Reply to Christopher Lebron." *Journal of Social Philosophy* 54 (3): 292–315.

Obama, Barack H. 2009. "Interview with Al-Arabiya." Interview by Hisham Melhem. NBC News. January 27.
Rawls, John. 1999a. *A Theory of Justice*. Cambridge: Harvard University Press.
Rawls, John. 1999b. *The Law of Peoples*. Cambridge: Harvard University Press.
Rawls, John. 2001. *Justice as Fairness: A Restatement*. Edited by Erin Kelly. Cambridge: Harvard University Press.
Rawls, John. 2005. *Political Liberalism*. New York: Columbia University Press.
Shapiro, Ian. 2016. *Politics against Domination*. Cambridge: Harvard University Press.
Shelby, Tommie. 2016. *Dark Ghettos: Injustice, Dissent, and Reform*. Cambridge: Harvard University Press.
Stannard, David E. 1992. *American Holocaust: Columbus and the Conquest of the New World*. New York: Oxford University Press.
Stoler, Ann Laura. 2011. "Colonial Aphasia: Race and Disabled Histories in France." *Public Culture* 23 (1): 121–56.
Wallerstein, Immanuel. 1974. *The Modern World System: Capitalist Agriculture and the Origins of the European World Economy in the Sixteenth Century*. New York: Academic Press.
Westmoreland, Mark William. 2021. "White Supremacy: Will the Present Be Prologue?" *Perspectives on Global Development and Technology* 20: 168–85.
Wolfe, Patrick. 2016. *Traces of History: Elementary Structures of Race*. New York: Verso.
Young, Iris Marion. 1990. *Justice and the Politics of Difference*. Princeton: Princeton University Press.

2

CURDLED CONTRACTS

Reading Mills through a Lugonesian Spirit

Taylor Rogers

The Formation of a Gesture

Charles W. Mills has often gestured toward the importance of embodied experience for constructing and resisting racialized oppression and ignorance. In his most well-known work, *The Racial Contract*, he says, "there is the micro-space of the body itself (which in a sense is the foundation of all other levels), the fact, to be dealt with in greater detail later, that the persons and sub-persons, the citizens and noncitizens, who inhabit these polities do so embodied in envelopes of skin, flesh, hair" (1997, 51). Throughout the corpus of his work, there are many other brief remarks of this kind, remarks which name but do not substantially engage the role of embodied experience in racism and anti-racism.[1] In his newest book project, however, Mills more explicitly thematizes the racist "*body* politic" as he draws new theoretical resources from the most materialist of the social contract theorists, Thomas Hobbes. Mills brings together Hobbes's materialism alongside Jean-Jacques Rousseau's contractualism—one that takes social life as a transformative process. More specifically, in *White Leviathan* (forthcoming), Mills gives an account of "materialist constructivism," which highlights how society is created by "interactions [that are] nonetheless bodily ones, phenomenologically experienced and cognitively and affectively interpreted through a politicized flesh, shaped throughout by social domination" (Chapter 3). While the book expands our understanding of how embodied experience might be theoretically situated within social contract theory, I argue that Mills's aim of "retrieving" a racist contract tradition for radical emancipatory ends requires an even more serious turn to the body than *White Leviathan* gives us. To make my case, I turn to the work of María Lugones.

The chapter proceeds in four parts. Section One outlines Mills's account of the "domination contract" and raises a critique by Alison Bailey (2007), who argues, drawing on María Lugones, that theorizing within the contract tradition undermines logics of resistance. In Section Two, I outline Lugones' account of purity and curdled logics as they relate to categories and concepts within racialized and gendered epistemologies of ignorance. In Section Three, I offer a reading of Mills through this framework which offers new insights about the way his commitment to the historically racist tradition can be read as successfully resistant,

DOI: 10.4324/9781003349983-3

while in Section Four, I expose the limits of Mills's strategy. I argue that the process of social contracting, even in Mills's modified formulation, maintains a commitment to rational abstraction as a normative methodology for generating principles of (corrective) justice. I end with a gesture toward how Mills might activate greater liberatory potential within his radicalized liberalist framework.[2]

The Domination Contract

According to Carol Pateman, "The most famous and influential political story of modern times is found in the writings of the social contract theorists" (1988, 1). Thomas Hobbes, John Locke, Jean-Jacques Rousseau, Immanuel Kant, and more recently, John Rawls, have had widespread influence both inside and outside of the academy using a very simple but powerful idea meant to explain or justify (or both) the basic structure of society (or the State): the social contract. In Rawls' widely influential formulation, one is to imagine an "original position" from which the social contract is forged. Here, one sits behind a "veil of ignorance" in which one knows nothing about the social position one might occupy in society, whether privileged, oppressed, or somewhere in between. As such, all contractors have a long-term self-interest, which is distinct from the kind of short-term self-interest that guides the prudential reasoning in Hobbes's contractarianism (Mills, forthcoming, Chapter 3), in generating principles of justice that would secure the best possible outcome for all groups of people once the veil is lifted. In this way, society can be understood as "a cooperative venture for mutual advantage" (Rawls 2009 [1971]).

Mills believes contract theory can and should be salvaged for the aims of social justice because it already enjoys such widespread authority in democratic political life. Therefore, he has spent much of his academic career aiming to "radicalize" the theoretical apparatus for liberatory anti-racist aims. To understand how this works, I want to remind us of what Mills means by the "contract" he wishes to salvage. He has a minimalist conception, with which Mills thinks all those fighting against oppressive structures would need to agree, that is, the "simple insight that humans create the sociopolitical, and in the process themselves" (2007b, 14). This is important because he does not think that it is toward *this* contract that critiques of contract theory should be directed. For this minimal sense is not refuted by the history of social oppression: humans are responsible for this history. And crucially, this conception helps us see that fact; without this model, we would be left with the alternative view that racism and sexism are *natural* (or biological), rather than human-made. (If we did not make the social world, how else would we explain such dramatic inequality?) And so, we should not "throw away contract theory" altogether but should assume its most minimal form—the human-created nature of society—which in turn is a conceptualization that can guide rectification: if humans created it, humans can change it. Secondarily, Mills wants to retain a normative dimension of the contract, namely, a commitment to "universal moral egalitarianism" in which the fact of all people being morally equal means we should strive toward political equality, or equal protection under the law for all.

The problem with social contract theory, then, is not the idea of a social contract per se, but with the contingent, historical contract (whether actual or theoretical), or the "thicker auxiliary shaping assumptions" (2007b, 86) which considered only property-owning white men to be "contractors" or "persons" at all. For this historical fact has meant that only some people have enjoyed basic political rights, are protected by the state, or are participants in the "cooperative" societal project at all. Given Rawls' aim to provide tools for generating principles of the just society, it seems odd that substantial engagement with issues of racism, sexism, xenophobia, homophobia, and the like is absent, given the role of these issues in preventing justice from emerging in the contemporary world. In his groundbreaking book, *The Racial Contract,* Mills argues that if the social contract is to serve anti-racism or other forms of social justice, it must avoid the kind of idealizing that Rawls' thought experiment requires. Abstracting away from the historical realities of domination and subordination obscures how such realities have shaped both the descriptive and normative dimensions of any social contract conceived or forged thus far. But this *perpetuates* injustice by promoting ignorance of it, thereby undermining the purported aims of the tradition.

And so, Mills gives us a modified contract, namely, the Domination Contract, which is the genus to more particular instances such as the Racial Contract, the Sexual Contract, the Racia-Sexual Contract, and others.[3] In all forms, the Domination Contract describes the historical contract as one forged in and by conditions of domination and subordination, building into its very framework an acknowledgment of the way by which moral and political status has been denied for most people, and also the way by which such exclusion has created and justified today's global white supremacist state (in the case of the Racial Contract). The Domination Contract is thus reparative to deceptive conceptualizations of the social world which include "everyone" as willing political actors, resisting the (white) ignorance, which follows from such "race-neutral" understandings, and supporting a shift from ideal to non-ideal theorizing. In this way, Mills's formulation functions as a consciousness-raising device, making complete sense of the fact that we find ourselves in a social world where women and non-white people are subordinated and ill-protected by laws and policies never meant to serve them. By illuminating the gap between historical and contemporary material realities and the social contract as it has been conceived of both descriptively and normatively, the Domination Contract provides the conceptual tools needed to seek *corrective* justice within the already widely influential contracts framework. However, insofar as "the mainstream version of the contract fails to acknowledge its racist [and more generally oppressive] foundations, it sabotages the radical potential of the apparatus" (Mills 2007, 89); without such a reckoning, we are thwarted in our ability to take responsibility for this history.

On Mills's version of the famous Rawlsian thought experiment then, one sits behind only a partial "veil of ignorance," because one has knowledge that includes the history of European expansionism in modernity, and the creation of white settler states (i.e., the workings of the Domination Contract). One then generates principles of rectificatory justice from this viewpoint.[4] In this way, Mills identifies and corrects for the racist epistemology at the foundation of social contract theory:

> So it is not, at least for me not [...] a matter of rejecting the contract figure as an illuminating way of encapsulating the truths of human equality and the human construction of the sociopolitical, but of *complicating it* so as to register the history of the exclusion of the majority of the population from the promise of liberal modernity.
>
> *(2015b, 546, my emphasis)*

His acknowledgment of these foundations, however, raises questions about his continued commitment to the tradition, and many of Mills's critics remain doubtful that his intervention goes far enough in securing a framework hospitable to gendered and racialized minorities.[5]

Representative of what I take to be a common critique of Mills's work, namely, that the resistance potential of Mills's philosophical apparatus is limited by its embeddedness in a deeply racist tradition of thought.[6] Alison Bailey in "Strategic Ignorance" critiques Mills's decision to theorize "within the language and logic of social contract theory" (2007, 78), arguing it undermines logics of resistance due to the inadequacy of centering stories and frameworks of non-white subjectivities. Bailey's view is resonant with Kristie Dotson's (2014) idea that resisting the harmful resilience of oppressive epistemological systems requires going "outside" of them. Here, the "oppressive epistemological system," is contract theory itself. While I agree with Bailey's specific claims, I would like to consider the resistance potential of Mills's attempt to write from *within* social contract theory, despite the racist foundations that he himself identifies. For, drawing on María Lugones' work, Bailey agrees that "there are ways of using the dominator's tools that do not [only] replicate dominance" (2007, 87) and that one can "strategically act in ways that conform to white expectations" (88) as a clandestine way of resisting.

What new insights emerge when we read Mills's Domination Contract in this Lugonesian spirit? On my view, we can notice how Mills is effective as a resistant actor through the way he complicates mainstream conceptions of "contract," as well as traditional and racist conceptions of "personhood." Given the widespread worry about the limits of Mills's emancipatory ambitions, my hope is to offer a new way of thinking about what resistance might look like in this context. This is not to diminish the content and stakes of these common critiques, ones I am often sympathetic with, but rather to create new opportunities for coalition-building as well as more expansive conceptions and avenues for resistance.

Purity and Curdled Logics

In "Purity, Impurity, and Separation," María Lugones writes about two different kinds of logics: "purity logic" and "curdled logic," both of which can be described by different modes of *separation*. Lugones explains purity logic as separating through splitting, using the metaphor of split-separating yolk from egg white. "The intention is to separate, first cleanly and then, in case of failure, a bit messily, the white from the yolk, to split the egg into two parts as cleanly as one can" (2003 [1994], 121). The intention of purity logic is thus to exert control over the messiness of multiplicity through fragmenting things into "pure elements" or pure parts, apart from their actual metaphysical inextricability from other parts. To be fragmented means to be "in fragments, pieces, parts that do not fit well together; parts taken for wholes." Crucially, the underlying assumption for the "lover of purity" is that *unity underlies multiplicity*. In this case, the fact of the impure multiple messy egg composed of impure multiple messy parts is understood as (pure) Egg—composite of (pure) Egg Yolk and (pure) Egg White—an assumption which guides and justifies the process of split-separation; the less "white" the yolk is, the more perfectly "Yolk" is, even if such separation is entirely unnatural, and in the end, impossible to completely achieve (and thus fictitious).

Within a social world in which purity logic dominates, not only things but individuals and groups are split-separated into "pure" elements or parts. This impacts what, who, and how we can know (the epistemic dimension of purity logic), often guided by what and who we assume exists at all (the ontological dimension of purity logic). Although we are all messy multiple beings on Lugones' view, she centers her discussion on those whose multiplicitous identities are fore-fronted by dominant conceptual frames, as is the case with Mexican-Americans.[7] Lugones argues that the purity-dominant Anglo imagination conceptualizes Mexican-Americans as being constituted by two essential yet fully separable "pure" parts: the authentic Mexican self and the fully assimilated American self. Any special knowledge that might be afforded to those with the distinctive in-between or hybrid identity of "Mexican/American" is thereby disregarded through this conceptual process which split-separates the Mexican half as inessential to the American half and the American half as inessential to the "authentic," "traditional," and "ornamental" Mexican half. "The ornamental nature of the Mexican self resolves the contradiction" because the Mexican self, crucially, is "over there," and so irrelevant, conveniently privileging the viewpoint of the illusory fully assimilated American self (2003, 135). This process of conceptualizing people harmfully limits what knowledge is available for uptake, guided by limited ontological assumptions about the kinds of beings that exist. In this case, purity logic protects the resilience of white supremacy by dismissing the distinctive knowledges multiple beings and hybrid experiences hold—knowledges needed for obtaining a more accurate, less racist, understanding (and ontology) of the world.

In contrast, curdled logic resists this "pure" way of categorizing and approaching the world, and is compared by Lugones to a different kind of separation, *curdled/separation*, this time using the metaphor of making mayonnaise:

> I place the yolk in a bowl, add a few drops of water, stir, and then add oil drop by drop, very slowly, as I continue stirring. If I add too much oil at once, the mixture se *separa*, it separates. [...] In English, one might say that the mayonnaise curdled [...] When an emulsion curdles, the ingredients become separate from each other. But that is not altogether an accurate description: rather, they coalesce toward oil or toward water, most of the water becomes separate from most of the oil—it is instead, a matter of different degrees of coalescence.
>
> *(2003, 122)*

When mayonnaise separates, "you are left with yolky oil and oily yolk." Curdled logic thus embraces complexity, ambiguity, and tension—something or someone is neither/nor, but kind of both, not quite either" (122)—and in doing so resists the control of possibilities that purity logic's attempted hard-edged split-separations seek. There is no "pure Mexican" or "pure American." There are only ever multiplicitous persons and groups of persons whose parts are overlapping and inseparable. Curdled understanding resists ignorance when embraced and practiced because it is simply an epistemically superior, or truer, perspective on reality. In other words, purity is a fiction, falsified by diverse bodily experiences and material conditions themselves. This point will end up being especially important for the latter part of my analysis; if bodily experience can falsify harmful purity, then epistemic norms, which dismiss the importance of bodily experience might inadvertently promote it.

For Lugones, then, instead of Mexican-American, one is *mestiza*, "ambiguous given the available classification of things" (122), thereby defying "control through simultaneously asserting the impure, curdled multiple state and rejecting fragmentation into pure parts ...

she has no pure parts to be 'had,' controlled." Many other concepts emerging from various literatures also illustrate this idea of curdling, threatening by their "very ambiguity the orderliness of the system, of schematized reality" (122). Interventions like "intersectionality" (Crenshaw 1989),[8] "queer," "quare" (Johnson 2001), "assemblage" (Puar 2018), "curdle" (Lugones 2003), "mestiza" (Anzaldúa 2015 [1987]), "matrix of domination" (Collins 1990), and many more are united in their desire to better track the complexity and diversity of bodily experience and the material world, grounding such concepts *within* the messiness or impurity of experience rather than abstracting away from it. In doing so, they resist reductive and colonial imaginations, which attempt to tame and control multiplicity, in turn germinating a non-oppressive consciousness, which is non-oppressive insofar as it opens further possibilities for coalition-building.

Curdled Contracts

Equipped with Lugones' analysis, I believe we can read aspects of Mills's account as effectively resistant, curdling the critique that theorizing within contracts discourse undermines logics of resistance. Mills shows what Lugones (2003, 133) calls "against-the-grain creativity" in his (re)conceptualization of the social contract as one of domination; this intervention has the result of complicating and curdling contract theory itself, as well as its conception of personhood. To see this, I would like to first note that purity logic itself cannot be pure; or rather, purity logic cannot be split-separated from curdled-logic as if these are two separate and essentialized ways of cognizing the world. This is because the problem with purity logic is its denial of multiplicity. As such, resisting its harmful dominance will require holding purity logic itself as "impure," or as coexisting interdependently, multiply, with other logics. *This is just the curdled/resistant nature of curdled-/logic.*

Resistance will require something more complex than a simple splitting away from purity logic, however appealing the imagining of such separation, as if

> I could go away with my own people to our own land to engage in acts that were cleanly ours! But then I ask myself who my own people are [...] being in the middle of either/or [...] separation into clean, tidy things and beings is not possible for me because it would be the death of myself as multiplicitous and a death of community with my own. I understand my split or fragmented possibilities in horror. I understand then that whenever I desire separation, I risk survival by confusing split separation with separation from domination, that is, separation among [other] curdled beings who curdle away their fragmentation, their subordination.
>
> *(Lugones 2003, 134)*

In other words, for Lugones, resistance is not simply a matter of split-separating from domination, either physically or conceptually. This would only reify harmful either/or thinking, thus making it impossible to form deep coalition with impure others, who inhabit themselves and the world somewhere in between this dualistic thinking and being. Crucially, solidarity requires "curdling away one's fragmentation." But what does this mean? She goes on:

> When seen from the logic of curdling, the alteration of the impure to unity is seen as fictitious and as an exercise in domination: the impure are rendered uncreative, ascetic,

static, realizer of the contents of the modern subject's imagination [for example, the Mexican-American]. Curdling, in contrast, realizes their against-the-grain creativity, articulates their within structure-inarticulate powers.

(2003, 133)

The remarks above could apply to any reduction of a multiplicitous person or viewpoint. And one such reduction might be that someone or something, like Mills or contract theory, is "resistant" or "oppressive," when in fact, most people and things, including Mills and contract theory, contain elements of both. Equipped with this insight, what I would like to suggest is that Mills, by choosing to write within a tradition that has excluded Black persons in the past, exemplifies a curdled activity within that tradition. He resists a split-separation which might look like denouncing contract theory wholesale due to its racism. By saying this, I do not mean to suggest that leaving inhospitable spaces cannot also constitute an act of curdling. Lugones points out that "withdrawing our services from the pure or their agents whenever possible and with panache" is an act of curdling (2003, 122). I am rather suggesting that sometimes remaining within such spaces can also be a resistant act.[9]

Mills seems to share the view that both approaches may well have benefits and costs worth considering:

> Subordinated social groups trying to develop an emancipatory politics routinely face the problem of how to relate to the frameworks, principles, and ideals officially promulgated by those who dominate the social order. Should they seek to adapt these frameworks, principles, and ideals to their own ends, or should they attempt to devise alternatives? The former strategy has the (seemingly) obvious virtue of self-positioning within the mainstream, taking up a conceptual and normative apparatus already familiar and socially hegemonic, albeit for unfamiliar and anti-hegemonic purposes. The possible downside is that this apparatus—shaped, after all, by long-established exclusionary practices—will turn out to be more refractory than hoped to any such appropriation. The latter strategy has the (seemingly) obvious virtue of jettisoning altogether the oppressor's creation, the master's tools, for one's own original liberatory vision.
>
> *(Mills 2018, 1)*

In his academic career, we see Mills's commitment to making radical interventions within the mainstream whether it be Kant, Marx, or Rawls. In doing so, he shakes up (stirs around, curdles), but does not pull out, the colonized ground upon which the discipline stands. Given that Mills himself recognizes the unconscious influence of contracts discourse on much of the US (and global) populace, he may be skeptical that we could "do away with contract theory" even if we were to consciously denounce and withdraw our attention from it.

Mills reflectively advocates for his own approach to racist philosophical traditions in "Black Radical Kantianism" (2018). Here, he argues that ignoring the racism inherent in Kant's enterprise by attributing it to irrelevant historical prejudices is problematic, as is doing away with Kant's work altogether. Mills invites a third alternative: apply the critique to the theoretical apparatus itself to reveal insights that otherwise might be occluded. By doing so, Mills produces a "color-conscious Kantianism," which curdles traditionally sexist and racist notions of personhood[10] and resolves contradictions between Kant's proclaimed universalism on the one hand, and his racism on the other. Rachel Zuckert puts Mills's contribution like this:

> Mills is driven by, and eloquently elicits in his readers, a recognition of painful incongruities: between Kantian moral and political ideals of respect for all persons and the modern Western history of racially structured subordination and disrespect, continuing to this day; between those ideals and Kant's own hierarchically structured—white supremacist—race theory.
>
> *(2022, 526)*

Despite the "painful incongruity," Mills reveals "there is no actual contradiction once we recognize that the egalitarian assumptions and pronouncements in the moral/political/teleological writings are really referring to the (male subset of the) superior race (i.e., whites)" (2018, 8). Applying anti-racist understandings of personhood to Kant's system in this way highlights the Domination Contract at work through a purity logic in which white men are harmfully split-separated out from the rest of humanity, yet simultaneously taken to be the Whole (or at least the pinnacle) of it. More specifically, Mills (2005) controversially proposes that Kant understands non-white people to be humans but not full persons, that is, "untermenschen." This idea is empirically supported by policies like the Three-Fifths Compromise that considered Black men three-fifths of a person for the sake of representation. Importantly, the use of purity logic is not unique to Kant but historically permeates the tradition. Insofar as we fail to bring conscious attention to how theory and practice have been shaped by such racism and sexism (often systemically), contemporary scholars remain vulnerable to inheriting and unconsciously perpetuating that harm and its supportive purity logic today.

Through his conception of the Domination Contract, Mills resists such harm and logic by staying within the tradition, within its non-ideal conditions, in order to change it/them. If taken seriously as a theoretical intervention, the modified contract is immanently corrective by honoring personhood where historically it has been disregarded—one cannot describe or perceive violations of social and political rights if one does not honor those who have been violated as persons in the first place. Mills gives us the new, necessary starting point for any social contract theorist serious about their liberatory aims and commitments: the actual domination and subordination in our shared social/political/theoretical worlds. Only from here can we move toward actual justice through the creation of reparative social contracts.

Mills's intervention indeed moves us toward such repair. As Linda Martín Alcoff puts it:

> There is no question that his writings helped to set in motion a new period of intense debate and analysis over the ways in which race and racism have operated implicitly in today's mainstage developments in normative political theory and ethics. And he won a wide multi-racial audience around the world who were persuaded that neither Kant nor Rawls should be taught in the old way, ever again.
>
> *(2024, 217)*

Mills's intervention has transformed the tradition's literature, methodology, and framework. The definition of "contracting" is no longer naïve about autonomous subjects making decisions with other autonomous subjects, and personhood cannot be taken for granted in the same way it could within previous "race-neutral" and "gender-neutral" analyses. Neither throwing away social contract theory wholesale nor utilizing it uncritically offers this same seed for resistance. And while there is continued resistance to Mills's framework within mainstream social and political philosophy, it is also true that philosophy as a discipline has not been the same since Mills's intervention. The field is richer, more complex, more accurate, and more hospitable because it considers issues of oppression.[11] By working within structures never meant to accommodate them, Lugones and Mills created new emancipatory possibilities, inspiring new alliances in the fight for justice along the way.

Let's Keep Stirring

While Mills "reveals the [oppressive] process of producing order" within contracts discourse, he "cannot help [but re-] produce it" himself (Lugones 2003, 145). What still cannot be heard within a contract theory modified by Mills? I argue we can get an even deeper transformation of the idea of contracting than Mills has so far provided by thinking about the importance of embodied experience for producing principles and policies of corrective justice within his modified Rawlsian framework. Unfortunately, the chapter of Mills's forthcoming book in which he works out the details of his newly theorized material constructivism within the modified thought experiment, remains unfinished. As such, the shortcomings I aim to highlight in this section speak less to the shortcomings of his most up to date views and more (I imagine) to the direction he was heading.

First, let's consider Lugones' reminder that split-separating is not just something that happens "out there" to objects or subjects of analysis or recognition but is also something that is done to ourselves as inquirers. Specifically, we do this when we aim to split-separate cleanly our rational parts from our embodied parts, a "purity logic of the self," which has pervaded "mainstream" conceptualizations of good inquiry and deliberation in the tradition. Contractualists, for example, often characterized and even assessed their own personhood and that of others in terms of rational capacity, whereby the distinctive value of persons concerns the capacity to give and assess reasons. Since rational deliberation is at the heart of generating principles for a just society, those believed to lack rational capacities are de facto excluded from any such political process. Occupying this "rational standpoint" which constitutes personhood, however, concurrently requires an attempted split-separation from one's direct, unabstracted, embodied experience, an experience which is often messier and more contradictory than our clean split-separated concepts would have us admit. As Lugones puts it:

> purification into someone who can step squarely onto the vantage point of unity [i.e. Reason] requires that his remainder become of no consequence to his own sense of himself as someone who justifiably exercises control over multiplicity. [...] And it is important to his own sense of things and of himself that he pay little attention to the satisfaction of the requirements of his sensuality, affectivity, and embodiment.
>
> *(2003, 130)*

While Mills quite consciously does not ascribe to this Reason-defined personhood, and aims to combat the egregious social hierarchies such understandings of personhood have supported, we can locate vestiges of this harmful ideology, I think, in his re-imaginings of Rawls' original position.

In *Contract & Domination*, Mills argues that contractors should know the history of racial domination and subordination behind the veil of ignorance. This is an important modification, which works to avoid the kind of ignorance about the world which follows from prescriptions for idealized abstraction. However, Mills also claims that contractors should remain ignorant of their own identity characteristics, including race, gender, sexuality, class, ethnicity, religion, and so on. Armed with such ignorance, policies of corrective justice can be forged without bias since one then reasons according to the equal possibility of being a member of some subordinate or dominant group. As such, one has a (long-term) self-interest in securing the most advantageous principles for all groups, considered together, thereby promoting the best possible outcome for whatever group one finds oneself in when the veil is lifted:

> What would you choose behind the veil on prudential grounds (worried that you might turn out to be, say, black) if you knew your options were limited to non-ideal societies shaped by the legacy or white supremacy, and regulated respectively by corrective public policy measures ranging from non-existent to very strong?
>
> *(Pateman & Mills 2007, 22)*[12]

Such a move, again, allows Mills to avoid idealized abstraction about the social world; however, by requiring an ignorance of one's identity, he remains committed to an idealized *method* of rational deliberation in which one split-separates from one's own social embodiment and experience to generate principles of corrective justice. But within such a conception of contracting, contractors appear "homogeneous in their ability to comprehend and communicate"; or simply, "postcultural," (Lugones 2003, 130) occupying precisely the kind of fictitious "neutral" philosophical standpoint Lugones is worried about. Difference appears flattened by an idealized vantage point, which abstracts away from the realities of particular bodily lives.

Mills might reply that his prescription for self-ignorance does not preclude the relevance of embodied experience behind the veil. Experiential knowledge could still be considered by contractors; this would not be first-hand phenomenological data, since one does not know one's own identity, but rather knowledge achieved through testimony, art, and other cultural artifacts, which depict the experiences of dominant and subordinated groups of people under the non-ideal social conditions we have access to within the modified thought experiment. On this line of argument, understanding the subjective experience of various groups of people is an important facet of what occurs behind the veil. Mills says something along these lines in his response to a related objection raised by Chris Lebron (2013) which concerns whites not having the subjective experience of racial domination behind the veil. Without such information, on Lebron's view, whites will be unable to imagine themselves as Black, and so will not be able to make judgments according to such a possibility. In response, Mills argues.

> That knowledge, deriving from R2 testimony [or the testimony of those who have been racially subordinated), is indeed going to be crucial to the prudential decision making of the R1s [or those who are part of the racially dominant group, but who do not know

> what group they are part of behind the veil] as they weigh the possibility of turning out to be R2s once the veil is lifted. But it is allowed entry, not precluded, by my revisionist reframing of Rawls's set-up as a way of deriving principles of justice for a non-ideal, ill-ordered racist society, which will require an informed picture of what such a society is actually like.
>
> *(2019, 17)*

In other words, Mills seems to agree that understanding what it is like to live in a society of domination and subordination, not just descriptively, but in a way that is richly perceived, plays a necessary role in arriving at the best principles of corrective justice. "Ignorance about one's [and others'] identity is only supposed to preclude self-serving biases, not critical awareness of racial inequality itself," says Mills. But, does ignorance about one's own identity have the capacity to preclude such biases? And furthermore, can such a normative standpoint for generating principles of corrective justice accommodate the transformative potential of embodied experience that Lugones and other feminist and queer theorists highlight as central to social justice? Let us consider an example to ground our analysis.

We could imagine that contractors are aiming to generate corrective anti-discrimination policy. Armed with Mills's political framework, contractors or policymakers would have access to information regarding the shortcomings and harm of anti-discrimination law as it has been formulated under white supremacy and patriarchy. Perhaps they have access to, for example, Kimberlé Crenshaw's (1989) work, which outlines how anti-discrimination law defined through a single-axis framework disproportionately harms women of color by making them problematically choose race *or* gender discrimination for their legal claims (but not both). Importantly, Crenshaw's work is empirical, guided by the actual experiences of women of color trying to navigate anti-discrimination law toward social and legal protection. In addition to such information, let's assume contractors also have access to art and other cultural artifacts, and also testimony from women who have directly experienced the harm of this inadequate legal landscape. In the best of cases, policymakers are given all external information for understanding what living under such a doctrine "is actually like" for those who are most vulnerable to its violence. Would such data points, coupled with ignorance about one's own identity characteristics and those of other contractors, be sufficient for generating the right corrective policies? After all—anyone could be in the least advantaged position since no one knows who they are (or will be) on Mills's criteria of self-ignorance. Could anti-discrimination law as it (still) stands be corrected by such a process, so that it finally meets the demand for universal protection social contract theorists espouse?

At first glance, I think "maybe." But upon deeper consideration, I find the idea that one could generate corrective anti-discrimination principles for a just society without knowing one's own socialized embodiment to be implausible, and for at least two reasons. First, without having access to one's own or others' identity characteristics, contractors are precluded from doing the necessary reflective and communicative work needed to correct for the very kinds of self-serving biases that worry Mills in the first place. This is because our identity characteristics dictate so much of our *unconscious* experience of self and others, as well as our interpretations of those experiences. Second, Mill's prescription for self-ignorance within the Rawlsian apparatus precludes genuine empathy or care for others as a primary motivator of justice. We should briefly consider both lines of response.

First, I am assuming we can agree that this kind of self-ignorance is impossible to achieve outside of thought experiments; we can never actually split-separate our "political" or "rational" parts from our embodied parts (which include things like our gender and race). Just because this is an impossible goal, however, doesn't mean we shouldn't try. Whether or not we should try depends on the benefits and harms of the attempt. Given this, we might ask what the benefit of aiming toward such a standpoint could be despite its impossibility. On Mills's view, the benefit is that it can preclude self-serving biases. But I am not sure I agree. Isn't it by aiming to attend to one's own socially situated identity, and that of others, that we can best correct for possible biases? Consider a juror who is from the South aiming to remain unbiased upon hearing testimony from a fellow Southerner whom he feels a "natural affinity" toward. Wouldn't understanding his own situatedness and that of the testifier be precisely the information he needs to attempt toward neutrality? Couldn't aiming to remain ignorant about these facts just result in them "slipping in through the back door" to determine judgment after all?

I think so. And this is because much of racism and sexism is experienced unconsciously, as embodied habits (Sullivan 2006, Mills forthcoming).[13] Since we cannot split-separate our rational and embodied parts away from one another, simply not knowing one's own identity will fail to correct for the different ways embodied beings take in data points for generating principles of justice. Given this impossibility, unless we assume contractors are merely the kind of "post cultural" subjects about which Lugones worries, we cannot assume art and other cultural artifacts, coupled with testimony, which seeks to share experiences of the inadequate anti-discrimination law, will elicit the same (i.e., appropriate or "reasonable") affective, rich understandings for all contractors. If we could imagine this, then without disagreement or productive epistemic friction (Medina 2013), it's hard to imagine what "rational *deliberation*" would look like at all—we'd need merely a single contractor who has all the relevant information needed for "discovering" corrective justice, which would be the most reasonable principles that follow from such information alongside self-ignorance. More realistically, contractors will experience differential cognitive and physical dissonance upon engagement with the art, cultural artifacts, and testimony under consideration. Given this, we should aim to responsibly bring awareness to unconscious (racialized) responses, or to how our bodies are taking in these rich data points—if I find myself feeling skeptical or overly identificatory, judgmental, angry, or confused, etc. when engaging with testimony regarding the single-axis framework, then as a responsible contractor, I should reflect on those feelings with myself and with others, asking why they might be coming up and what they might be telling me about potential biases I need to correct for. But this will require attending to, rather than overlooking, facts about social identity.

Moreover, aiming to be ignorant of one's social situatedness is *already* aligned with the prescriptive norms of impartiality which supposedly guide contemporary social contracting, both judiciously and legislatively. But these norms has failed. Consider how aiming to operate from a "reasonable" or "unbiased" standpoint is often what justifies biased questions which undermine the credibility of those who have experienced sexual assault: "You did a lot of partying in college, right?" (an attorney for Brock Turner in 2015 who questioned a woman who claimed that Turner sexually assaulted her while she was unconscious), "Did you twerk" (an attorney for R. Kelly who questioned a woman who met Kelly at 17 during a concert and later testified that he sexually assaulted her), "What were you wearing," or most recently, "You didn't scream for help?" (an attorney for Donald J. Trump who questioned E. Jean Carroll in her rape case against the former president).[14] Or consider again the malconstruction of current anti-discrimination law—it was precisely by failing to attend to social identity that policy makers were able to take their own single-axis framework of identity as the policy guiding "norm." As Mills himself puts the idea, "Indifference to concerns about race and sex makes subjects white and male rather than genderless and raceless" (forthcoming, Chapter 3). A corrective law will therefore require a different approach—one which attends to social identity to assess various possibilities of differential impact. This might require an intentional consultation of diverse perspectives outside of the legislative body or a diversification of the legislative body itself (which would be my own prescription). In either case, knowledge rather than ignorance about one's own identity and that of other contractors will be needed.

My second response concerns the motivation behind Mills's prescription for self-ignorance behind the veil. On Mills's picture, following Rawls and others, it is *self-interest,* which drives contracting toward just outcomes. In other words, it's because *I could be the least disadvantaged person* when the veil is lifted that I create policies, which protect that possible self; to appropriately consider this possibility, self-ignorance (or an attempt at self-ignorance) is required. It is then my rich perception of what being disadvantaged under the current anti-discrimination policy which yields the judgment: "I do not want to suffer in that way." And this fear of suffering produces the "justness" of any corrective principles. Notice a contrast case: I richly perceive what it is like to live under current inadequate anti-discrimination policy, and this yields the judgment: "I don't want anyone to have to suffer like that!" This care for others' experience produces the "justness" of corrective principles. Whether or not the same results are obtained, there is a notable distinction between the motivations guiding justice in the two cases. I leave the question open regarding whether self-interest is a necessary, strategic, or palatable starting point, but note that placing such individualism at the heart of justice should, on my view, leave even the most conservative feminist uncomfortable. Any radicalization of contract theory that Mills has accomplished so far has not been accomplished by this commitment to individual self-interest as the driver of social justice.[15]

Gesturing toward Liberatory Potential

Armed with a curdled lens, Charles Mills's work on the Domination Contract can be interpreted as both successfully resistant and problematically limited. Multiplying conceptions of contracting and personhood within social contract theory has made social/political philosophy more hospitable as a discipline. But we need further modifications of the contracting process, a more "curdled conscious Rawlsianism" than Mills has so far given us if embodied experience is going to play its rightful role in co-creating a just world.[16] And co-creation should be the goal. As Mills himself (forthcoming, Chapter 3) puts it: "Only by admitting the ineliminable corporeality of the racialized (and gendered) body in the American body politic will we fully be able to understand its politics," and presumably, how to move from these politics to corrective justice. Furthermore, only by attending more seriously to the importance of embodied experience in the generation of a just world might a greater coalition between Millsian critical philosophy of race and feminisms, which emphasize the importance of embodiment for responsible knowledge production, be forged (especially women of color and decolonial feminisms). I believe Mills would be sympathetic to these new possibilities for coalitional scholarship.

On both interpretations of his work then, we need our complex, embodied, messy, oppressive, resistant, multiple selves to properly orient us toward ourselves and each other; we need to pay attention to and acknowledge, rather than dismiss, the fullness of ours and others' curdled beings. Given that Mills certainly does not advocate for the thought experiment as the only way one might go about generating corrective justice, he might agree that we can do away with the approach I have outlined toward rectificatory justice within contracts discourse. Alcoff notes that a serious reading of Mills's critical engagement with Kant or Rawls lends itself to the idea that "lines of argument from their work [can] be lifted [...] but the significant alterations required to make their massive moral theories truly inclusive forbid us to name the subsequent theory 'Kantian' or 'Rawlsian'" (Alcoff 2024, 217). And so, a truly "Millsian" account of justice will likely not require a process that split-separates contractors from the actual social world. Instead, they/we should stay exactly where they/we are, and stir. This is a starting place for justice I would fight for.

Notes

1 For example, among others, see Mills's remarks drawing on Alvin Goldman's work (1997, 95, 120), or his remarks in *Blackness Visible* (2015a, 190).

2 Thank you, first and foremost, to Charles Mills, who I was lucky enough to learn from intellectually and personally. May we carry on his legacy by engaging in brave scholarship, open hearted mentorship, and playfulness. I am also particularly grateful to José Medina, Rachel Zuckert, Linda Alcoff, and Emmalon Davis, who read and commented on full drafts of this chapter. I have also benefited from conversations with Carmen De Schryver, Whitney Lilly, Lauren Guilmette, Abigail Iturra, Cristiana Eltiste, Staci Slattery, Jennifer Nash, and Allen Wood.

3 Here, Mills is following in the footsteps of both Rousseau (1984 [1754]) and Pateman (1988), theorizing that society corrupts human nature, rather than the other way around, as theorists like Kant, Locke, and Hobbes claim.

4 However, the veil remains thick enough to bar knowledge of one's own identity characteristics, such as one's gender, race, class, etc., in Mills's view, to prevent biasing one's own social group in the generation of corrective principles. More on this in Section IV. According to Mills, one would also not have demographic racial ratios in the society (for example, am I in 1920s USA, where whites constitute 90% of the population, or in 1960s South Africa, where whites constitute 13% of the population), thereby ruling out the maximization of expected utility as a decision-making strategy.

5 See, for example, Pateman (2007, 15). According to one of Mills's imagined critics in Black Rights/White Wrongs (2017a): "American Liberalism in Particular Has Been so Shaped in its Development by Race that Any Emancipatory Possibilities Have Been Foreclosed." His reply: "It is precisely such shaping that motivates the imperative of recognizing the multiplicity of liberalisms, not merely for cataloging purposes but in order to frame them as *theoretical* objects whose dynamic requires investigation" (26–27). It is important to distinguish between the social contract as a tradition and the social contract as an idea. There is obvious overlap, but whether one can hold onto the idea of a social contract without "staying in the tradition" is an open question, and critiques toward Mills, as well as his response to those critiques, often conflate the two.

6 Mills (2017a, 14–27) considers ten types of critics (both real and imagined) who think his framework cannot be "radicalized" toward emancipatory ends. Mills clearly takes the critique very seriously.

7 Lugones uses slashes and hyphens intentionally, where slashes refer to split-separations (as in hard-edged), and hyphens refer to curdled/separation (as in either/or). See Lugones (2003, 122). I will follow her lead on these usages.

8 One can see how these ideas are taken up by intersectionality, where "additive approaches" to complex identities are critiqued. Women of color are not a composite of "Women" and "Black or brown" in ways that enable split-separation. Rather, these parts are entangled, enmeshed, and mutually constitutive. Mills has been critiqued for having an additive approach in his version of the domination contract which considers racial and gender oppression together in the racia-sexual contract. See Sullivan (2017) and Gines (2017) for these critiques, see Mills (2017b) for his response, and Pateman & Mills (2007) for the relevant chapter.

9 Thank you to Linda Martín Alcoff, who pointed out that one of Mills's primary reasons for holding onto some aspects of liberalism was motivated by his concerns about vanguardism (Mills 1990).

10 In Mills's latest work, he distinguishes between personhood as objective in the moral sense, and personhood in the social/political sense, which comes about through social recognition. Regarding the latter, "personhood needs to be recognized as a technical term, a term of art, whose defining characteristics are generally so devised as to make whiteness a prerequisite for personhood. Non-whites fall under an array of alternative categories—'savages,' 'barbarians,' 'natives'—whose common feature is generally their normative inequality" (Forthcoming, Chapters 2, 5). He therefore distinguishes between personhood as an attribution within political economies versus personhood as a moral fact.

11 Mills notes the progress which has been made despite the persistence of racism and sexism in the discipline:

> So there is a flurry of activity in multiple spheres, which—for those of us old enough to have been around in the 1980s and 1990s—is quite astonishing by comparison with those hard times. We are a long way from the period when Leonard Harris was unable to find any regular philosophy press for his pioneering book on Afro-American Philosophy, Philosophy Born of Struggle, and had to go with Kendall/Hunt, or when APA sessions on race and Africana philosophy were confined to the deadly late-night group program, with only a handful of diehards in attendance.
>
> *(Mills 2017b, 31)*

12 Given Mills commitment to something like Derek Bell's (1980) view of "convergent interests," where moral suasion will always be insufficient for moving whites or other dominant groups to act outside of their personal interests for aims of anti-racism, this mandated ignorance of one's own social positioning makes some sense: "materialism rules out moral motivation as a prime social mover, so it would have to be *perceived* group interest" (2017a, 9; my emphasis). In the revised thought experiment, one's perceived group interest is any possible group's interest given one's self-ignorance about group membership.

13 Mills takes this view as central to his project in *White Leviathan*, highlighting how the larger social body politic shapes these habits through attributions of personhood or sub-personhood.

14 These quotes and descriptions of them were drawn from Bennett (2023).

15 Mills (forthcoming, Chapter 1) makes clear that he is committed to moral individualism, or taking the individual as the locus of value for contract protections, but this doesn't, in his view require a descriptive individualism which denies the fundamental relationality of individuals.

16 This is consistent with Mills's claims that the "autonomous epistemic agent needs to be replaced by a 'community of knowers'" (2015a, 33).

Bibliography

Ahmed, Sarah. 2013. *The Cultural Politics of Emotion*. New York: Routledge.

Alcoff, Linda Martín. 2024. "The Life of Charles Mills, Radical Philosopher Extraordinaire." *Critical Philosophy of Race* 12 (2): 215–233.

Anzaldúa, Gloria [1987]. 2015. "Borderlands/La Frontera: The New Mestiza." In *This Bridge Called My Back: Writings by Radical Women of Color*. Edited by Cherríe Moraga and Gloria Anzaldúa. Albany: State University of New York Press.

Bailey, Alison. 2007. "Strategic Ignorance." In *Race and Epistemologies of Ignorance*. Edited by Shannon Sullivan and Nancy Tuana. Albany: State University of New York Press.

Bell, Derrick A., Jr. 1980. "Brown v. Board of Education and the Interest-Convergence Dilemma." *Harvard Law Review* 93 (3): 518–33.

Bennett, Jessica. 2023. "Why Didn't She Scream? And Other Questions Not to Ask a Rape Accuser." New York Times. May 2, 2023.

Collins, Patricia Hill. 1990. *Black Feminist Thought: Knowledge, Consciousness, and the Politics of Empowerment*. Boston: Unwin Hyman.

Crenshaw, Kimberlé. 1989. "Demarginalizing the Intersection of Race and Sex: A Black Feminist Critique of Antidiscrimination Doctrine, Feminist Theory, and Antiracist Politics." *University of Chicago Legal Forum* 1: 139–67.

Dotson, Kristie. 2014. "Conceptualizing Epistemic Oppression." *Social Epistemology* 28 (2): 115–38.

Gines, Kathryn T. 2017. "Black Feminist Reflections on Charles Mills's "Intersecting Contracts"." *Critical Philosophy of Race* 5 (1): 19–28.

Johnson, E. Patrick. 2001. "'Quare' Studies, or (Almost) Everything I Know About Queer Studies I Learned From My Grandmother." *Text and Performance Quarterly* 21 (1): 1–25.

Lebron, Christopher J. 2013. *The Color of Our shame: Race and Justice in Our Time*. New York: Oxford University Press.

Lugones, María. 1987. "Playfulness, 'World'-Travelling, and Loving Perception." *Hypatia* 2 (2): 3–19.

Lugones, María. 2003. "Purity, Impurity, and Separation." In *Pilgrimages/Peregrinajes: Theorizing Coalition Against Multiple Oppressions*. Lanham: Rowman & Littlefield Publishers.

Medina, José. 2013. *The Epistemology of Resistance*. New York: Oxford University Press.

Mills, Charles W. 1990. "Getting Out of the Cave: Tension Between Democracy and Elitism in Marx's Theory of Cognitive Liberation." *Social and Economic Studies* 39 (1): 1–50.

Mills, Charles W. 1997. *The Racial Contract*. Ithaca: Cornell University Press.

Mills, Charles W. 2005. "Kant's Untermenschen." In *Race and Racism in Modern Philosophy*. Edited by Andrew Valls. Ithaca, NY: Cornell University Press.

Mills, Charles W. 2007. "White Ignorance." In *Race and Epistemologies of Resistance*. Edited by Shannon Sullivan and Nancy Tuana. Albany: State University of New York Press.

Mills, Charles W. 2014. "Kant and Race." *Redux: Graduate Faculty Philosophy Journal* 35 (1-2): 125–57.

Mills, Charles W. 2015a. *Blackness Visible*. Ithaca: Cornell University Press.

Mills, Charles W. 2015b. "The Racial Contract Revisited: Still Unbroken after All These Years." *Politics, Groups, and Identities* 3 (3): 541–57.

Mills, Charles W. 2017a. *Black Rights/White Wrongs: The Critique of Racial Liberalism*. New York: Oxford University Press.

Mills, Charles W. 2017b. "Intersectional Meditations: A Reply to Kathryn Gines and Shannon Sullivan." *Critical Philosophy of Race* 5 (1): 29–50.

Mills, Charles W. 2018. "Black Radical Kantianism." *Res Philosophica* 95 (1): 1–33.

Mills, Charles W. 2019. "Theorizing White Racial Domination and Racial Justice: A Reply to Christopher Lebron." *Journal of Social Philosophy* 54 (3): 292–15.

Mills, Charles W. Forthcoming. *White Leviathan*. New York: Oxford University Press.

Pateman, Carole. 1988. *The Sexual Contract*. Cambridge: Polity Press.

Pateman, Carole, and Charles Mills. 2007. *Contract & Domination*. Cambridge: Polity Press.

Puar, Jasbir K. 2018. *Terrorist Assemblages: Homonationalism in Queer Times*. Durham: Duke University Press.

Rawls, John. 2005. *Political Liberalism*. New York: Columbia University Press.

Rawls, John. 2009 [1971]. *A Theory of Justice*. Cambridge: Harvard University Press.

Rawls, John. 2021. "Knowing How to Feel." *Hypatia* 36 (4): 725–47.

Rousseau, Jean-Jacques. 1984. *A Discourse on Inequality*. New York: Penguin Press.

Sullivan, Shannon. 2006. *Revealing Whiteness: The Unconscious Habits of Racial Privilege*. Bloomington: Indiana University Press.

Sullivan, Shannon. 2017. "'Smadditizin' Across the Years: Race and Class in the Work of Charles Mills." *Critical Philosophy of Race* 5 (1): 1–18.

Sullivan, Shannon, and Nancy Tuana. 2007a. *Race and Epistemologies of Ignorance*. Albany: State University of New York Press.

Sullivan, Shannon, and Nancy Tuana. 2007b. "Introduction." In *Race and Epistemologies of Ignorance*. Edited by Shannon Sullivan and Nancy Tuana. Albany: State University of New York Press.

Zuckert, Rachel. 2022. ""Memorial Introduction about Charles Mills," in the special issue "Radicalize Kant?"" *Kantian Review* 27 (4): 525–27.

3

CORRESPONDING CONTRACTS

The Intersectional Mills

Corey Reed

The Framing of the Framework

At the beginning of a dialogue between Charles W. Mills and Carole Pateman in *Contract & Domination*, Mills responds to Pateman with the following statement:

> The complexities of race, class, and sex, yes. It's so difficult to think them all together—like the many-body problem in mechanics—because they're all interacting with one another. My own case is interesting (to move to the personal level), since it's not just class, gender, and race, but nationality and ethnicity also, and how they affect the translation of these three across national boundaries.
>
> *(2007, 10)*

Mills, throughout his corpus, is concerned with, and attempts to build his frameworks alongside, intersectionality. However, three questions are apparent from his work: (1) To what extent is his work successful at being intersectional? (2) Are his critics correct in finding limitations to his work regarding certain oppressions? and (3) Can Mills's addendums to the traditions of contract theory and liberalism work with intersectional interests?

To answer these questions, and to get a broad understanding of how his work engages various forms of oppression beyond race, I organize this chapter in the following way. First, a distinction must be made regarding intersectionality's definition, as I will argue that one approach will describe Mills's work as less successful for intersectional objectives than another. Second, Mills's critics, especially those of the *racia-sexual* contract, illuminate some of the weaknesses of his theories for intersectional projects. By addressing those worries, the utility of Mills's work for intersectional concerns becomes more apparent. Third, a cross-analysis between his utilization of contract theory and liberalism will show both the strengths and weaknesses of using Mills's work for intersectional concerns.

Before I engage in these outlined points, I first want to explain three terms: sub-person, the domination contract, and contractualism. Mills defines sub-persons in *The Racial*

DOI: 10.4324/9781003349983-4

Contract as "humanoid entities who, because of racial phenotype/genealogy/culture, are not fully human and therefore have a different and inferior schedule of rights and liberties applying to them" (1997, 56). In *Contract & Domination*, not only does Mills explicate that a sub-person can qualify for both women and racialized people in the social contract, but he then describes the social contract as a *domination contract* and states that "under cover of egalitarianism, the domination contract generates norms, and stipulations about how to apply these norms, that will themselves reinforce domination, and so which need to be interrogated by those seeking to end their subordination by the contract" (2007, 90). For Mills, there are various kinds of interlocking contracts—racial, sexual, class, colonial, and the like. In all instances, the *domination contract* is one of exclusion.

To understand Mills's approach to intersectional issues, we must capture what he means by *contractualism*. Following Stephen Darwell's distinction between *contractarianism* and *contractualism* (where *contractarianism* derives from the social ideal of Thomas Hobbes, and the contract is about bargaining), Mills argues in favor of *contractualism*, via Immanuel Kant, whereby "morality is an object set of other-regulating rules, and the 'contract' is really (in [John] Rawls' phrase) a 'device of representation' for getting at what those rules are" (2007, 15). This is a critical starting point because despite his analysis of the social contract being political, moral, epistemological, etc., his reasoning behind utilizing this tradition for contemporary theorization, even with its vast critiques, derives from its moral value. The social contract is the theoretical vehicle that demonstrates what the rules should be for everyone in a social landscape. As he states in *The Racial Contract*, the contract illustrates "a schedule of rights, duties, and liberties that shapes a citizens' moral psychology, conceptions of the right, notions of self-respect, etc." (1997, 10). For Mills, the moral evaluation of a society is a complex relation between rights (positive and negative), duties, and how the psychology of the agents therein is shaped by the two former notions. With these definitions out of the way, let us turn to the question of how successful he is regarding intersectionality.

Crenshaw, Collins, and Mills: Intersectionality and the Racial Contract

Kimberlé Crenshaw introduces intersectionality in her 1989 law article, "Demarginalizing the Intersection of Race and Sex: A Black Feminist Critique of Antidiscrimination Doctrine, Feminist Theory and Antiracist Politics" (1989). Using three case examples, Crenshaw articulates that in the law's scope, at that time, there were interventions to conceptualize racism (the absence of Black employees, for example) and sexism (the absence of women), but there was not a framework to conceptualize the absence of Black women. Intersectionality, then, became a model to understand how forms of oppression can *intersect*. In a latter article, she defines intersectionality as a *location* of women of color, a coordinate by which people are situated by various axes of oppression. She states,

> In the previous sections, I have used intersectionality to describe or frame various relationships between race and gender. I have used intersectionality as a way to articulate the interaction of racism and patriarchy generally. I have also used intersectionality to describe the location of women of color both within overlapping systems of subordination and at the margins of feminism and antiracism.
>
> *(1991, 1265)*

Crenshaw's *original* definition, or at least the original application, for intersectionality was primarily concerned with the social location of the agent between varying parts of their identity and how systems lacked nuance to describe and rectify ways in which injustices connected and overlapped with other injustices. My intention here is not to limit Crenshaw's original approach or isolate it from Patricia Hill Collins' later uptake of the term. The goal here is to see how a certain interpretation of intersectionality can be better suited to Mills's work. Collins, in both her inaugural text with Sirma Bilge, *Intersectionality*, and in her more recent text *Intersectionality as Critical Social Theory*, takes a much more robust approach, describing intersectionality as "a paradigm, concept, framework, heuristic device, and theory" (2019, 3). Collins' approach captures many more dimensions of individual experiences and the nuances of one's life because of various aspects of her being. Intersectionality, in its more recent developments, is not about "oppression A plus oppression B equals oppression AB," it is about the unique experiences of the agent and how, when oppressions intersect, they become something unique, namely X. A key example is Moya Bailey's concept of *misogynoir,* which is not just "racism plus sexism," but a descriptive term for the negative treatment of Black women because of their Black womanhood (2021, 1). Put differently, *misogynoir*, a portmanteau of misogyny and *noir* [Black], refers to the inimitable interlocking oppression that Black women face for distinctively being Black women. Those two features—racism and sexism—cannot be understood properly if treated separately.

I argue that Mills's approach to intersecting or interlocking issues caters more to the original interpretations of intersectionality than some of the more recent perspectives. First, it is important to note that Mills's *domination contract* is meant to engage misconceptions of social contract interpretations and address the issues of non-ideal theory (2007, 80). In describing the Western contract tradition as an "exclusionary manipulative contract deployed by the powerful to subordinate others in a society under the pretext of including them as equals," Mills, by extension, gives language to the paradox of egalitarian ideals and various oppressions' coexistence broadly (82). He then makes a clear path for an intersectional component to the domination contract in the following quote:

> Class society, patriarchy, and white supremacy come into being not 'naturally' but as the result of collective human causality—in which, however, some humans have a far greater causal role than others, and institutions thereby established. The social contract in its guise as the domination contract captures these crucial 'descriptive' realities while simultaneously, by emphasizing their 'artificial' genesis, bringing them across the conceptual border from the realm of the natural into the realm of the political.
>
> *(87)*

Not only does Mills capture how these oppressive systems are socially created and facilitated phenomena, but he also articulates how they are hidden in a framework that claims to offer equality and justice. As he states, "this egalitarianism has been denied to women and non-whites both in theory and in practice" (88). The problem with Mills's framework is that he also argues for a normative *racia-sexual* contract, where "pre-existing patriarchal structures are modified by the emergent new structure of racial domination" (172). In this framework, "Whites as a group dominate non-whites as a group, while within these racial groups men generally dominate women" (173). Using a tilted diamond model, white men are at the top, as full contractors and persons, white women sit slightly above non-white men as sub-contractors and sub-persons, and non-white women are considered non-contractors and non-persons.

This works well only in reference to what Crenshaw was observing in her early law articles, especially in the *DeGraffenreid v. General Motors* case from 1976, a case that discusses whether a Black woman can be discriminated against for being Black and a woman. In other words, rather than appealing only to race or only to gender, the court needed to determine if Black womanhood should be considered a unique identity—one that is intersectional. The court determined that a plaintiff could not combine statutory remedies; that is, one must seek a remedy that ignored intersectional identity. This kind of *locality* that can be neatly mapped at an intersection is what intersectionality, as a tradition, has moved beyond. Although his framework has clear conceptual difficulties when it comes to multiple dimensions of being (like being a poor or queer white man and still full persons in the domination contract, or the environment and context being crucial to the power dynamic of a non-white man or white woman as sub-persons and sub-contractors capable of being dominated and dominating), it has benefits. Mills outlines four targets of this framework: first, it addresses "color blindness and gender blindness as simple blindness" (2007, 175). Second, it conceptualizes a *certain kind* of white man as full person and contractor to conceptualize the social (domination) contract as one that centers a certain agent, makes them the human, and all others are evaluated in this metric regarding proximity to this central agent (178). The third and fourth points conceptualize white women and non-white men as sub-contractors and sub-persons, underscoring racism in feminist movements and sexism in marginalized communities.

All four of these objective points, to different degrees, represent intersectionality's aims. Mills would conceptualize both kinds of blindness as products of an epistemology of ignorance (1997, 18), and color blindness in particular as a kind of "white ignorance," which includes "false belief[s] and absence of true belief" (2007, 16). Nina Lykke describes critiquing gender blindness, for example, as an objective not just to women's studies broadly, but to intersectionality (2010, 16). An objective of intersectionality is to decenter white men (whiteness and maleness) as the exemplar of experience (see Hardy2022). Intersectionality, as Crenshaw noted, took on the burden to address the failures of feminist and Black movements in giving Black women proper uptake. Mills's work concurs and takes the lack of agency and autonomy in the domination contract as something that needs to be articulated in his framework. However, as Mills's critics note, there are some failures in this framework. In the next section, I focus on a few rebuttals most in line with intersectional concerns.

Mills and His Critics on Contract Theory, Liberalism, and Intersectionality

Mills, in the "Intersecting Contracts" chapter of *Contract & Domination*, acknowledges and continues Black feminists' discussions of phrases like "racial patriarchy, racist patriarchy, white supremacist patriarchy, and so forth" (2007, 169). His general position is that

> the interlocking nature of the systems means that one cannot speak of the 'contracts' in isolation, since they rewrite each other. Or perhaps better (since patriarchy predates white supremacy, and the sexual contract—assuming a premodern incarnation—precedes the racial contract), the racial contract is written on patriarchal terms, and the sexual contract is rewritten on racial terms.
>
> *(172)*

There are two important conditions of Mills's thought exemplified here. First, Mills takes these contracts to shape one another, but if the racial contract is written on patriarchal terms, then the racial contract is quintessentially and foundationally patriarchal, whereas the sexual contract *becomes* racial. Second, he suggests that these contracts are dynamic and change significantly when they are rewritten. He describes a *racia-sexual contract* which, following the preceding conditions, asserts that although patriarchy predates white supremacy, "racial subordination [...] generally trumps gender" (172). He argues against the symmetry of racial/gender oppressions and instead asserts a series of asymmetries. Mills gives the example of non-white men's lack of normatively dominating white women as a rationale behind defining "the white supremacist patriarchal polity," or a framework for us to see the interconnections between the sexual and racial contracts without doing a 1:1 calculus (173).

Mills's "critics" are wide-ranging, especially on his approach to intersectionality. Keisha Lindsey, in her text "The Racial Contract: A Feminist Analysis," praises Mills's analysis of how race intertwines with other forms of oppression (2015, 531). However, her observation is that Mills's most complete thought about intersectionality is limited to a footnote in *The Racial Contract*, where he writes that "we all have multiple identities, and, to this extent, most of us are both privileged and disadvantaged by different systems of domination" (1997, 138). Although one might defend Mills for noting throughout his seminal work that Black women are often affected the most by the *racial contract*, it would be fair to say that Mills does not do much intersectional work until his text with Pateman, that is, *Contract & Domination*, which necessitates the answers he gives in the later work.

Mills's non-ideal theory is utilized in intersectional feminist theory regarding Asian women in the work of Youjin Kong, with the addendum that a "strong" non-ideal theory is needed to achieve the aims of intersectional feminist theory (2022, 872). The usefulness of Mills's work for intersectional aims is clear in these two authors; however, Mills's work evoked stronger criticisms from Shannon Sullivan and Kathryn Belle (formerly known as Kathryn T. Gines).

Kathryn Belle, in my reading, has two general concerns: 1) the reiterated note that race generally trumps gender that Mills states multiple times in the "Intersecting Contracts" (2007, 184–87), and 2) that Mills does not give deep enough of an account of non-white men's privileges, powers, and patriarchal domination of non-white women (Gines 2017, 27). The first concern I take to be Mills's way of rectifying his first claim that gender precedes race chronologically. Mills is in conversation with Carole Pateman's historical account of marriage and the restriction of women in *The Sexual Contract*, which precedes his book *The Racial Contract*. It was necessary for him to address how race *transforms*, or as he puts it, *rewrites* gender relations; however, the problem that Belle is addressing is the term *trumps*. This is the problem that Crenshaw's early work on intersectionality addressed: that race and gender needed to be thought about in tandem because of gaps that exist when they are thought of separately. Mills, however, does not capture the more recent thoughts about intersectionality, that race and gender create new phenomena and unique experiences that would make it impossible to judge the oppressions separately. Race cannot trump gender or vice versa because for Black women, for example, these two phenomena are bound up in each other.

Belle's second concern is a broader concern for all of us who are Black men working on feminist issues. A detailed account of our own positionality is often looked for because it requires us to address, to the fullest extent, our own privilege in what we write. Belle finds his analysis of non-white men insufficient, and it was doomed to be so, because of the broad stroke it is written in. Black men, Asian men, Latinx men, Indigenous men, etc., all fall within that umbrella of non-white men, and it is easier to isolate them as general sub-contractors and sub-persons: holding privilege and domination simultaneously. I find this largely insufficient, especially if we are thinking beyond the original intervention of intersectionality. Although Belle's concern is that "non-white men can be patriarchal, too" (2017, 17), my question is more "how can big umbrella terms like *non-white men*, and a neat paradigm like the *racia-sexual* contract, capture the intersectional complexities of multidimensional lives"? (26). Belle's concerns are warranted, but neither she nor I take them as dismissive of what this framework offers: a description of the asymmetries between race and gender (22), nuance to the "white problem" (24), and an account about how non-white men and white women have often used race or gender to strive toward personhood at the expense of others (25).

Mills describes Belle's two major critiques of *Contract & Domination*: "(1) that my 'racia-sexual contract' 'does not register [...] other multiplicities,' and (2) that in claiming that 'race generally trumps gender' I end up stop[ping] short of describing non-white men as dominating non-white women, and thereby 'understating the interplay of oppression and privilege for non-white men'" (2017b, 37). To this, Mills agrees but is worried by the growing number of agent-types that come about when we expand past race and gender:

> A hypothetical racia-sexual-straight contract would require the demarcation of eight positions: straight white men, gay white men, straight white women, white lesbians, straight non-white men, gay non-white men, straight non-white women, non-white lesbians. Imagine trying to represent diagrammatically the inter-relations of all those positions in two-dimensional space. Add a fourth variable and you get sixteen positions, and so on. [...] Critics might conclude (like [Shannon] Sullivan), that this problem demonstrates the intrinsic limitations of a "domination contract" model for representing intersectionalist oppression, and we need to develop some other approach.
>
> *(38–39)*

His worry, however, is at the heart of intersectional objectives and it is a complication that intersectionality embraces. I take Mills's "infinite intersections problem" to be the result of wanting a practical, accessible, and applicable theoretical model. Difficult pluralities, however, are the inevitable outcomes of the *domination contract* if we accept that 1) multiple oppressions are written into the domination contract and race/gender are not exhaustive in capturing said contract, and 2) agents have multiple aspects of their identities that correspond with various forms of oppression. I think Mills should be read as attempting to be pragmatic in his sketch of the *racia-sexual* contract, knowing (and hoping) that his work would be continued and expounded with this same contractualistic-intersectional framework.

Her second concern focuses on the privilege and patriarchal power of non-white men. Her concluding thought in her critique was, "I am struck by the fact that Mills can cite all of these women of color, their critiques of white women, their critiques of non-white men, and their articulations of intersectional oppressions and identities, and yet he can still insist that race generally trumps gender" (2017, 27). As stated before, Belle's concern is a general concern for intersectionality, regarding the treatment of race and gender as phenomena that additively adjoin instead of merge. I do not take Belle's critique to insinuate the antithesis that gender trumps race; instead, I take her critique as a rejection of models that treat the two as distinct, mutually exclusive, and isolated phenomena. Mills took Belle to be misreading him, but I would argue that both Mills's "Intersecting Contracts" and its critiques yield an important conclusion: intersectionality is, by definition and objective, nuanced, multidimensional, and untidy. I do not mean *untidy* as non-systematic or anti-theoretical; I am claiming that in a framework like Mills's, intersectionality does not illustrate neatly into the diamond shape he formulates in the "Intersecting Contracts" chapter. I take Mills to be aware, even before his critique by Belle, that this proposition of connecting the racial and the sexual contracts is just a starting point. As he suggests in the "Domination Contract" chapter of *Contract & Domination*, the social contract is inherently flawed in multiple ways, and intersectionality is a response to these conditions of domination.

I turn now to Shannon Sullivan's critique of Mills regarding the class and economic dimensions of intersectionality. Sullivan argues that there is a shift in Mills's thought in the 1990s, where Mills takes on the issue of race more than his original passion for Marxist critiques of class. There are a few important notes to take from Sullivan's analysis. First, Sullivan points out Mills' rejection of the Oppression Symmetry Thesis (OST) and asserts what she labels as an Oppression Asymmetry Thesis (OAT) in the text "From Class to Race" (2017, 6–7). The OAT, as she notes, is more in line with an intersectional approach. She claims,

> Intersectionality is far richer than this streamline definition [OST] can capture, but the point is that intersectionality's claim about co-constitution is not a claim that different forms of oppression are morally or casually equal. From the perspective of intersectionality, the main problem with symmetry claims of OST is that to make those claims, OST implicitly considers race, gender, class, sexuality, and other axes of existence to be fundamentally distinct and separable from each other—and is precisely the position that intersectionality challenges. The same problem plagues OAT, which from the viewpoint of intersectionality turns out to be the flip side of the same coin as OST. Whether symmetrical or asymmetrical, the comparisons made by OST and OAT implicitly work with an additive model of oppression that intersectionality refuses.
>
> *(7)*

Here, again, we find Mills doing a quasi-intersectional project. As Sullivan highlights, Mills is correct to reject this symmetrical model that treats all injustices as morally and causally the same. However, his attempt to create a neat model of asymmetry falls into the inverse issue that intersectional concerns cannot be boxed into "additive" models. Perhaps it is a misreading of early Crenshaw that leads to this reoccurring theme of treating oppressions as additive, or at least interlocking, while maintaining distinct features? However, what Mills is successful at, in my view, is understanding how contracts (using his language via the social contract tradition) *correspond* with one another. They are dynamic phenomena, and Mills understands that race informs gender, and vice versa (even though he takes gender to *precede* race more than it is *rewriting* race). How well Mills's work achieves intersectional goals depends on what texts we are referring to and what kind of reading we take to intersectionality's earlier texts.

Sullivan argues that Mills's work was not always this stringently additive in his earlier analysis of class, Marx, and the Caribbean. She notes, via Mills's 1987 text "Race and Class" (reprinted in 2010), "The relationship instead is one of fusion: ideational patterns of class position and race/color become fused together, rendering them inseparable" (2017, 9). What happened that made Mills's work change? Sullivan's hypothesis is that a shift in his work occurred after *The Racial Contract*, where his last explicitly Marxist text is "European Specters" in 1999 (reprinted in 2003) and everything afterward focuses largely on Mills's criticism, defense, and radicalization of liberalism (10). Sullivan offers ending comments to Mills, and the last I take to be the most critical for this project:

> I am skeptical that the insights of intersectionality can be "translated" into contract theory (as Mills says in *Contract & Domination*) without dismantling contract theory's additive analyses. While I applaud Mills' reference to intersectionality in his work with Carole Pateman, I think that translation is the wrong relationship to establish between intersectionality and contract theory. Something important about intersectionality is lost when it is translated into the pop-bed logic of contract theory even if that process helps expand asymmetrically the number of contractual status positions from two (white and black) to four (white men, white women, black men, and black women).
>
> *(13–14)*

Sullivan's conclusion implores Mills to *remake* contract theory instead of *translating* intersectionality into contract theory (14). This challenge is critical in understanding why frameworks like contract theory and liberalism may fall short in achieving intersectional aims. From Sullivan's perspective, Mills reads as doing "additive" analyses of oppression because the grounding framework, *contractualism*, is additive. There are a few rationales behind Mills's move to preserve contract theory and liberalism. It may have been an issue of social and political philosophy at the time (requiring the use of these traditions in order to be understood as "doing philosophy" on race). In that case, Mills is analyzing through his philosophical training and writes both *The Racial Contract* (1997) and *Contract & Domination* (2007) before Patricia Hill Collins expands intersectionality (2019).

Sullivan, following Vivian May's *Pursuing Intersectionality, Unsettling Dominant Imaginaries*, argues that "intersectionality does not concern only black women, nor is it restricted to race and gender. Instead, it grapples with the various and entangled relationships of power, privilege, and oppression that help constitute all of us, whatever our gender or race" (2017, 1). This is where class becomes relevant as a potentially understated aspect of intersectionality.

Mike Cole, in his analysis of Mills's work, takes Mills to lack significant depth regarding capitalism and socialism in his assessment of race. He asserts that "given the massive advantages to capitalism of racialized capitalism, capitalism without racism (or sexism) [...] is almost inconceivable" (2009, 257). Although I disagree with Cole's dismissal of Critical Race Theory and his faith that "an anti-racist/anti-imperialist Marxism" (263) captures all issues regarding antiblack racism, for example, I take Cole's assertion that the later Mills shies away from a Marxist format for a liberalistic (neo-Rawlsian) approach. However, Mills claims to have left open the possibility that a critique of racial capitalism vis-à-vis Marxism could be fruitful. Mills writes, "I do think that a *modified* historical materialism might be able to carry out an adequate conceptualization of the significance of race" (2003, xvi–xvii). In *Racism: A Critical Analysis*, Cole suggests that Mills' reliance on the term "white supremacy" tends to "the homogenization of all white people," and that it fails to acknowledge that many whites are economically harmed by capitalism (2016, 16). Mills does, however, identify the concern that exploitation under racial capitalism can also harm some whites. The distinction that Mills thinks is salient is that even poor whites have racialized benefits within a white supremacist polity even if they do not share in economic benefits of that polity's economic machine.

In response to Sullivan and the general critique of Mills lacking a proper class account, Mills reiterates the importance of chronology in his work. He argues,

> Once the historicity of these variables is conceded, the possibility is at least opened up (if not proven) that some may have been central to the causal creation of, and this explanation for, some of the others. [...] Gender would seem to go back to the origin of the species, but class and class societies arise only in the last few thousand years, while the dominant postwar position on race (though it has recently been subjected to increasing challenges) is that race and racism are very new, products of modernity.
>
> *(2017b, 43)*

He gives a similar analysis of homosexuality. For him, "race generally trumped class as well as gender [and sexuality]" (42). The key difference of opinion between Mills and Sullivan is asymmetry vs. symmetry-lessness, or in other words, Sullivan's position would be that various oppressions do not just rewrite each other, but there are critical transformations that occur to the positionality of the agent because of various parts of their identity. As Audre Lorde would put it, "there is no hierarchy of oppressions" (1983).

Even in asserting that certain oppressions may have deeper, historical contexts than others, or more social relevance, it would be wrong to diminish how various oppressions create unique life-worlds for those that exist between them. As stated before, Mills helps us engage how various contracts correspond to one another, rewrite one another, and format our social and political landscapes, but his work is insufficient in describing how certain intersections, like Blackness, poverty, and womanhood in an antiblack, capitalistic, and patriarchal society, require nuance that an analysis via contracts cannot provide. It can be simultaneously true that *contracualism* helps us understand the historical and contemporary formations of our society, but falls insufficient in capturing the phenomenological experiences of the agent inside the world the contract(s) attempt(s) to organize.

Can Contract Theory and Liberalism Do Anything Meaningful for Intersectionality?

At this stage, Mills's commitment to revitalized versions of contract theory and liberalism, and rectifying various forms of domination, is evident. It is also clear, by his wide-ranging critics, that there are limitations of contract theory and liberalism when aiming to incorporate gender, class, and other axes of oppression. What does Mills take to be the benefit of these traditions to combat interlocking oppressions like misogynoir, Black queerphobia, racial poverty, and other complex phenomena? He claims that the issue that *Contract & Domination* highlights is that,

> Constituencies that we hoped to bring into dialogue showed that they were not interested in talking to each other. Mainstream contractarians aren't interested in race and gender; race and gender theorists are generally dismissive of contract theory[...] Male theorists who work on race don't follow feminist theory; white feminists don't (beyond the

> gestural) pay much attention to race; and people interested in intersectionality [...] are severely underrepresented in philosophy and generally not interested in contract theory.
> *(2017b, 36)*

His hope is that this work brings together these different schools of thought. Mills tests these traditions to see if they are compatible or not. Let us start with revisiting Mills' rationale behind the *racial contract*.

Mills states that "the account I favor conceives the Racial Contract as creating not merely racial exploitation *but race itself* as a group identity. In contemporary vocabulary, the Racial Contract 'constructs' race" (1997, 63). He emphasizes that race is invented and facilitated through explicit contracts like the law and implicit contracts like social taboos and cultural norms. This is not only a *histo-empirical social constructivist* approach to the metaphysics of race/gender, but it also conceptualizes how oppressions are facilitated explicitly and implicitly. The target of Mills's response is Sally Haslanger, who, in her rebuttal to Mills and other critics of her metaphysics of race, lists Mills's criticism as "race/gender should be studied historically/empirically and *a priori* stipulations cannot do justice to the phenomena" (2013, 2). For Mills, contract theory is a critical model for how racism and other forms of oppression continue to rewrite themselves, rewrite and correspond with other *contracts*, and persist over time through a literal or implied agreement between persons. This approach captures partial agreements via sub-persons and sub-contractors, and also demonstrates who lacks agency altogether. The sub-contracting component, alongside the beneficiaries/signatories dichotomy, does a good job in capturing how people can benefit from or *partially* subscribe to oppressive structures (Mills 1997, 11). In other words, Whites as a group receive differential treatment vis-à-vis the *racial contract* even if only some are signatories to the contract. The same holds true, Mills claims, with regard to gender, class, or other kinds of social identity.

This is where I take Mills's contract theories to be beneficial for intersectional aims. Effective analysis often gets lost in trying to think about oppression in absolute terms; however, there are many nuances to oppressive systems and the agents that help facilitate them, consciously or unconsciously. This framework allows us to think in some *middle* terms. However, my criticism is that contract theory is limited because it thinks in *agreement* terms with agents that could not (historically) be signatories and are very complex beneficiaries. For example, Black men can benefit from a patriarchal system, but their position in that system is extremely complex because of the effects of antiblack racism historically and contemporarily. Kathryn Belle's criticism of Mills's lack of addressing Black men as participants in sexism is valid but requires deep analysis, as they, too, can lack the ability to be signatories, and their benefit can be counterproductive or negated by antiblack racism. I find problems in Carole Pateman's analysis of "patriarchy as fraternity" in *The Sexual Contract* (1988, 3) when applied to marginalized men. Although they participate in and benefit from patriarchal structures, to claim that they have fraternal bonds with white men (*persons* in the contract) is largely inconsistent. For example, the "I Am a Man" campaign in Memphis, Tennessee, demonstrated that when it came to pay and treatment, white men would not stand with Black men collectively for fair treatment. To argue that they share a fraternal protection of one another is largely false, with examples both historical and contemporary. That coalition often breaks because of how race *rewrites* gender privilege.

Now, let us turn to his dedication to liberalism. Liberalism, as an theory, offers commitments to consistency in the application of the law and procedural norms, transparency, and the assurance of equal justice. Among citizens, rights and responsibilities are distributed equally, and there is parity of participation. Now, liberalism in practice is not so clean. There have always been practices of exclusion, whether they be ones of race, gender, class, or ability. For Mills, this does not mean that liberalism must be abandoned altogether. Although he critiques racial liberalism, he argues for a "Black Radical Liberalism," whereby "Black radical liberalism both (a) recognizes white supremacy as central to the making of the United States and (more sweepingly) the modern world, and (b) seeks to rethink categories, critical assumptions and descriptive and normative frameworks of liberalism in light of that recognition" (2017a, 203). Mills mentions that "orthodox Marxism, varieties of radical feminism and black nationalism, dominant strains of post-structuralist and post-colonial theory, exemplify the path of a principled rejection of liberalism" (xiv); however, he still believes that a revision of this framework is useful. One may ask, is Mills's account of liberalism necessary to his approach to intersectionality? For him, yes. Just as his contract theory account is predicated upon us shifting from Kantian/Rawlsian ideal theory to non-ideal theory, his concept of freedom is also bound up in individual agency, autonomy, and rights (37). His entire political ideology is informed by non-ideal theory: a conception of society as ill-ordered, a domination based social ontology, a view of epistemology as a domain of domination, a radically liberal and revised Rawlsian version of corrective justice, and a Black Radical Kantian approach (BRK) (206). Together, contract theory and liberalism make the polity that shapes intersectional experiences.

The tangible world in which we find ourselves is one constituted by the influence of a liberalism that obscures its tendencies toward race-hierarchies while simultaneously presenting itself as race-neutral. For example, Mills says, "Consider social contract theory, classically seen (Hobbes aside) as the main vehicle by which European liberalism challenged absolutism. Contractarianism grounds the polity on the consent of free and equal human beings" (1998, 128). To remedy the misleading presentation of liberalism, Mills's work addresses how classical liberalism does not capture those who are sub-persons or non-persons in the social contract as equal, and how the social contract assumes itself to be egalitarian and fails in that respect. His uptake of liberalism brought about various critiques, with one in particular worth noting by Lewis Gordon. Gordon argues the following:

> An objection that Mills does not consider, for instance, stems from his own admission of the artificiality of the constructions presumed by many contractarians, namely, the absoluteness of the material and economic framework and context of their reflection. Capitalism and its correlative liberal rationalizations, for instance, historically understood, is able to claim its end of history narratives not from any internal or systematic triumph but from de facto history of its proponent countries' conflicts with their alternatives.
>
> *(2009, 241)*

In other words, the systems of the West, like capitalism, contractualism, and liberalism, are considered dominant paradigms, not because of what they accomplish but because of the failures of their alternatives. Thus, we need to examine Mills's support of these traditional frameworks with colonization and other global factors that contribute to the failures of alternatives in mind. Yet, for Mills, that is a key ingredient if we examine oppressions *through* history. His reply to Sullivan states that "imperial expansionist capitalism, and the differential power of the privileged class, brings this new 'world-historical' identity into existence" (2017b, 43–44). Mills traces history differently than Gordon is suggesting. For Mills, history shows us how oppressions develop into one another over time, which is why chronology is so important. For Gordon, global history needs to be considered when employing these theoretical frameworks that have colonial remnants in them.

There is also a critique raised by Dilek Huseyinzadegan regarding Mills's "Black Radical Kantianism," which is connected to his account of "Black Radical Liberalism." In support of Mills's BRK, she states,

> Kant's ideal theory, via his non-ideal theory, is ultimately grounded and justified by a historical narrative of European civil and political progress, a cultural narrative of commerce and industry as chief achievements of humanity, and a racialized-gendered hierarchy of human beings. In other words, I believe that it is time that we Kant scholars and anyone working with Kantian ideas finally recognize, as Jennifer Mensch [2021] puts it, that we cannot "plausibly defend the hard boundaries between ideal and non-ideal positions in Kant, while ensuring that no cross-contamination from the so-called 'tainted' parts has taken place."
>
> *(2022, 261)*

Huseyinzadegan seems to find Mills's approach a satisfactory alternative to other approaches to Kantian theories; however, I am unsure of how well Mills's BRK escapes this same issue as it pertains to intersectionality. Could it be the case that, due to the limits of the Kantian liberalism that Huseyinzadegan outlines, any use of Kant would find issues with intersectionality? Mills focuses on non-ideal theory, but if non-ideal theory is also unsafe from "taint," then it is possible that even Mills's BRK is not radical enough to do what intersectionality proposes. However, I share Huseyinzadegan's praise that Mills's intervention is radical for Kantian studies, liberalism's traditions, and contract theory's traditions. He offers what may be the best way through contract theory and liberalism as it pertains to freedom from a variety of oppressions, so the critiques of Mills may be critiques for his utilized methodologies more than his philosophical thought.

He revises these two paradigms (contract theory and liberalism), but are those revisions sufficient for intersectional aims? Perhaps not in the applied sense of social justice. Although Mills's framework is a good starting place for conceptualizing how oppressions *intersect* or *interlock*, it may be insufficient for social justice projects that pertain to multiple axes of oppression (that create states of being outside of the additive model). Due to its additive nature, Mills's framework could improperly conceptualize situations like Audre Lorde's, where, as a poor, queer, Black mother, her identity requires an approach that captures all of that into a singular complexity (1984, 112). An additive model may prove improper when put into action in grassroots work of social justice. As Collins notes, "Uncoupling intersectionality from its commitment to social justice might gander academic legitimation for intersectionality, but it also might undermine the integrity of intersectionality's *critical* inquiry" (2019, 275), and Mills's work becomes complicated when applied as an ethic for social justice. Mills's framework would place Lorde as a non-person, which may capture her political position with regards to the domination contract, but it does not rectify that these marginalized agents are full persons *ascribed* non-personhood.

Conclusion

Like much of philosophy, especially philosophy that challenges its own traditions, the questions that constantly arise are "what project is being taken on, and is it attempting to modify, reconcile, dismantle, or destroy that which precedes it?" Mills's work is radical because of what it contributes to domains that have been employed in exclusionary ways (i.e., contract theory and liberalism). However, it is also not completely radical for the same reason: he utilizes rigid tools expecting a smooth product. I do not share Audre Lorde's full position that "the master's tools will never dismantle the master's house" (1984), but I do claim that they will not dismantle unless employed to. There is much that can be achieved with the master's tools, and anyone who takes that stance will likely find useful tools in Mills's work for intersectional objectives. Some tools, however, cannot achieve outside their design, like a saw aiming to do the work of a hammer. I take Mills to be radicalizing inside of two major traditions in social and political philosophy. That does not mean his efforts achieved everything they needed outside of those traditions, but he moved classical traditions to confront multiple oppressions and injustices within themselves. That includes bringing intersectional thoughts into European theoretical models. It may not hit every note for the intersectional projects outside of the traditions, but it certainly shook the foundation of those traditions, and for that reason, I find his work critical, vital even, for philosophy.

I end by examining a quote by Mills in *Blackness Visible* (1998). He states, in reference to "racialized reason":

> Like gender, then, this reconceptualization provides a framework for illuminating and explaining the silences, evasions, misrepresentations, and double standards of (most of) the important figures of modern Western political theory. These phenomena can appropriately be seen not as marginal deviations uninterested to a later and (supposedly) more sophisticated audience but as a part of the general project of justifying the global white racial polity and the exploitation of the rest of the planet for the benefit of Europeans home and abroad. *(128)*

For some, how important Mills's intervention is to philosophy is insufficient, due to the nature of intersectionality being focused on social activism beyond the armchair. However, I assert that his intervention is critical, even with the issues of contract theory and liberalism to this feminist theory. He is largely successful at giving language for Critical Race Theory (CRT) and addressing the range of influence regarding white supremacy, as Cole suggests (even though he finds CRT ineffective compared to Marxism). He diagrams issues that many would not, or could not, diagram. He is critically aware of how race, gender, class, etc. correspond to one another, even if we take his method to be insufficient, and he gives uptake to Black feminism regarding the injustices of the world in ways many social and political scholars do not. Although there is warranted caution in utilizing Mills's "intersecting contracts" framework, it does great work in helping us understand how systems of oppression influence one another, historically and contemporarily.

Bibliography

Bailey, Moya. 2021. *Misogynoir Transformed: Black Women's Digital Resistance*. New York: New York University Press.

Cole, Mike. 2009. "Critical Race Theory comes to the UK: A Marxist Response." *Ethnicities* 9 (2): 246–84.
Cole, Mike. 2016. *Racism: A Critical Analysis*. London: Pluto Press.
Collins, Patricia Hill. 2019. *Intersectionality as Critical Social Theory*. Durham: Duke University Press.
Crenshaw, Kimberlé, 1989. "Demarginalizing the Intersection of Race and Sex: A Black Feminist Critique of Antidiscrimination Doctrine, Feminist Theory and Antiracist Politics." *University of Chicago Legal Forum* 139: 139–67.
Crenshaw, Kimberlé, 1991. "Mapping the Margins: Intersectionality, Identity Politics, and Violence against Women of Color." *Stanford Law Review* 43 (6): 1241–99.
Gines, Kathryn. 2017. "Black Feminist Reflections on Charles Mills's 'Intersecting Contracts.'" *Critical Philosophy of Race* 5 (1): 19–28.
Gordon, Lewis. 2009. "On Pateman and Mills's Contract and Domination." *The CLR James Journal* 15 (1): 235–47.
Hardy, Kenneth. 2022. *The Enduring, Invisible, and Ubiquitous Centrality of Whiteness*. New York: W.W. Norton & Company.
Haslanger, Sally. 2013. "Race, Intersectionality, and Method: A Reply to Critics." *Philosophical Studies* 171 (1): 109–19.
Huseyinzadegan, Dilek. 2022. "Charles Mills's 'Black Radical Kantianism' as a Plot Twist for Kant Studies and Contemporary Kantian-Liberal Political Philosophy." *Kantian Review* 27 (4): 651–65.
Kong, Youjin. 2022. "Intersectional Feminist Theory as a Non-Ideal Theory: Asian American Women Navigating Identity and Power." *Ergo* 9 (33): 848–77.
Lindsey, Keisha. 2015. "The Racial Contract: A Feminist Analysis." *Politics, Groups, and Identities* 3 (3): 524–40.
Lorde, Audre. 1983. "There Is No Hierarchy of Oppressions." In *Homophobia and Education*. New York: Council on Interracial Books for Children.
Lorde, Audre. 1984. "The Master's Tools Will Never Dismantle the Master's House." In *Sister Outsider: Essays and Speeches*. Berkeley: Crossing Press.
Lykke, Nina. 2010. *Feminist Studies: A Guide to Intersectional Theory, Methodology and Writing*. New York: Routledge Press.
Mensch, Jennifer. 2021. "Review of Kant's Non-ideal Theory of Politics." *Society for German Idealism and Romanticism Review* 4 (1-2): 127–32.
Mills, Charles W. 1997. *The Racial Contract*. Ithaca, NY: Cornell University Press.
Mills, Charles W. 1998. *Blackness Visible: Essays on Philosophy and Race*. Ithaca: Cornell University Press.
Mills, Charles W. 2003. *From Class to Race: Essays in White Marxism and Black Radicalism*. Lanham, MD: Rowman & Littlefield.
Mills, Charles W. 2007. "White Ignorance." In *Race and Epistemologies of Ignorance*. Edited by Shannon Sullivan and Nancy Tuana. Albany: State University of New York Press.
Mills, Charles W. 2010. *Radical Theory, Caribbean Reality: Race, Class, and Social Domination*. Mona, Jamaica: University of West Indies Press.
Mills, Charles W. 2017a. *Black Rights/White Wrongs: The Critique of Racial Liberalism*. New York: Oxford University Press.
Mills, Charles W. 2017b. "Intersectional Meditations: A Reply to Kathryn Gines and Shannon Sullivan." *Critical Philosophy of Race* 5 (1): 29–50.
Pateman, Carole. 1988. *The Sexual Contract*. Cambridge: Polity Press.
Pateman, Carole, and Charles Mills. 2007. *Contract & Domination*. Cambridge: Polity Press.
Sullivan, Shannon. 2017. "'Smadditizin' Across the Years: Race and Class in the Work of Charles Mills." *Critical Philosophy of Race* 5 (1): 1–18.

4

TOWARD THE BOURGEOIS REVOLUTION

Situating Mills's Liberal Turn

Rafael Vizcaíno

The Time Has Come

Over the past few years, the work of Charles W. Mills has finally received the wider recognition that it deserves across the humanities and the social sciences. The year 2017 saw his induction into one of the most prestigious academic societies in the world: the American Academy of Arts and Sciences. Then, in that most tumultuous year of 2020, Mills delivered the famous Tanner Lectures on Human Values at the University of Michigan, a distinction that placed him alongside canonical figures in the discipline such as Karl Popper, Michel Foucault, Jürgen Habermas, John Rawls, and many others. This significant occasion gave Mills a global platform to defend a systematic outline of his "radical liberalism" approach to political philosophy and racial justice. Then in 2021, just a few weeks before his untimely passing, Mills received the Benjamin E. Lippincott Award, honoring the legacy of his landmark publication *The Racial Contract* (1997) as an exceptional contribution to the field of political theory. At the time of his death, Mills was working on several promising publications, while also overseeing the publication of his Tanner Lectures and the 25th anniversary edition of *The Racial Contract* (2022), the text that launched his career as the influential political philosopher that he became. It seems that Mills's time had finally come.

It is not difficult to relate such long overdue recognition of Mills's work to the increased relevance that the social and political movement for racial justice has had in the United States in recent years. Indeed, it has been in the era of Black Lives Matter that such discourses of racial justice and anti-racism have been embraced by the liberal political mainstream, if often in a perfunctory fashion. The summer of 2020 witnessed an unprecedented national reckoning with the history and legacy of racism in the social fabric and political institutions of the United States—one not seen since the years of the Civil Rights and Black Power movements of the 1950s and 1960s. At last, anti-racism had come into the mainstream; or, at least, a certain brand of anti-racism palatable for the liberal foundations of Americanity.[1] For those interested in preserving such liberal foundations while responding to the demands for the inclusion of the rhetoric of racial justice, the work of Charles Mills now appeared like the most adequate interlocutor to bring into the conversation table.

DOI: 10.4324/9781003349983-5

This historical conjuncture was certainly not lost on Mills himself, who, in his off-scripted remarks delivered as part of his Tanner Lecture, reflected on the character of the mainstream ideological assimilation of radical ideas to question the normative grounds of his own work. Of course, this was done in that uncannily witty and sharp humor that characterized him, a humor for which there is a present need to understand how it plays out in Mills's thinking and writing. All who knew him personally can attest to how humor often led to significant developments in his scholarship. I quote his remarks at length:

> When I got this invitation, I was flattered, I felt honored, but I was also shocked, because I thought of myself—you know, we like to sort of position ourselves with various delusions—I thought of myself as this radical oppositional guy, and I said, you know, radical oppositional guys don't give the Tanner Lectures, that's something like a blot on your CV. So maybe I have to think this over. And then they mentioned the honorarium and I said: "Well okay, I guess I will have to give up my principles just this once."[2]

Parsing through Mills's humor, I dare to say that there is a certain truth to the joke (as perhaps all good jokes have). This truth has to do with something that preoccupied Mills throughout his entire career: the extent to which his work can be said to be truly radical, or "oppositional" (as he always preferred to put it), by which he unequivocally meant "endorsing pro-egalitarian structural change to reduce or eliminate unjust hierarchies of domination" (2017a, 11); and the extent to which his work could be interpreted, in contrast, in a reformist way that would avoid the radicality of structural change.

Since the publication of *The Racial Contract*, the radicality of Mills's work has indeed been a constant topic of debate among academics and students alike. Most of these debates, however, if not nearly all of them, tend to focus on this first pioneering and provocative book, and a few also include the last book published during his lifetime, *Black Rights/White Wrongs: The Critique of Racial Liberalism* (2017). Of course, both texts explicitly seek to build on, or perhaps better yet, seek to actually realize, a liberal theoretical framing. By "liberal," the late Mills meant an "anti-feudal ideology of individualism, equal rights, and moral egalitarianism" inclusive in practice of roughly everything between left-wing social democracy and conservative liberalism (2017a, 12). Evidently, an initial point of confusion might be this expansive definition of liberalism, which is much broader than the colloquial understanding of the term in the United States, the latter usually referring to center-left social liberals. For Mills, it is in this wide-ranging sense that liberalism is the ideological mainstream of the modern world. It, therefore, includes positions such as classical liberalism and, even more polemically, what in the United States is called "neoconservatism," as in the tradition of Bayard Rustin and other disenchanted socialists.

Confining the assessment of Mills's work to *The Racial Contract* and *Black Rights/White Wrongs* might be all fine and good up to a certain extent. However, it is evident that one cannot get the full picture of this question without contextualizing the entirety of Mills's work. And to the surprise of many relatively recent readers of Mills, this includes Mills's early work on none other than Marxist social and political philosophy. In fact, in the introduction to the book dedicated to tracing his intellectual "evolution," an evolution conceived both in terms of "focus" and of "approach" as evidenced in its very title *From Class to Race: Essays in White Marxism and Black Radicalism* (2003), Mills already prefigured the "revelation" that this fact would bring on the "left-wing readers and reviewers who were critical of [*The Racial Contract*] for its failure to engage with, let alone utilize, a historical materialist framework" (2003, xiii). The present chapter aims to contribute to this debate by situating Mills's late "liberal turn" within a radical interpretation of his whole theoretical corpus. In short, I argue that Mills's earlier, more explicitly Marxist work can help to re-interpret or re-evaluate his later, more explicitly liberal work.

Of course, the radical potential of Mills's later work depends on the theoretical relevance and political utility that such early work on Marxism can provide to the present historical conjuncture.[3] Said differently, what is at stake is the degree to which such early work could successfully be retrieved to reinforce aspects of Mills's later social-contractarian work that may be at risk of co-optation by a reformist bourgeois liberalism. It is this task that I wish to explore in this chapter.

I therefore begin by examining Mills's "early" (1984–1994) and "middle" (1994–1997) attempts to grapple with race through the lens of a Marxist historical materialist approach. Since middle-period Mills claims that "a *modified* historical materialism might be able to carry out an adequate conceptualization of the significance of race" (2003, xvi–xvii), I hope to at least outline some points of contact where one could develop such connection. Doing so, I argue, could end up "radicalizing" Mills's work in a way that, perhaps even against his own mature position of seeking a "deracialized" liberalism (2017a, xxi), could ultimately go beyond what he once called that "classic piece of bourgeois ideology" (2003, xiii).[4]

Revisiting Mills's Early and Middle Periods

By the early period of Mills's career, I have in mind the first ten years of his intellectual production, approximately between the years of 1984 and 1994, the large majority of which were spent working within the fields of Marxist social and political philosophy, specifically in the tradition of Analytical Marxism. An initial attempt to develop a historical materialist account of racial dynamics can thereby be found in his 1987 essay appropriately titled "Race and Class: Conflicting or Reconcilable Paradigms?" Anthologized in a slightly revised version in the 2010 volume *Radical Theory, Caribbean Reality: Race, Class, and Social Domination*, this is an essay that develops a Marxist social-theoretical critique of the work of the Jamaican anthropologist M. G. Smith and his "cultural pluralist" framework to understand Caribbean societies. Looking back from the 2020s, Smith's cultural-pluralist framework could not be said to have passed the test of time, and Mills's own contribution contains an insightful review of such critical reception across various theoretical perspectives.

The opening question of this essay is the following: "Should race and class paradigms be regarded as absolutely counterposed, or are any of their insights complementary?" (2010, 72). Against Smith's overly autonomous conception of culture, which is largely dissociated from any material and economic forces, early-Mills here offers a Marxist analysis that aims to do justice precisely to how material and economic interests largely overdetermine certain cultural formations (83). Largely drawing from the work of the Italian philosopher Antonio Gramsci, the point is to conceive of culture as a "dual" ideological formation, a contradictory battleground where material and economic interests are expressed at the level of ideas and popular consciousness with different degrees of clarity and sophistication (82). Gramsci is particularly helpful for Mills at this point, as the Italian philosopher was interested in overcoming a vulgarly reductionist Marxist approach to culture (paradigmatically represented in the works of Georgi Plekhanov and, to a lesser extent, György Lukács and Lucien Goldmann) that conceived of cultural phenomena as mere epiphenomenal or "superstructural" ideological illusions lacking in the real materiality that constitutes the "base" of society. Gramsci was instead interested in theorizing the ways in which culture not only expresses class interests but is also reciprocally capable of affecting and transforming the material and economic "base" of society (Lucente 1989, 169).

Mills's assertion that culture has a "dual" and contradictory ideological character thus expresses the fundamental Gramscian thesis that cultural phenomena have a specific function in the development of hegemonically manufactured "common sense," or "the traditional popular conception of the world" (Gramsci 1971, 199). It is in this sense, for instance, that Mills conceives of race as a "dominant ideological framework—the prism through which people [understand] the world," and also "the foundation for the 'common-sense' of society" (2010, 93–94). In short, race is a cultural-ideological phenomenon that contributes to the maintenance of bourgeois hegemony, no less by the "'spontaneous' consent given by the great masses of the population," as Gramsci would put it (12).

This Gramscian conception of race as an ideological element of common sense within a particular struggle for hegemony recalls the formulation of yet another Jamaican Marxist-Gramscian who was certainly familiar to Mills, Stuart Hall, who famously argued in the late 1970s that race is "the modality in which class is 'lived'" (1980, 341). In fact, and no doubt to the surprise of the selective readers of his later work, Mills approvingly cites the work of Hall in this 1987 essay and even defends Hall from criticisms received by Smith himself that the historical materialist analysis of race presumes a too neatly aligned correlation between class and race (2010, 95). Mills is unequivocal in his insistence that such correlation is neither innate in the structure of each category nor temporally unchangeable.[5] The point is rather simply to argue that "the coincidence of class and race under slavery, and the massive extent of the continuity in the structure of the Caribbean social pyramid in the century and a half since Emancipation, have generated and sustained racialist ideologies which fuse colour and class position" (95).[6]

However, while this Gramscian conception of culture was deployed to evade a reductionist Marxist analysis of race in which race is conceived as a mere ideological effect lacking independent material reality, it is notable that years later, as part of the preface to *Radical Theory, Caribbean Reality*, a mature Mills would nonetheless retrospectively conceive of this preliminary approach as a kind of *failed unintentionally reductionist approach* (2010, xiii). In other words, rather than reconciling race and class, the conclusion of this first 1987 essay becomes the subsumption of race *into* class. We see this in the claim that "racist perceptions, even if they are 'modally decisive for distributions of economic, educational, political and social opportunities,' may themselves be secondary variables originally determined by a class analysis" (97). Or in the even broader claim that "the differential *significance* we [Marxists] attach to racial difference is socially determined, primarily by class variables" (97).

Mills's early period can thus be characterized as an unintentionally Marxist reductionist approach to the analysis of racial phenomena. Promisingly, however, Mills would not so easily abandon the attempt to develop a proper Marxist analysis of race that builds on the historical synthesis between class and race under slavery. In my view, the rectification of this failed attempt characterizes the brief period of his career that I call his "middle period," encompassing the years between 1994 and 1997. In a sense, it is this period that also begins to signal the incoming transition "from class to race."

A characteristic piece from Mills's middle-period would be his "Under Class Under Standings." Originally published in 1994, seven years after the previous intervention from 1987, this is an essay that explicitly aims to defend the import of the concept of race within what is now called a "modified" historical materialist framework (2003, 124). Seeking to bypass, if not outright debunk, the stale "race versus class" debates of the 1970s and 1980s, Mills seeks here to develop a materialist analysis of global capitalism that accounts for the "internal dynamic[s]" and "normative rules" of racial identity (128). This is to say that the globality of capitalism needs to be explicitly understood in relation to the whiteness of the colonial project that produced it. After surveying the positions on this debate from various figures across the ideological spectrum, Mills flips the Old Left's view on how to deal with racism to make the case for the significance of race for the critique of such white supremacist capitalism. That is, "it would not be that socialism is needed to eliminate the problem of racism," as the Old Left once maintained, but rather that "antiracism is needed to eliminate the problem of capitalism" (144). In short, the historical materialist framework, as a theory of society and political change, is revised simply by accounting for the ways in which race and processes of racialization are at the core of the accumulation and preservation of private property in capitalist modernity.

To be clear, this revisionism would not entail the abstract subsumption of racial experience under strict class-based historical materialist analyses. Indeed, this was the failure of Mills's early period. Rather, the task in question would require the epistemic reworking of what is taken to be the *real* historical record on the material foundations of the global political economy. In Marxist terms, it would be about deepening the Gramscian insight concerning the materiality of culture by shifting the place of race from a *super*-structural position (as an ideological or cultural appendage to economic factors) toward placing it at the base of the social ontology, that is, in an *infra*-structural position (central to economic concerns).

Mills clarifies this point in a following essay titled "European Specters." First published in 1999, but also included in slightly revised form as part of the *From Class to Race* volume, this essay is noteworthy for being Mills's last scholarly intervention fully and explicitly committed to a historical materialist framework—thereby delineating the middle-period Mills from the later, more definitive Mills. Acknowledging that, like other modern political thinkers of their time, Marx and Engels had "no perception on their part that the peculiar situation of people of color required any conceptual modifications of their theory" (2003, 151), Mills here goes on to provide an infrastructural account of how race is, in fact, the "primary contradiction" of modernity (156) through which freedom and equality entangled with domination and exclusion.

Mills is emphatic that by the "primary contradiction" of modernity, he does not imply that race is either the "oldest" oppression, the "progenitor of all other oppressions," the most exploitative of oppressions, or even the "only important oppression" (2003, 156–57). Instead, it indicates that race is simply, at least in the horizon of Western modernity (or even more narrowly: in the New World), "the central identity around which people close ranks," therefore being "what ties the system together" (157). Such significance is what needs to be rendered back into the historical materialist analysis if the latter is to be of any use for the purposes of social justice. Rather than defending a regression toward upholding a biological understanding of race, however, we are talking about the social, and more specifically politico-economic elements of how race structures value—the "wages of whiteness," in DuBois's terms, or, in the terms of the contemporary critical race theorist Cheryl Harris, "whiteness as property," that is, as a kind of differential entitlement (166–67).

Unfortunately, Mills would never go on to explore this specific conjuncture at any point in his subsequent academic career. That is, this is as far as Mills's middle-period attempts to develop an adequate historical materialist analysis of race and racism goes. This might be the case because, by the time of the publication of "European Specters" (1999), Mills was already well in the course of turning away from such focus and approach to instead theorize white supremacy as a political structure in the tradition of classical social contract theory. This is a transitional process that can be said to begin with the essay "Revisionist Ontologies: Theorizing White Supremacy," also from that very prolific year of 1994, a year which we can confidently claim to mark the beginning of Mills's conceptual "evolution."[7] In other words, the brief but intense middle-period of Mills's career can be said to consist of two parallel and competing tracks of research, the racial revisionism of historical materialism and the exploration of social contract theory for the analysis of race, the latter of which would triumph to engender the radical contractarian Mills of *The Racial Contract*, who would end up becoming, in the view of the large majority of his readers, the definitive Mills.

Curiously enough, however, in an autobiographical essay published in 2002 as part of George Yancy's edited anthology *The Philosophical I: Personal Reflections on Life and Philosophy* (also anthologized as the introduction to Mills's *Radical Theory, Caribbean Reality*), Mills would retrospectively pronounce this conceptual evolution as nevertheless being an "unconscious" application of the "theoretical apparatus [he] knew best—Marxism"—though at the level of form and not the level of content (2010, 22). That is, after all his deviation from Marxism at the level of content, now primarily focusing on white supremacy as opposed to capitalism as an object of study, he *still* only managed to theorize white supremacy *like a Marxist would normally theorize capitalism*.[8] It is such a momentary reflection that lends credibility to Shannon Sullivan's claim that Mills's move from class to race actually committed him further "to certain key tenants of Marxism, such as its base-superstructure model" (Sullivan 2017, 5).[9] Consequently, I take such a reflection as an opportunity to articulate a more radical historical-materialist interpretation of Mills's later work.

On the Radical Retrieval of Liberalism

While, in my view, the definitive Mills begins to be apparent in a publication such as *The Racial Contract*, for the purposes of this chapter I will simply fast-forward to the late Mills, specifically his last major publication, *Black Rights/White Wrongs: The Critique of Racial Liberalism*—bound in that clever tradition of his to assemble revised versions of previously published articles. It is in this last major publication of his that we encounter the most well-defined version of the conundrum that is the point of departure of my assessment. For it is in this text that the clash between a radical or oppositional interpretation of Mills's work comes into most direct conflict with what could be said is an alternative reformist interpretation that eschews the consequences of the material ways in which race (as the "primary contradiction") structures the politico-economic order of modernity. The radical "principled rejection of liberalism" associated with "Orthodox Marxism, varieties of radical feminism and black nationalism," as well as "dominant strains of post-structuralist and post-colonial theory," is now contrasted with a project of retrieval, based on "social democracy and feminist liberalism," that seeks to "reclaim" liberalism as a "liberatory political philosophy" (2017a, xiv). It is this now explicitly liberal agenda that puts into question the radical and oppositional potential of Mills's work.

Rather than seeing the alliance between racism and liberalism as "a matter of a preordained logic of liberalism itself," as the aforementioned radical frameworks often do, Mills now argues for seeing such a connection as being merely historically "contingent" (2017a, xv). This conceptual maneuver has the consequential repercussion of facilitating the normative retrieval of liberalism for *anti-racist* purposes. In short, delinking the historically contingent racist baggage from the norms of liberal political philosophy can, according to Mills, produce a "color-conscious, racially reflexive, anti-racist liberalism" (xv). It is clear that under such liberal anti-racism, the liberal foundations of modernity are not only preserved, but they are even further strengthened and expanded to include those subjects historically excluded from them. Rather than overcoming that "classic piece of bourgeois ideology" (2003, xiii), the aim of Mills's project has now become simply to "deracialize" liberalism (2017a, xv).[10] In short, it would appear that the radical goal of structural transformation explicitly present in Mills's early work has been given up in the name of a more reformist tactic in which liberalism is plainly here to stay for the foreseeable future.

Of course, as he indicated in his autobiographical reflections from 2002, and more recently in his off-scripted remarks at his 2020 Tanner Lecture, Mills generally rejected the characterization that his later work is reformist in character. Indeed, in *Black Rights/White Wrongs*, he explicitly deploys the label "Black radical liberalism" to describe his mature theoretical stance (2017a, xx). The clear advantage of such nomenclature is its ability to bypass the ostensible opposition between radicalism and liberalism upheld in the global political spectrum—a move perhaps not unlike Mills's earlier attempts to bypass the ossified debates between race and class, where interlocutors mostly managed to talk past each other. Therefore, if what is at stake in my assessment of Mills's work is that even older debate between reform and revolution, then the conceptual validity of this new political amalgamation of "Black radical liberalism" is what needs to be evaluated.

Fortunately, there is one place where Mills neatly spells out the foundations of such amalgamation. In 2011, during the peak of the Occupy Wall Street days that brought to the American public sphere a revived interest in radical and progressive politics around class and inequality, Mills wrote an essay that sought to justify his retrieval of the liberal framework for the purposes of a radical anti-racist agenda. Initially titled "Ten Reasons Why Liberalism Cannot Be Retrieved for Radicalism (And Why They're All Wrong)," this essay would go on to become chapter two of *Black Rights/White Wrongs*.[11] The two primary reasons articulated here to validate the radical reclaiming of liberalism are: (i) liberalism's mainstream ideological positionality as the dominant framework that mediates political activity in North America (again, liberalism broadly defined as inclusive of everything between left-wing social democracy and conservative liberalism), thereby providing any radical agenda with a higher likelihood of appealing to more people if presented in these terms; and (ii) the aforementioned alleged "contingent" complicity of liberalism with systems of domination such as "plutocracy, patriarchy, and white supremacy" (2017a, 10–12). It is the latter point that Mills aims to systematically defend by countering common radical arguments for the intrinsic (*i.e.*, not merely contingent) complicity between liberalism and said systems of domination.

In his defense of this broad liberal umbrella, Mills dispels the postulation that liberalism depends on an asocial, atomistic individualist ontology, as well as rejects the assumption that liberalism cannot recognize group oppressions in its framework. His claim is that while this may be the case for *some* liberalisms, it is also the case that not all liberalisms do this (2017a, 14–17). Similarly, responding to the structuralist and post-structuralist critiques of liberalism's naïve understanding of subjective agency, Mills defends the latter as an irreducible "locus of *value*" (18). While the conception of the self in classical liberalism as absolute self-creation is certainly absurd, the structuralist and post-structuralist rejections of human agency go too far in the opposite direction, being fundamentally inconsistent with the political history of resistance to systems of domination (20).

An anti-racist radical liberalism would thus "affirm the value of the individual" while at the same time "recognizing how the individual is socially molded, especially when the environing social structures are oppressive ones" (2017a, 18). It would be a specifically materialist liberalism that understands how concrete material forces make possible the complex machinations of structures of oppression and domination in the social order, thereby avoiding the overestimation that classical liberalism places on "rational argumentation and moral suasion" (23). Perhaps most importantly, however, it is a liberalism that takes "political struggle" as the engine of progressive pro-egalitarian structural change, which does not take for granted empty teleological abstractions about its accomplishments or the inevitability of its successes. And this is precisely what makes this kind of liberalism a radical one. For it is a liberalism that is theoretically grounded on the realm of the *real*, which is to say, in the jargon of mainstream analytic Anglo-American political philosophy, the "*non-ideal*" (22, 26).[12]

Right from the outset of its publication, responses to Mills's defense of a "Black radical liberalism" have largely rejected its main premises. Some, for instance, have called into question the radicality of any liberalism that theoretically insists on the centrality of the individual and its concomitant notion of private property rights. In the very first published responses to this essay, which appeared in symposium format in the *Radical Philosophy Review*, Nancy Holmstrom (2012, 326) called out the politico-economic ambiguity of this position, which conveniently says nothing about the question of capitalism. On these lines, Richard Schmitt commends Mills for at least redrawing the division between liberal and radical for the twenty-first century, a century in which (unlike the nineteenth century of Marx and Engels) the "*inevitability of capitalist collapse*" no longer seems to be on the horizon (334). For Schmitt, the problem in Mills's position is less the question of capitalism per se, and more the character of actual liberal practice. Specifically, Schmitt takes issue with Mills's separation between a normative liberalism and a historically contingent instantiation of it because, according to Schmitt, at the core of liberalism there is a commitment to making "false empirical claim[s]" about "equality and inequality in capitalist society" (333). According to Schmitt, confronting these epistemic distortions leaves nothing of liberalism worth retrieving.[13]

In his initial response to Holmstrom and Schmitt, Mills admits to self-consciously avoiding the mention of capitalism, mainly because in the political context of the United States, "the declaration of an anti-capitalist agenda will immediately isolate and marginalize you" (2012, 337). The politico-economic ambiguity highlighted by Holmstrom thus now appears as part of a strategic move to facilitate the point of the entire intervention: the retrieval of liberalism for a radical agenda *as the radical infiltration of liberalism*. In short, this initial reply puts emphasis on the first of the two reasons that Mills gives in the 2011 essay for validating said retrieval, which, to be sure, Mills only mentions in passing in both this essay and its ensuing 2017 minor revision for *Black Rights/White Wrongs*: the mainstream ideological positionality that liberalism already holds in the public sphere.

To put it plainly, the *strategic* validity of the retrieval project relies more on liberalism's mainstream positionality, rather than on the normative conceptual resources of liberal theory. Said otherwise, the focus on liberalism in Mills's later work would have less to do with the exhaustion of radical values than with the mere empirical fact that liberalism is the ideological norm that conditions ordinary political activity, thereby giving radicals an opportunity to leave the musty echo chambers of radical spaces by simply "occupying" liberalism. Indeed, one of the subarguments that Mills makes for the radical retrieval of liberalism is that the core values of liberalism, such as equality and freedom, are also found at the center of radical projects for social and political transformation. His initial reply to Schmitt thus calls into question Schmitt's assertion that liberalism necessarily produces epistemic evasions—Mills's point (once again) is that these evasions are historically contingent, not demanded by the normative core of liberal values (2012, 342). Radicals need to begin, Mills contends in his response to Holmstrom and Schmitt, "where people's heads are," and only then "try to move them further left" (2012, 337). This is, in the end, why Mills always saw himself as doing radical "oppositional" work in the interest of "pro-egalitarian structural change" (2017a, 11), and not ultimately ending up endorsing some form of bourgeois reformism. The point is not to clumsily merge or combine radicalism with liberalism, diluting the former into the latter, but to occupy the latter so that, from within, radicals can steadily transform it into the former.

This argument is clarified one last time in the epilogue to *Black Rights/White Wrongs*, where Mills explicitly contrasts Black radical liberalism to Black mainstream liberalism on the one hand and Black radicalism on the other. If Black mainstream liberalism shares with Mills's approach an endorsement of liberalism as a political philosophy, its character as mainstream is its evident differentiating factor. By mainstream, Mills denotes going along with the refusal to recognize the political reality of white supremacy as a system of domination, when not simply "[giving] lip service" to its reality in a way that assumes that liberalism already contains all the answers to the eradication of racial oppression (2017a, 203). In this sense, by presupposing the reality of white supremacy, Mills's Black radical liberalism undoubtedly shares more with Black radicalism than with Black mainstream liberalism. Black radicalism is here a broad umbrella inclusive of subvariants such as Black nationalism and Black Marxism. Differences aside, these subvariants uphold a theory of white supremacy rooted in the project of European colonialism and its practice of racial slavery (202). Now, it is on the other end of the spectrum that Black radical liberalism differs from these other Black radical approaches, as the latter assume the aforementioned principal rejection of liberalism that places them at the fringes of the ideological spectrum (*i.e.*, outside the mainstream), a situation that Black radical liberalism aims precisely to strategically avoid.

In short, Black radical liberalism lives at the confluence of both Black mainstream liberalism and Black radicalism. It is a *synthesis* of both approaches, drawing from each what is most valuable: ideological normativity and a critique of white supremacy, respectively

(2017a, 202–03). Elsewhere, particularly in response to Sullivan's intersectional critique, Mills represented this position as starting "at the very least" from the spectrum of a "left, social-democratic liberalism," à la John Rawls (2017b, 42). It would be from there, therefore, that through the political struggle of occupation, such a position would do the work of moving the needle "further left" (2012, 337) toward the goal of "pro-egalitarian structural change to reduce or eliminate unjust hierarchies of domination" (2017a, 11).

Toward a Revised Historical Materialism

As stated earlier, the purpose of the present chapter is to contribute to the ongoing debate concerning the radicality of Mills's work. I am interested in charitably defending the general intentions and ambitions of Mills's work against those critics that might see in his late liberal turn either a reactionary sign of "ideological defeatism" that is race-reductionist and supportive of bourgeois liberalism (Ferguson II 2022, 11) or a contradictory attempt that fails to be critical enough and that never succeeds in putting forward an alternative to liberalism's weak handling of racial justice (Darby 2019; Slack 2022). Of course, I am by no means expecting to refute these criticisms in their entirety, some of which will surely apply to my own interpretation. All I wish to accomplish is the reconsideration that Mills's liberal turn is a direct abandonment of the earlier radical aspirations of his work.

To be clear, I am not interested in defending Mills from *within* the premises and objectives of liberalism itself. Rather, my aim is to defend Mills in conversation with Mills's earlier, more explicitly radical (historical materialist) work. In a sense, I want to take seriously the "radical" in Mills's Black radical liberalism, as well as his assertion that his liberal turn aims to strategically synthesize the best that radical frameworks have to offer, all with the point of eventually being able to develop and offer a more feasible radical theory of political transformation for the twenty-first century and future generations. His earlier work, I contend, offers vital resources not only to understand but to further deepen the radical aspect of his seemingly contradictory later work.

For the sake of brevity, I shall only bring up one early instance that helpfully recontextualizes Mills's subsequent liberal turn within a wider radical agenda. Such an instance can be found in the last scholarly intervention of his that is explicitly and fully committed to a historical materialist framework, already partly analyzed above: the 1999 article "European Specters." Not only is this the place where Mills offers an infrastructural account of how race is the "primary contradiction" of modernity, as we saw above, but this is also the place where the triangulation that becomes Black radical liberalism perhaps first comes into full view. For it is here where a Marxist historical materialist critique of modern capitalism is explicitly supplemented with a Du Boisian analysis of racial domination, all while endorsing the rubric of social contractualism as the new theoretical terrain of political philosophy. The crucial point here being that a historical materialist framework remains central, if only in "*modified*" form (2003, xvi).

At one decisive point in "European Specters," Mills candidly narrates how in 1996, at the second national conference of the Radical Philosophy Association, he planned to develop the theoretical consequences of making race the primary contradiction of modernity. Part of such intervention involved a now-largely-forgotten damning 9-point critique of the epistemic ignorance of white Marxism that argues for centering the analysis of race for the sake of keeping alive the hopes for a future Marxist revolutionary socialism—also very much in line with the conclusions of the earlier publication "Under Class Under Standings." A quick look at this 9-point critique underscores the radicality, scope, and vast objectives of Mills's eventual takeover of liberalism.

The critique starts by articulating what it means to argue that race (and, say, not class or gender) is the primary contradiction of modernity. As we saw above, this is to say that race is "the central identity around which people close ranks," therefore being "what ties the system together" (2003, 157).[14] The critique then proceeds to articulate how white people are "cognitively-handicapped" when it comes to perceiving the reality of racial domination (157), in a sense anticipating arguments that would be further developed in *The Racial Contract* (1997, 19) and the later very influential essay "White Ignorance" (2007). It is for this reason that an orthodox (white) Marxism is unable to conjecture the significance of race in its theories of oppression and liberation.

Significantly, it is at this point that we encounter the moment that a later Mills would retrospectively conceive as an "unconscious" application of Marxism (2010, 22). Mills makes the heretical claim that abstracting from the frameworks of Marxist theory, the realities of race-based group domination can be attested "with *far greater ease*" than those of class-based domination (2003, 157). At least as it pertains to the United States, the claim is that it is far less controversial, for instance, to assert the racial character of the state and its apparatuses (such as the legal system) than it is to make the claim that the state is controlled by the bourgeoisie (158). After making analogous claims regarding the nature of exploitation and ideological hegemony, Mills stresses that anyone willing to defend a traditional class-based analysis of domination should, thereby, be able to extend the analysis to race-based domination—unless one risks falling prey to the ideological mysticisms or cognitive impediments of whiteness.

Perhaps most interestingly for the purposes of my argument, however, is the amusing and ironic way in which Mills concludes this 9-point critique. It humorously announces a "500-Year Plan," asserting that the struggles for social democracy and socialism envisioned by Marx and Engels for the nineteenth and twentieth centuries would occur only *after* the anti-racist movement manages to instantiate the thus-far-missing bourgeois-liberal-democratic revolution. Because race is the primary contradiction of a white supremacist colonial modernity, Mills argues, a true socialist revolution has to wait for the complete bourgeois revolution that thus far has been averted by a racial *Herrenvolk* liberalism (2003, 171).[15] "[O]ne could say," Mills continues "half-jokingly" (and this "half" is key), that Marxist revolutionary socialists need "to persuade white proletarians to lose their chains of whiteness and inscribe on their banners: 'Toward the bourgeois revolution!'" (171).

Circumnavigating through Mills's humor, I dare claim there is a serious point to be made here: the bourgeois-liberal-democratic revolution has failed in large part due to the persistent fact of racism, and such failure is the ground upon which a later Mills seeks to genuinely occupy liberalism from a radical perspective without incongruity. The enduring incompleteness of the bourgeois revolution is then why, for Mills, the fight against white supremacy must take place primarily in the terms of the ideological political norm of liberalism. And when one takes a hard look at the history of modern social change, what we are talking about is a long-term struggle that easily promises to take no less than 200 years. If this assessment is correct, it is only then, in the twenty-third century, once racial liberalism has been dismantled by a true (and thus, anti-racist) bourgeois-liberal-democratic revolution, that the political movement would be able to be taken "further left" toward a non-racial or trans-racial democratic socialism. For just as global modernity took almost five centuries to consolidate, these last two struggles promise to take no less than 300 years—hence the "500-year plan."

While it might be easy for some to simply dismiss this instant in Mills's intellectual trajectory as an example of his ever-prevalent satire, taking it seriously actually opens the possibility to develop a holistic account of his entire life's work. In other words, if the achievement of a revolutionary socialism is dependent on the completion or further advancement of the "bourgeois revolution," a central topic of debate in the tradition since the earliest publications of Marx and Engels, then Mills's attempts to formulate a Black radical liberalism are not necessarily a complete contradiction in terms.[16] Rather, such an attempt might very well be taken to be a serious contribution to this long conversation within the tradition of Marxist historical materialism as a theory of society and political change, reconsidering the coordinates of radical structural change for the third millennium.

If anything, if we re-route this point through *The Racial Contract*, which Mills still characterized as being in the tradition of Marxist *ideologiekritik* (1997, 129), where one exposes the limitations and contradictions of an ideology from within, with the ultimate aim of overcoming it, then it is not out of the question to also consider the retrieval of liberalism as an illustration of *ideologiekritik*.[17] In this sense, the occupation of liberalism would not be an end in itself, but rather would have the function of immanent critique, through which new political possibilities could be opened depending on the actual practice in question. The task of *ideologiekritik* would be part of the political struggle of occupation needed to do the work of moving the needle "further left" (2012, 337) toward the goal of "pro-egalitarian structural change" (2017a, 11).

Conclusion

In this chapter, I have examined parts of Mills's "early" and "middle" periods to contextualize, supplement, and re-interpret the later Mills's "liberal turn." Staying with his middle-period claim that "a *modified* historical materialism might be able to carry out an adequate conceptualization of the significance of race" (2003, xvi–xvii), my hope is to have outlined some points of contact where one could now go on to develop what Mills himself was unable to do: more radical interpretations of what it means to "occupy" liberalism for the purposes of a radical agenda, especially one that is expressed in the terms of an anti-racist Black radical liberalism. I find it imperative to do this hermeneutic operation to challenge interpretations of Mills's work that aim to reduce it to a reformist bourgeois liberalism in the service of mainstream discourses of diversity and multiculturalism. When read in relation to his earlier work, which Mills never claimed to have abandoned, his later liberal turn appears more clearly as a pragmatic means toward a more radical end.

The more speculative conclusion of this chapter is that Mills's liberal turn could ultimately be seen as a revisionist contribution to the theory of historical materialism, aiming to update the theory not only for the twenty-first century but perhaps for the entire third millennium. Accordingly, given liberalism's privileged position as the ideological norm of the contemporary political field, its occupation by radicals could be deployed as an exercise of *ideologiekritik*, where one exposes the limitations and contradictions of racial liberalism from within, with the ultimate aim of overcoming it (going "further left").

Rather than abandoning historical materialism, I argue that a synthetic reading of Mills's work offers a revised theory of historical materialism, which presumes that the bourgeois-liberal-democratic revolution needs to be first fully instantiated (the struggle to deracialize liberalism) before the struggle for social democracy and, eventually, socialism can be considered once again *as mainstream projects*. It is in this sense that, for Mills, the call "toward the bourgeois revolution!" is the entry point toward more *feasible* possibilities of "pro-egalitarian structural change."

To close, I must clarify that my objectives in this chapter have been purely exegetical and interpretative. In other words, I have only aimed to give a potential radical interpretation of Mills's Black radical liberalism, one which is made possible in connection to certain elements in Mills's earlier, more explicitly Marxist-influenced work. I have, therefore, only intended to reconstruct a latent possibility within the unity of Mills's work, all the while deliberately avoiding making a normative judgment regarding the limitations of such an approach. Evidently, my interpretation hinges on the strategic validity of "occupation" and the historical necessity to "complete" the bourgeois revolution. If either of these two premises are faulty, then Mills's critics would be right to interpret the liberal turn as either a sign of "ideological defeatism" (Ferguson II 2022, 11) or a contradictory attempt that simply fails to be critical enough (Darby 2019; Slack 2022).

Nonetheless, as any Marxist would agree, the test of a political theory is the realm of practice, and not the abstractions of theory (even "non-ideal" theory). So, for the label of Black radical liberalism to not "fly apart from centrifugal forces," as Mills self-critically put it (2017a, 205), its coherence must ultimately be put to the test on the ground. But at least within the parameters of the philosophical debate, Mills's forthcoming posthumous writings promise to keep this conversation alive for the years to come.

Notes

1 For the concept of Americanity, see Quijano and Wallerstein, 1992.
2 These remarks are available in the video recording of Mills's Tanner Lecture. See https://www.youtube.com/watch?v=78wzAfQu9Mw
3 Recent contributions on this front have been provided by Jorge Montiel (2022) and Gregory Slack (2022), both of which appeared in an issue of *Radical Philosophy Review* honoring Mills's life and work.
4 My account of Mills's trajectory overlaps with, but is ultimately more succinct than, Shannon Sullivan (2017)'s otherwise very fruitful critical account of Mills's conceptual evolution from the perspective of intersectionality.
5 Mills's own systematic engagement with Hall's work first appeared somewhat belatedly in 2007, in the anthology *Culture, Politics, Race and Diaspora: The Thought of Stuart Hall*, edited by Brian Meeks (which itself gathers contributions from the 2004 Caribbean Reasonings Conference in Mona, Jamaica)–this essay is also anthologized as chapter seven of Mills's *Radical Theory, Caribbean Reality* (2010). In this almost forgotten piece, Mills traces the long arc of Hall's theorizations of race, from a heavily materialist Marxist commitment to a culturally "postmodernist" one, to conclude that Hall's late work could be conceived as "classically *idealist*," essentially going "way too far in the opposite direction" (2010, 205, 207). In short, one of Mills's claims is that there are better resources to theorize race in the earlier Marxist-Gramscian Hall than in the later postmodern Hall. The fact that this argument is taking place in the late 2000's, and not in the 1980's, is significant for the purposes of my own claim regarding the radical horizon of Mills's overall theoretical corpus. For a contemporary assessment of Hall's work in light of our "post-postracial" historical conjuncture, see Vizcaíno 2024.
6 It is worth noting just how geographically contextual this early theoretical intervention of Mills is supposed to be. It is meant to address not even Caribbean societies as a whole, but most

specifically, Jamaican society and its relatively simple racialized national culture–as opposed to more complex Caribbean cultures, such as Guyana's and Trinidad and Tobago's (Mills 2010, 100, n. 4).

7 In 1994 alone, Mills published six articles in respectable peer-reviewed journals. By then, he was already a tenured Associate Professor at the University of Illinois Chicago.

8 This point is not to be confused with the aforementioned assessment of Mills's early attempts to theorize race within a Marxist framework as being an instrumentalist reduction of race into class dynamics. Montiel (2022) has traced how Mills's mature materialist account of racial domination constitutes the core of Mills's radicalism.

9 For Sullivan, the "additive model of social structures and identities" is another concrete instance of the Marxist legacy in the later Mills, a commitment that she finds problematic from the perspective of intersectionality (Sullivan 2017, 8).

10 It is remarkable the extent to which this position largely parallels, but ultimately differs from, the diagnostic offered by another prominent contemporary Jamaican thinker: Sylvia Wynter. For Wynter, a radical project of decolonization must indeed not deny the emancipatory legacies of modernity, which in her case is best represented by the liberal-secular political critique of theocentric orthodoxy. However, Wynter's conclusion, even with its dialectical subsumption of the secular revolution, is clearly more radical than Mills's eventual strategic occupation of a deracialized liberalism. That is, Wynter's goal remains unapologetically radical in form, content, tactic, and strategy: to go *"beyond Man"* and his liberal-secular genre of being human (Wynter 2003, 2015). For an assessment of such radical project, see Vizcaíno 2022.

11 This essay was notably presented in an alternative panel titled "Philosophers Respond to Occupy Wall Street," at the 2011 American Philosophical Association Eastern Division annual meeting. Attendees to such event reported an electrifying and highly polemic atmosphere that developed as a result of Mills's essay. The journal *Radical Philosophy Review* subsequently published this essay with short responses from Nancy Holmstrom and Richard Schmitt, and a reply from Mills himself–pieces which I engage below.

12 Chapter five of *Black Rights/White Wrongs*, titled "Ideal Theory as Ideology," is a masterful example of how Mills's later work reappropriates his earlier radical historical materialist framework to dismantle fundamental presuppositions in liberal political philosophy.

13 Most recently, Slack (2022) has also pushed back against Mills's characterization of Marxism as an unviable mainstream terrain for future political struggle.

14 This is the argument that is the target of Sullivan's (2017) critique.

15 The later Mills uses the term "*Herrenvolk* socialism" to similarly describe a white supremacist form of socialist theory and practice (2017a, 27).

16 The conclusion to their *Manifesto of the Communist Party*, for instance, claims that "the bourgeois revolution in Germany will be but the prelude to an immediately following proletarian revolution" (Marx and Engels 1976, 519). Of course, this claim has been interpreted in vastly different ways by many Marxists of different stripes in the last 150 years. For a recent re-evaluation of what is at stake in this thesis, see van Ree 2013.

17 I thank Cristina Lafont for a conversation that made me see this specific point with more clarity. Our conversation took place after I first presented an earlier and shorter version of this chapter at the "Racial Contract at 25" conference, held in honor of Mills at the University of Illinois Chicago, in September of 2022.

Bibliography

Darby, Derrick. 2019. "Charles Mills's Liberal Redemption Song." *Ethics* 129 (2): 370–97.

Ferguson II, Stephen C. 2022. ""Black Radical Liberalism" and the Retreat from Class: The Life and Legacy of Charles W. Mills." *APA Studies on Philosophy and the Black Experience* 22 (1): 4–12.

Gramsci, Antonio. 1971. *Selections from the Prison Notebooks*. Translated by Quintin Hoare and Geoffrey Nowell Smith. New York, NY: International Publishers.

Hall, Stuart. 1980. "Race, Articulation, and Societies Structured in Dominance." In *Sociological Theories: Race and Colonialism*. Paris, France: UNESCO.

Holmstrom, Nancy. 2012. "Response to Charles Mills's 'Occupy Liberalism!'." *Radical Philosophy Review* 15 (2): 325–30.

Lucente, Gregory L. 1989. "Yesterday, Today, Tomorrow: Notes on Gramsci's Theory of Literature and Culture." *Forum Italicum: A Journal of Italian Studies* 23 (1-2): 168–77. https://doi.org/10.1177/001458588902300111

Marx, Karl, and Frederick Engels. 1976. *Marx and Engels Collected Works Volume 6: Marx and Engels 1845-48*. London, UK: Lawrence & Wishart.

Mills, Charles W. 1997. *The Racial Contract*. Ithaca, NY: Cornell University Press.

Mills, Charles W. 2003. *From Class to Race: Essays in White Marxism and Black Radicalism*. Lanham, MD: Rowman & Littlefield.

Mills, Charles W. 2007. "White Ignorance." In *Race and Epistemologies of Ignorance*. Edited by Shannon Sullivan and Nancy Tuana, 13–38. New York, NY: State University of New York Press.

Mills, Charles W. 2010. *Radical Theory, Caribbean Reality: Race, Class, and Social Domination*. Mona, Jamaica: University of West Indies Press.

Mills, Charles W. 2012. "Reply to Nancy Holmstrom and Richard Schmitt." *Radical Philosophy Review* 15 (2): 337–43.

Mills, Charles W. 2017a. *Black Rights/White Wrongs: The Critique of Racial Liberalism*. New York, NY: Oxford University Press.

Mills, Charles W. 2017b. "Intersectional Meditations: A Reply to Kathryn Gines and Shannon Sullivan." *Critical Philosophy of Race* 5 (1): 29–50.

Mills, Charles W. 2022. *The Racial Contract*. 25th Anniversary ed. Ithaca, NY: Cornell University Press.

Montiel, Jorge. 2022. "Charles Mills's Radicalism." *Radical Philosophy Review* 25 (2): 265–75.

Quijano, Aníbal, and Immanuel Wallerstein. 1992. "Americanity as a Concept, or the Américas in the Modern World-System." *International Social Science Journal* 29: 549–57.

Schmitt, Richard. 2012. "Comment on Charles Mills, "Occupy Liberalism!"." *Radical Philosophy Review* 15 (2): 331–36.

Slack, Gregory. 2022. "Black Radical Liberalism or Black Marxism?" *Radical Philosophy Review* 25 (2): 277–92.

Sullivan, Shannon. 2017. "Smadditizin' Across the Years: Race and Class in the Work of Charles Mills." *Critical Philosophy of Race* 5 (1): 1–18.

van Ree, Erik. 2013. "Marxism as Permanent Revolution." *History of Political Thought* 34 (3): 540–63.

Vizcaíno, Rafael. 2022. "Sylvia Wynter's New Science of the Word and the Autopoetics of the Flesh." *Comparative and Continental Philosophy* 14 (1): 72–88.

Vizcaíno, Rafael. 2024. "Strategic Anti-Essentialism: Stuart Hall's Dialectics of Maneuver and Position." In *Creolizing Critical Theory: New Voices in Caribbean Philosophy*. Edited by Kris F. Sealey and Benjamin P. Davis. New York, NY: Rowman & Littlefield.

Wynter, Sylvia. 2003. "Unsettling the Coloniality of Being/Power/Truth/Freedom: Towards the Human, After Man, Its Overrepresentation–An Argument." *CR: The New Centennial Review* 3 (3): 257–337.

Wynter, Sylvia. 2015. "The Ceremony Found: Towards the Autopoetic Turn/Overturn, its Autonomy of Human Agency and Extraterritoriality of (Self-)Cognition." In *Black Knowledges/Black Struggles: Essays in Critical Epistemology*. Edited by Jason R. Ambroise and Sabine Broeck, 184–252. Liverpool, UK: Liverpool University Press.

5

MILLS ON CLASS IN RELATION TO RACE

Lawrence Blum

White Supremacy as a System

Charles W. Mills made at least two great and permanent contributions to political theory and philosophy. One was to promote the recognition of "racial justice" as a fundamental form of social justice, so theorizing about social justice must take account of racial justice as a central concern. The second was to establish that a system of race-based injustice has reigned inside most countries in the West, and the globe more generally, for several centuries. This system, which he plausibly calls "white supremacy," has deeply shaped the modern world, and philosophers must pay attention to it. The sources of white unjust advantage are built into the characteristic ways national and international institutions function. Mills also argues, and I think establishes, that although race as a social phenomenon came to exist as a largely after-the-fact rationalization of economic exploitation and domination, once on the scene, its subsequent manifestations, including in the present, can no longer be understood fully in class terms (2003, xvi; 2017a, 7–8). To say that race cannot be reduced to class is not the same as denying the possibility of a Marxist account of race, since the resources of Marxism go beyond centering class. Indeed, Mills regards himself as offering a "materialist" account of race, in what he argues to be the Marxist sense of this concept—one that includes the aspiration to explain society-wide structural oppression.

In addition to white supremacy, Mills recognizes other comparable overarching systems of domination and advantage as features of our world, the most prominent being gender and class (2003, 182). Mills's understanding of white supremacy is "intersectional" in the sense that he sees it as interacting with these other systems, and they with each other. Individual persons' life situations can be fully understood only in relation to the interactions of all the relevant domination systems. Nevertheless, Mills (explicitly borrowing an insight from feminist political theory) comes to treat white supremacy as a relatively autonomous system in its own right rather than an abstraction from, for example, class (181). For Mills, white supremacy is a system in itself—one that has radically shaped the modern world.

I will be critical of various aspects of Mills's writings but want to affirm and honor the permanent value of his work for political philosophy. He will be remembered as one

DOI: 10.4324/9781003349983-6

of the great philosophers of the late twentieth and early twenty-first centuries, and I am deeply grateful and fortunate to have known him and to have lived when he did. Although Mills does sometimes explicitly recognize class as fully analogous to race and gender as a domination/advantage system, I will argue that, once he stopped explicitly writing as a Marxist and turned his attention to race, on the whole his writings do *not* portray class as a system of domination and advantage analogous to race (and gender). Several times in the last 23 or so years of his life, Mills explicitly states that he is no longer trying to provide an account of class as an overall domination system (2003, xvi–xvii). In "Intersectional Meditations: A Reply to Kathryn Gines and Shannon Sullivan," Mills explains that it was coming to the United States that affected his understanding of the relation between race and class (2017b, 42). This shift occurred due to the historical evidence of white supremacy in the shaping of the United States, the weakening of Marxism in higher education and the US landscape, and the fact that liberalism was the "globally triumphant" worldview of the time (2007, 115).

In his writings after this shift, Mills fails to portray class as a pervasive force and system affecting every domain of life, as race and gender are. Nor does he provide an unequivocal sense of class as a distinct locus of moral wrongfulness, both analogous to race and gender, and like them, contributing to the overall normative character of the larger processes in society that involve them all. However, he does sometimes contrast class and race normatively, arguing that race involves a more serious moral violation than does class. I will argue that his argument does not establish this. In addition, though Mills believes he can pursue his project of theorizing white supremacy without attending to class considerations, I will argue that he cannot successfully do so. For race, I will argue, is not a stand-alone domination system, even one that interacts with other (allegedly) stand-alone ones, such as class and gender. Rather, our understanding of race already incorporates (though only in part) class concepts and processes. In this way, Mills's failure to provide an accurate account of class detracts from his conception of race and white supremacy. For example, he fails to recognize that white supremacy as an actually existing socio-economic-political system can actually harm the legitimate interests of large numbers of whites. My argument requires preserving both race and class as domination systems with their own (though necessarily intersecting) character. Thus, I will be following Mills's strictures in avoiding a "class reductionist" way of thinking about the connections of race and class.

Race's Relation to Class

Both class and race are normatively complex domains. There are several distinct forms of both racial and class wrongfulness and even of the "racial injustice" and "class injustice" subsets of that wrongfulness. In the racial area, for example, racial discrimination, racial inequality, racial insensitivity, racial microaggressions, racial stigma, racial oppression, and racial misrecognition all name distinct (if sometimes partly overlapping) categories of wrongfulness.

Although this internal complexity is itself sometimes lost sight of in discussions of race, it is also quite common for a comparable complexity in the class domain not to be recognized. I want to give some indication of that latter complexity here. The following are all distinct forms of class-based injustice: (1) lack of access to a basic minimum of fundamental human goods such as food, shelter, and health care; (2) unequal family economic and social resources undermining equality of opportunity (understood here as the possibility for occupational success) for the next generation; (3) the gap between different tiers in the economic hierarchy is too great; (4) class standing affects the social valuing (the "social bases of self-respect," in John Rawls's terminology [2001, 60]) generally attached to economic and occupational positions in ways that are unjust and sometimes damaging to their occupants' sense of self-worth; and (5) owners of enterprises exploit their workers. These five categories of injustice are distinct from one another, although there can be overlap among them (e.g., part of the wrongfulness of the inequalities in (3) is that persons in the lower tiers lack the basic minimum in (1)). But all involve "class" broadly construed. Mills does not articulate this complex normative structure of class-based injustice and wrongfulness.

One familiar way class plays an essential role in understanding race is that some of the concepts we use to characterize familiar forms of racial wrongfulness are of a class character. For example, it is generally regarded as in some way unjust or wrong that in the US, whites' median household (family of four) income is $79,000 while Blacks' is $48,000.[1] Comparable racial disparities involve wealth, health, worth and quality of home, and education—all standardly regarded as class phenomena. What makes these disparity-related injuries racial is that the source of the deprivation is the sufferer's racial identity. But what the sufferer is *deprived of* is a good standardly understood in class terms. Not all race-based ills and wrongs are class-based, however. The injury of being stigmatized because of one's race—for example, as a terrorist for being Muslim, or a "foreign" carrier of Covid because of being Asian—is not. Suppression of the Black vote by Republicans is not (Anderson 2019). Nevertheless, many race-related wrongs do involve a class-based dimension. And *some* particular racial stigmas incorporate class-related elements, for instance, a stereotype of Blacks as low-income.[2]

Because some racial injustices involve class categories, class-based processes can contribute to generating them. For example, the degree of (racial) disparity between, and the degree of racial injustice of, the median or mean overall incomes of Blacks and whites are affected by many economic or economic policy factors, such as salaries of different occupations, tax rates for different incomes, the robustness of the society's welfare system that provides public support to people of lower income, and neoliberal economic processes that increase income inequality overall. These processes shrink or exacerbate racial disparities and their degree of injustice but are not driven by an explicit racial logic or intent. ("Disparate impact" is a normative legal term expressing this phenomenon.) Indeed, we can construe "white supremacy" as a scalar concept. That is, a social order can be white supremacist *to different degrees*, depending on degrees of unjust advantage of whites over non-whites, in different domains or overall (in addition to its primary "binary" use referring to a social order with *any* significant degree of white advantage).

This point does not reduce race to class. Economic factors can only exacerbate a racial disparity that has already been created by at least partly racial processes, such as direct racial discrimination or the legacy of race-based structures such as Jim Crow segregation. Nor does the sometimes-causal dependence of racial disparities on class processes imply that in some overall way, class is causally more important than race or vice versa in our current global or national order. Mills plausibly argues that in at least some social orders, such as Nazi Germany and Jim Crow segregation, race was clearly "more important" than class (2003, 163; 2017b, 46; 2003). I am making the more modest claim that in the current social order globally and nationally in the US: it is impossible to give an adequate account of white supremacy without taking account of class. As bell hooks puts it, "It is impossible to talk meaningfully about ending racism without talking about class" (2000, 7).

Let us now turn to Mills's explicit presentations of class, in its own right and in relation to race. There is no single place where Mills provides an account of class that fully covers his accounts elsewhere, but an important discussion, more extended than his usual references to class, is the following passage from "Retrieving Rawls for Racial Justice?" a comparison between race and class with respect especially to the moral character of their ideological underpinnings.

> As such, racial discrimination can be condemned across the liberal spectrum since it breaches the norm of equal personhood and respect upon which liberalism qua liberalism is supposed to rest—the "equal rights" of all "men" trumpeted by the American and French revolutions against the premodern world, the ancien régime of ascriptive hierarchy and differentiated status. [...] Racial injustice is, most fundamentally, a refusal to respect equal personhood, whether in the original rights violations or in the legacy of such violations. *Racial injustice is antiliberal.*
>
> Contrast that with class disadvantage arising out of market workings. In a modern class society, as against a premodern caste society, the white (male) working class is not being kept down by antiliberal laws and discriminatory social practices. Rather people compete on the market, some do worse than others, and the children of the latter grow up in homes and neighborhoods where family resources are thinner and the schools are worse. Presuming the competition was fair by capitalist norms, children will be disadvantaged in escaping their parents' status, but not barred. But a racist society where through discrimination, segregation, etc., poor black kids do not get an equal chance *does* violate capitalist market norms. To be on a lower rung of the social ladder because of bad luck in the social lottery is different from being on a lower rung because of social oppression that denies equal personhood. *Class injustice is anti-left-liberal.*
>
> *(2013, 20)*

This passage sets up a contrast that frames much of Mills's thinking about race and class normatively. It is that racial injustice is a much more substantial moral violation than class injustice, and thus generates a much greater moral claim for prevention, mitigation, and rectification. This is so because, at least in the "classic" period of white supremacy, when it took the forms of colonialism, imperialism, and slavery (and Mills generally counts Jim Crow segregation and South African apartheid in this general category), it consisted in treating and regarding the non-white other as a "sub-person" (1998, 6). He claims there is no counterpart on the class side; the working class were not viewed as sub-persons but rather had a kind of equal status in capitalist societies, as both market agents and citizens. Workers do suffer from the inequities of a capitalist economic and social order, but at a qualitatively lesser moral level than people of color under white supremacy.

Mills identifies treating persons as "sub-persons" with denying them basic rights (often called "negative" rights) such as life, liberty, and property, as colonial, slave, imperialist, and segregationist orders did. He argues that class injustice does not involve such deprivation of basic rights. He sees this distinction as another expression of the way the wrong/injustice involved in white supremacist orders is much greater than that involved in class injustice.

In the quote above, Mills emphasizes that the existence of these race-based social orders in the modern period (at least from the late eighteenth century on) challenges the standard

Enlightenment view that (1) the "liberal" revolutions (French and American) established social orders in which liberal rights were honored across all populations; (2) ascriptive hierarchies (ones in which characteristics at birth [such as race, gender, and ancestry] determine one's position as adults in the hierarchical social orders of the society in question) were rejected; and (3) all members of those societies were regarded as persons. These "modern" societies did do away with these ascriptive hierarchies, but only for the white population, not for the subject and enslaved populations. So modern societies remained stratified ones in which persons of color (and women) were not accorded an equal civic status reflective of being regarded as equals. However, it is not clear that the *current* post-colonial (even if neo-colonial) and post-segregationist form of white supremacy dominant in Western countries and indeed on the global arena is still accurately characterized as resting on treating people of color as sub-persons.

Different Regimes, Different Foundations

Mills sometimes explicitly recognizes that "white supremacy" can name historically and normatively significantly different variants. In "Racial Exploitation" (an important source for his views related to class) he says, "Here [i.e., the US or Europe in the present] the inequity does not arise from R2s still being stigmatized as of inferior status, or at least such stigmatization is not essential to the process [presumably, the process resulting in the inequity]. White supremacy is no longer overt, and the statuses of R1s and R2s have been formally equalized (for example, through legislative change)" (2017a, 125).[3] This is a quite normatively/morally significant difference from classic white supremacy as he understands it. No longer is the polity pervaded with, and regarded by the white population as resting on, the sense that R2s are inherently inferior in a manner captured by the idea of "sub-persons," as it was in the slavery, segregation, and colonial eras. Yet it is still very racially unjust.

A second formulation of the normative difference between different historical white supremacist regimes:

> The present period of de facto global white supremacy is characterized by a more complicated normative arrangement, an abstract/formal extension of previously color-coded principles to the nonwhite population. [...] Even though such an extension is a real normative advance, by no means to be despised, it does not constitute a genuine challenge to white supremacy unless and until the means to correct for the effects of past racial subordination are included in the rewriting.
>
> *(1998, 107)*

As in the prior passage, Mills does not supply a positive characterization of the present normative order, only that it involves an "abstract/formal" extension of former principles applicable to the white population to people of color. That characterization seems to deny that replacing the laws of Jim Crow segregation with non-discriminatory and anti-discrimination laws is *substantive*, not just abstract and formal. Genuine rights were extended to people of color that they did not have before. Mills wants to emphasize rights and their honoring as the important marker for whether a group is treated as persons rather than sub-persons. And the shift from Blacks having few rights under Jim Crow to having a full panoply of rights after the civil rights legislation of the 1960s that undermined the legal foundations of Jim Crow seems an important step forward normatively. Because Mills makes rights acknowledgment a measure of whether personhood is being recognized, it seems he cannot think the *current* racially unjust regime rests on a sub-personhood ideology.

Of course, the point Mills is emphasizing in this quote is that the possession of these rights by R2s does not undermine white supremacy as a systemic advantage system; to do that would require rectification of the socio-economic disadvantages created by the prior white supremacy system and not addressed by the kind of rights provided (e.g., civil rights such as the right to vote). That is an important point and shows the limitations of a rights regime that does not address economic or welfare issues. But it does not speak to whether the racial injustices that remain unaddressed are best understood as now resting on a sub-personhood ideology, and in these two passages he seems to be, if unclearly or ambivalently, saying it does not. Mills claims that there is little difference between de jure and de facto regimes of rights, but he may be conflating whether the society remains white supremacist in both cases with whether there is a significant difference in their moral character (and thereby ignoring the latter issue, the one I am concerned with here). Mills builds a case for reparations partly on the "rights violation" idea he connects with classic white supremacy, together with the notion that our current social/racial order is a "legacy" of the classic period. I cannot deal with this complex issue here but want to note that the legacy idea is perfectly consistent with the notion that the current order has a different normative character than classic white supremacy. Just because B is a legacy of A does not mean B has the exact same normative character as A, only that it shares *some* important empirical and normative features (e.g., being racially unjust), in addition to being a causal descendant of A. If we are to compare current white supremacy's moral character to that of the class-based system of injustice, we need a more positive characterization of the former than Mills provides. Material racial injustices continue to characterize our social order. How do we understand the racial attitudes that underlie them, if they are not an attribution of sub-personhood to R2s?

Social psychologists and philosophers have devoted a good deal of attention to this question. By and large, they have produced explanations, some competing, some complementing, that encompass morally problematic attitudes and sentiments. "Aversive racism," "laissez faire racism," "cultural racism," "implicit bias," "microaggressions," and "colorblindness" are all wrongful race-related attitudes, sentiments, or ideologies. They involve neither fully regarding the racial other as a sub-person nor a robust sense of equality with racial others, but something in between.

So the difference between these current objectionable racial attitudes and the earlier sub-person forms, like the difference between them and fully egalitarian attitudes, is one of degree, but a degree that constitutes a qualitative difference. Like white supremacy itself, these problematic racial attitudes have a scalar character. A white person who does not embrace strict equality with people of color has morally objectionable views, but ones that do not necessarily fall within the "sub-person" ideological framework. I think the notion of disrespect well captures the intermediate attitudinal terrain of today's white supremacy, somewhere between equality and the severe degree of inequality of moral status expressed by "sub-person," and Mills implies this when he writes of violations of the "norm of equal personhood and respect" (2013, 20).[4]

In an attempt to channel Mills's famous use of diagrams, I suggest a picture that looks something like the following, where ">>>>" means "more morally objectionable than":

A. regarding the racial other as a sub-person >>>>
B. disrespecting the racial other >>>>
C. regarding the racial other as a full equal

A is more morally objectionable than B, and B is more morally objectionable than C. It is a scale of attitudes differentiated by their moral objectionability. It is also partly historical in that A and B represent different historical periods in white supremacy. Often we want to emphasize how distant both the middle and its extreme counterpart are from the egalitarian attitudes and social order that justice demands, thereby establishing that white supremacy in Mills's sense still obtains in our current world. And sometimes, as in the discussion here, we have reason to focus on the moral difference *between* the two non-egalitarian categories (regarding sub-persons and racial disrespect). Because Mills is often concerned to make the former point, the latter one is often left insufficiently addressed. Respect, Mills claims, is "linked to a certain positioning in the racial polity" (2018, 159). The mistake I find in Mills is that he has already described the polity in a way that makes social positioning binary in nature—leaving no room for a scalar understanding. Put differently, Mills discusses respect in the spirit of my suggestion here, though without making an explicit distinction between the classic and contemporary forms of white supremacy in which "racial disrespect" operates. In general, Mills treats "racial disrespect" in a binary way, emphasizing the contrast with racial respect and not clearly leaving room for qualitative differences within racial disrespect.

Material Situations of People of Color

In addition to changes in whites' racial ideology and attitudes, the socio-economic-political situations of people of color in Western societies, though far from just, are of an entirely different order than in the societies of classic white supremacy. To deny this is, for one thing, to deny that the struggles Blacks, Indigenous people, Latino/a's, and Asian-Americans fought for in their particular movements for civil rights, equality, and freedom (in the US) had a significant impact on the normative character of the resultant social order. For example, people of color are now a much higher proportion of the professional-managerial class than they were before these movements. People of color are routinely in positions of authority over whites. Prohibitions on racial discrimination are often codified or constitute norms of behavior in organizational settings, permitting challenges to unequal treatment (though far from stamping it out). People of color have the right to vote and can challenge failures of their societies to protect that right.[5] None of this was possible in colonial, slave, or de jure segregated societies. If we acknowledge that white supremacy can have a scalar character (as described above), it would be accurate to say that white supremacy today is distinctly less severe than its classic form.

To repeat, I am in no way questioning whether our current order is white supremacist in Mills's sense of a structure of unjust race-based advantage/disadvantage resting on a historical legacy of a white supremacist society with a sub-person ideology, not only in the sense of its being a causal antecedent but that something of classic white supremacy's character continues to play a role in its contemporary manifestation. I entirely affirm that characterization and share Mills's sense of the moral urgency of fighting against that (current) injustice.

Thus, to summarize, Mills occasionally explicitly recognizes, and recognizes in theory, that the current form of white supremacy rests on a normative foundation distinct from its classic form, in which white supremacy was rationalized by the imputed sub-personhood of Blacks and other people of color.[6] Overall, in its current form, Blacks are not seen as full equals with whites, but they are not seen as sub-persons either. Mills is putting this discussion in service of a contrast between the moral character of class and race; but the relevant contrast requires the absence with respect to class of an ideology or set of attitudes comparable to those of the *current* white supremacist regime. Prior to inquiring into what might be a comparable normative entity on the class side, my point here is that the entity on the race side has to be the contemporary version, not (necessarily) the sub-person version of classic white supremacy.

However, although sometimes recognizing the modern shift to a non-sub-personhood ideological foundation, Mills has a stronger tendency to blur this distinction and to assert that the current form of white supremacy also rests on the denial of personhood, and on a violation of the libertarian rights reflective of that form. For example, in one of his last essays, Mills writes, "If the wrong has involved the systematic denial of personhood [...] as racial wrongs typically do, then correction requires that this denial be retracted through a reaffirmation of racial personhood" (2019, 117). Recall the previously quoted claim that "racial injustice [common to both classic and contemporary social orders] is, most fundamentally, a refusal to respect equal personhood" (2013, 20). And that is what he means by his summary statement of the paragraph: "Racial injustice is antiliberal," meaning it violates the basic rights attached to personhood. And Mills implies that this is true of the present.

This view is connected with Mills's thinking, as he says in the long quote (p. 77), that racial injustice in general, thus in the present as well, would be "condemned across the liberal spectrum," i.e., including libertarian liberals, in contrast to class injustice, which can, he claims, only be condemned by left-wing liberalism but not by libertarians. Mills implies here that this contrast provides a more secure footing, at least in the sense of a wider spectrum of ideological buy-in, for the condemnation of racial injustice than class injustice. But that view is somewhat at odds with his conceding in his 2018 "Racial Justice" that in fact libertarian-liberals do not look at it this way in that they virtually never subscribe to the reparations argument Mills sees as flowing from the libertarian premise of the denial of fundamental "negative" rights to slaves and colonized peoples (81). It also seems inconsistent with his grounding of his own preferred racial justice principles in Rawlsian, "left-liberal," principles, implying that he regards this foundation as fully intellectually sound, and his observation that the Rawlsian version of liberalism (rather than the libertarian) has become hegemonic among liberals (82). Mills's ambivalence or unclarity about the normative foundation of the differing regimes of white supremacy is a problem. If he wants to compare race and class with regard to their normative character, it matters which normative characterization of racial injustice he uses.

Keeping this ambivalence in mind, let us turn to what Mills says about class injustice in the long quote. He supplies no moral critique of the workings of capitalism there and almost implies that the market allocates rewards fairly—assuming the competition was fair (and challenging the labor theory of value; see 2017a, 119; 2018, 28; 2007, 125). In the long block quote above (p.77), he recognizes no distinct injustice suffered on the basis of class by low-income or working-class adults, noting injustice only in relation to the workers' offspring's lack of equal opportunity.[7]

Lack of equality of opportunity for the working-class offspring's socio-economic success, and in particular "advanc[ing] beyond their parents' socio-economic situation," is, indeed, an important injustice. Nevertheless, the way Mills characterizes this class injustice in comparison to race is misleading. He says the working-class offspring are "disadvantaged" but not "barred" from escaping their parents' socio-economic lot, implying the Black children are barred. However, Black working-class or low-income children are no longer "barred" from advancement the way they were during the segregation era, where they were excluded by law from well-resourced (white) schools and from many avenues of occupational attainment and success. In the present, a low-income Black child is severely hampered from advancement by attending inferior schools, but not really barred. Though in general *more* disadvantaged than the low-income white student (see below), both are disadvantaged rather than barred.

But in addition, the Black child whose opportunities are being contrasted with the white child is, in Mills's statement, a specifically "*poor* Black kid" (my emphasis). Mills would not think an upper-middle-class Black student today would be "barred" from advancement, as such a student would have been under Jim Crow segregation. By bringing in the Black child's poverty, Mills is no longer comparing the appropriate categories. The pertinent comparison is race vs. class—Blacks *of all classes* vs. low-income working-class whites. But in fact, he compares low-income Blacks and low-income whites. He is thus tacitly acknowledging class processes as part of what disadvantages the "poor black kid," and that the disadvantage is not purely racial. And he is drawing on but not acknowledging a sense of class injustice as part of what he is portraying explicitly as a purely racial injustice.

In addition, the spirit of the long quote does not convey the pervasive and systemic ways class on its own constitutes a barrier to equality of opportunity—for example, that predominantly white working-class schools, e.g., in rural areas, have nothing like the resources and cultural capital of well-resourced white-dominated upper-middle-class schools.[8] Students in those schools (on average—of course, there are many exceptions, as there are in the race case as well) have less qualified teachers, lesser cultural cachet to help students get into good colleges, a weaker culture of achievement, fewer resources for educational programs, and so on. In addition, upper-middle-class students have other life advantages not located in the schools themselves, from their parents' social, cultural, and financial capital. These class-based injustices are greater in the US than in most European countries (Bradbury et al 2015). These injustices are comparable to those of race where class is held constant.

Race and Class in Relation to Exploitation

Another context in which Mills explicitly contrasts class and race is that of exploitation. He says that the proletariat in the metropole is exploited only at the point of production, while the colonized (and also, he claims, the Black and brown inhabitants of the white supremacist metropole) are further economically disadvantaged in all domains of life. He cites, as examples of the latter, Blacks paying more for inferior goods in ghettos, paying higher rent for housing, and Black enterprises not being permitted access to white markets (2003, 188; 2017a, 127–29). Mills refers to this wider disadvantaging as "exploitation."

If we are to understand exploitation in that broader, beyond-the-workplace way, then class exploitation has to be understood in the same way. Low-income workers are disadvantaged not only inside their workplaces but also by the insufficient wages they receive, so that they have to contend with inferior housing, neighborhoods, education, health care, and the ability to provide their children with what they regard as decent life prospects. The intensified inequality of the last 40 years or so has reduced the working class's relative socio-economic position in society across all of its domains (as Mills recognizes elsewhere [2003, 147]).[9]

So, class is a source of pervasive disadvantage, entirely analogous to the pervasive disadvantage in Mills's "racial exploitation," even if the specific forms and processes of disadvantage are partly different in the two contexts. Of course, it is true that Black working-class persons suffer greater disadvantage than working-class whites because they suffer from both class and racial disadvantage ("exploitation" in this context). Well-off Blacks, who may experience some forms of disadvantage (job discrimination in their higher-level workplaces, for example), do *not,* for the most part, experience the forms of disadvantage involved in what Mills means by "exploitation." They are not living in food deserts, paying for inferior goods in ghettos, or paying higher rents (since they are largely homeowners). Mills misstates when he claims that race exploitation is much worse than class exploitation on the grounds that the former goes far beyond the workplace while the latter is limited to the workplace. Both go far beyond the workplace. This is another context in which Mills, without noting it, includes class disadvantages as part of what he portrays as racial disadvantage.

Thus, to summarize, Mills misportrays the comparative character of contemporary race and class injustice by (1) (albeit not consistently) portraying contemporary race obstacles as having the same character they had in classic racially ordered societies (resting on sub-personhood ideology); (2) incorporating class characteristics and processes into the characterization and implied normative assessment of racial disadvantage but without noting this; and (3) failing to articulate class as a deep and pervasive structure of disadvantage and injustice, including the range of such forms mentioned (inadequate access to fundamental goods, too great disparities in economic resources, inequality of opportunity, social devaluing, exploitation in the workplace).[10] He thus understates the character of current class injuries and (though not consistently) overstates the character of racial ones, and does not establish that racial injury is morally much worse than class injury, as he is claiming in the long quote above (p.77).

We can plausibly regard class-related harms as often comparable to race-related harms in character. Many such harms are straightforwardly material—inadequate nourishment, housing, health care, and job opportunities. In addition, there are harms of what are often called "recognition," which Mills refers to as "respect." Being regarded as a sub-person, even apart from any material exploitation and deprivation flowing from that, is a serious personal harm, as Mills emphasizes. In its non-sub-person form, racial disrespect is harmful. But low-income people of any race, including whites, are subject to those harms as well. Low-income people are often disrespected by higher (upper middle and upper) class people, often (especially in the US) seen as failures, their low socio-economic status being taken as reflecting their inferior "merit" and capability. As in the racial situation, for the economically disadvantaged, disrespect therefore adds insult to (material) injury, and low-income people often internalize that disrespect as shame for their class position (see hooks 2000; Sayer 2005; Sandel 2021; Sennett and Cobb 1973).[11]

This is not to say that every comparable harm has the exact same character and severity in the race and the class case. For example, because of its history, current anti-Black stigma may well be more severe, on average, than anti-low-income stigma (for whites). But this average difference in degree (in *some* cases, class stigma will be greater than racial stigma) does not make them of entirely different kinds, as Mills's argument implies (see Blum 2023).

If class and race harms and injustices are comparable, this has implications for Mills's claim (echoed in much of the literature on white supremacy) that white supremacy benefits all whites, a claim he qualifies in this way: "The claim that racial exploitation [of Blacks by whites] exists does not commit one to the claim that its benefits are all necessarily distributed equally" (2017a, 121). Indeed, it may seem true by definition—white supremacy as a system of white advantage—that all whites must benefit from it. But some whites may be better off than some relevantly comparable Blacks yet without themselves benefiting from the white supremacist social order. Aspects of the complex white supremacy structure can work against the interests of particular subgroups of whites.

For example, seeking to retain advantage over people of color can blind some whites to their shared interests with people of color in circumstances that can be quite important for their well-being, such as securing more robust health care, preserving social security benefits in the face of attempts to weaken them, or having a union or not. Whites can be misled into thinking that their belief that they are superior to people of color is a genuine good to them when, based on a falsehood, it is illusory and interferes with their ability to seek common class-based goods through concerted action (see Tanchuk et al 2021). Their white supremacist belief that Black people are unworthy sometimes expresses itself in hostility toward government assistance for vulnerable people generally—for example, Southern state governments' declining to expand their Medicaid programs permitted under the Affordable Care Act that would have benefited low-income whites in those states. (As of February 2024, 10 US states had not accepted federal funding to expand Medicaid that would provide health coverage to low-income adults in their state.) In these ways, institutional forms and ideologies of white supremacist societies can systematically disadvantage low-income people of every race, and thereby whites.

Mills's recognition of the differential benefit of white supremacy to whites does not provide a principled way of holding that benefit at zero. The differential benefit logic opens up the possibility that some whites not only benefit minimally but are actually harmed in an overall way (if not, of course, in every single respect) by white supremacy. Mills does sometimes recognize that white workers might do better either in a non-racist social democratic or a socialist social order than they are doing in their current form of white supremacist capitalism. He suggests that a "convincing case can be made that though they [i.e., white workers] do gain in this present order, they lose by comparison to an alternative one" (2017a, 133). He thinks about what might be done to help white workers recognize this so as to join in an interracial alliance to bring about that more beneficial social order. But saying that white low-income workers could benefit in a non-racist social order is not quite to acknowledge that the current white supremacist order actually harms them. It does so because features of white supremacy harm their class-related (among other) interests.[12]

Class is deeply implicated in the white supremacist order, and in the racial order more generally. It helps to situate our understanding of what it does and does not mean to say that a given social order is "white supremacist." We cannot take that to mean that it automatically benefits all white people. And we cannot examine its racial dynamic purely on its own, as Mills said he thought he could do, for class considerations are internal to white supremacy and to its normative character.

Oppression Asymmetries

Mills argues on substantive grounds that race is a stronger determinant of people's life conditions than class or gender. At one point, he makes this argument in the context of a more general rejection of the "Oppression Symmetry Thesis" (OST), the view that all forms of oppression are equally "morally bad" or equally causally significant (2003, 161–64; 2017b, 47). Mills is partially defending Marx's implicit rejection of OST, but also saying Marx was wrong to accord class the asymmetric primacy over other social dominance axes. Rather, Mills argues, race has that primacy.

I will not examine Mills's view on this issue further, except to say that my argument in this essay does not require OST, and I agree with Mills in rejecting it. Indeed, I think my own view is even compatible with Mills's granting race primacy over class in some significant respect (though not in every respect). I am arguing only that class is very important in the life situations of people of color, that what we think of as "race" is already entwined with class considerations, and that Mills fails to give class its due, both in itself and in relation to race. I am not explicitly arguing that class is "more important" than race overall, and I am not certain a clear meaning can be attached to that claim.

We can shed light on Mills's inadequate account of class and its relationship to race by reminding ourselves of the historical context of the colonialist, slavery, and imperialist systems that constituted the initial, classic forms of white supremacy in our world. Mills's account of these systems emphasizes their racial character, which, as we have seen, he frames as whites treating people of color (as slaves, colonial, and imperial subjects) as sub-persons. But these historical systems of oppression were not only racial and racist projects but capitalist (and nationalist) ones as well. The capitalist dimension combined an extreme form of coerced labor exploitation and resource extraction in the "periphery" with market-based exploitation of workers in the metropole (in settler colonialism-with-slavery, as in the US, both processes took place in the metropole). These systems not only denied personhood in the recognitional/evaluative sense but, as Mills also often notes, relied on the sub-personhood ideology to justify their exploitative and extractive economic practices (2017a, 124). But the capitalist dimension also combined with the racial dimension to send the extracted wealth of the colonies back to the metropole, advantaging the (then white) proletariat in the metropole, though of course to nothing like the degree it enriched the capitalist class (Rodney 2018).

In the post-colonial world, former colonial subjects immigrated to the (former) metropoles (UK, France, Belgium, Netherlands, etc.), seeking economic advancement. Joining white workers as citizens in those societies, they enjoy some of the benefits of the prior colonialist wealth transfer, lifting them substantially above their fellow workers in their former homelands in the periphery, as they seek to do through immigrating to the metropoles. In that way, they benefit to some degree from the capitalist/nationalist dimension of the colonial project.

But as (descendants of) racialized former subjects, they are also often discriminated against in the metropoles and so do not experience that capitalist/colonialist benefit to the same degree as the white workers. Nevertheless, they also share with the native white proletariat the pervasive material disadvantage and multiple forms of class injustice of at least a substantial, low-income segment of the proletariat under capitalism. Mills is, of course, aware of all these processes, but his focusing only on the purely racial character of white supremacist capitalism often leads him to overlook both the ongoing structures of class domination and injustice that operate on former colonial subjects and their descendants now in the metropole and also the benefits of prior capitalist colonialism that the proletariat-of-color accrues by living in the metropoles.

Mills generally fails to bring into view these capitalist and nationalist dimensions of colonialism, slavery, and imperialism, and of the post-colonial social order, and therefore how those features continue to interact with its distinctly racial dimensions. He very clearly recognizes the economic dimensions of white supremacy (2003, 187–89, 204–10). However, he seldom attaches economic disadvantage and exploitation to a distinctly Black, Latino/a, and Indigenous segment of the low-income working class in the present, whose simultaneous location as people of color in a white supremacist system and members of a significantly disadvantaged class in a class domination system renders them disadvantaged along those two distinct but very intertwined axes of disadvantage. This lacuna, and his more general failure to keep both the capitalist and the white supremacist systems in his analytical field of vision, are reflected in Mills's inadequate account of class in contemporary white supremacist orders.

Conclusion

We should also situate Mills's published work on class and race, and what I am arguing are some of its inadequacies, in historical political context, noting two particular recent developments. The first is the greatly increased public attention to racial justice issues, occasioned partly by the Black Lives Matter movement founded in 2013 and ramped up by the enormous, global, public response to the killing of George Floyd in 2020. Many Western countries, in addition to the US, have seen the kind of public attention to racial injustice Mills called for.[13]

A second pertinent development is the rise of a post-communist socialist or social democratic presence in American political life, a result of several different factors, one certainly being the disenchantment with neoliberal capitalism, initially occasioned by the Great Recession of 2008–09, another, noted specifically by Mills, a degrading of the life and work conditions of many sectors of the proletariat (Dawson 2019). Mills's earlier turn away from class-related concerns, and from Marxism, had been occasioned *in part* by his sense that the socialist and Marxist political traditions were, at least for the foreseeable future, nowhere on the horizon. Mills stated this point of view quite starkly in 2012: "It seemed (and seems) to me that at the present time period, in this country [the US], given its history, the declaration of an anti-capitalist agenda will immediately isolate and marginalize you" (2012, 337). As we have seen, for some years Mills had looked to the liberal tradition for the intellectual resources to engage with race politically and to bring race into the mainstream of political philosophy and thought. I am not here able to assess his specific project of founding anti-racism on liberalism (see Darby 2019), but nor is it clear to me how fully intellectually (as contrasted with strategically) attached he was to that project. However, the combination of his abandonment of Marxism and socialism, and liberalism's weak foundation for an understanding of class, surely contributed to Mills's own pulling away from a focus on class that had informed some of his earlier work on race.

But as Mills began to recognize, at least with the Occupy movement of 2011, these new progressive and even (from the perspective of the 2000s) radical forces in American political life could ground hope for wider movements for progressive change than he had seen in the prior 30 years or so. In his occasional remarks about the possibilities of interracial political alliance and movement, Mills criticized a traditional class-based approach that ignored race and hoped racial division would be overcome by a focus on shared class interests (Dawson 2019). He did not remark on, and may not have been aware of, a fairly recent development in interracial organizing that brings an explicit anti-racist focus into a class-anchored approach. This approach calls out racism but also emphasizes ways that racism hurts whites as well as people of color, rather than leading with a demand that low-income and working-class whites abandon their (alleged) white privilege (Haney-Lopez 2019). Very occasionally, one sees in Mills's late writings a suggestion that more decisively left traditions could speak to the possibility of an anti-racist future in the context of definitively progressive and even socialist political movements (Dawson 2019; Mills 2018). Perhaps if he had lived longer, he might have turned more toward a synthesis of race and class (possibly in its Marxist form), bolstered by a greater hopefulness for the possibilities of an interracial movement for progressive and radical change.[14]

I have argued that Mills is correct to see white supremacy as a sociopolitical order with its own character and logic, not reducible to, nor a mere expression of, a more fundamental class-based social order. But I have argued that neither is white supremacy as autonomous from the structures of class injustice as Mills implies. I have argued that, in his writings, Mills fails to portray class as a domination system with its distinctive forms of harm and injustice that are inextricably intertwined with the racial domination system and its particular normative character. He fails to recognize clearly how class interests can result in white low-income workers, overall, being harmed rather than benefiting from white supremacist structures and ideologies.

Race cannot be understood apart from class, and Mills's attempt to do so weakens his account of race. But Mills's permanent contribution to contemporary political philosophy and political thought more generally was to press a recognition of race as a social system structuring, and rendering unjust and wrong, the national and global social orders of our time—thereby requiring of political philosophy that racial justice be a core concern of social justice.[15]

Notes

1 United States Census Bureau, *Current Population Survey, 2021 and 2022 Annual Social and Economic Supplements.* https://www.pgpf.org/blog/2022/11/income-and-wealth-in-the-united-states-an-overview-of-recent-data (Peter Peterson Institute).

2 I will sometimes follow Mills in speaking only of Blacks with regard to racial injustice, but he often means Blacks to stand in for people of color in general. And yet his overall project is concerned with the specificity of the Black experience in the modern world. I will sometimes, but not always, also treat the cited example of Blacks in that general way.

3 Mills often uses the "R1/R2" terminology to refer to racial domination systems in general, with R1 implied as white and R2 as people of color, or sometimes Blacks in particular. I will sometimes follow him in that usage. When Mills says that "white supremacy is no longer overt," he presumably means that white advantage is no longer officially declared to be morally appropriate. He does not mean to deny that white advantage is a matter of empirical and visible sociohistorical fact (as "no longer overt" might be thought to imply).

4 I am indebted to my former student Hannah Carrillo for the idea that there could be a form of racial disrespect rendering the racial other less degraded than what is involved in "sub-personhood."

5 Recent attempts by several Republican-dominated legislatures in the United States to restrict voting by people of color—though never acknowledged explicitly as the actual target of that legislation—reveal that large swaths of the American political class do not fully accept (but nor do they fully reject, as in the Segregation era) the equal right to vote for citizens of all racial groups. (See Anderson 2019).

6 Another periodization Mills sometimes articulates concerns the rise of Enlightenment egalitarianism mentioned earlier. Prior to that, slavery and colonialism did not rely as much on a "sub-personhood" ideology because those domination systems were by and large not challenged and were not regarded as requiring a morally-based ideological justification. Mills accepts George Frederickson's view that the sub-personhood ideology degraded the slave to a lower human status than in the pre-Enlightenment period (2018, 15).

7 I will generally use "low-income" (standardly defined in the US as double the poverty line) to characterize the generic class-disadvantaged category.

8 I am avoiding the terminology of "middle class" because its use in general American discourse is so imprecise. While, as in educational contexts, it is often used to contrast with "working class," in other contexts, many working-class people also (or instead) identify as "middle class," and that usage is also entirely familiar in popular discourse. For my purposes in this essay, the designation "upper middle class" will serve well enough.

9 I do not define "working class" here. While it matters how one defines it, the broad-stroked categories I am employing in the context of Mills's argument may not require it. In the US, lack of a college degree might be a rough and ready definition, which would also include "low income" persons. I generally use "working class" when referring to the proletariat, or in a distinctly Marxist intellectual context, and "low income" when referring more specifically to class disadvantage.

10 In the long quote (2013, 20), Mills refers to "the white (male) working class." He may be thinking of the working class in Marx's time, and perhaps also the view of the working class in the literature he calls "white Marxism." But the context here should be pulling for the actual working class of contemporary American society. I think it is fair to say that in Mills's writing in general, there is little recognition that the working class in the US is composed, and disproportionately so, of women, Blacks, Latino/as, and Indigenous women and men. Was Mills aware of this demographic fact? Of course. But this awareness almost never makes its way into his theorizing about class and race.

11 Bell hooks, a prominent Black feminist, writes poignantly about her mother's sense of class-based shame, summarizing it: "[H]er sense of shame around class was deep and intense" (2000, 28).

12 An example of *non*-class-based white interests harmed by white supremacy is Southern US cities in the 1960s shutting down their municipal swimming pools rather than comply with a directive to integrate them, thereby depriving white families of public access to swimming. (McGhee 2021, chapter 2).

13 It is not clear how much the actual situation of disadvantaged Blacks, browns, and Indigenous peoples in the US has been significantly improved by the public attention mentioned. I am grateful to Mickaella Perina for calling my attention to this point.

14 But Mills always thought of himself as a "radical," including when he was working within a liberal framework, as expressed in his preferred designation for his own position, "Black radical liberalism" and his close association with the Radical Philosophy Association (Jones 2022, 245).

15 I am grateful to both my "race/class" group (Mickaella Perina and Christopher Lewis) for feedback on an earlier draft of this paper and for conversations on these issues over the past four years, and my Race and Philosophy group (Elvira Basevich, Jorge Garcia, Sally Haslanger, Adam Hosein, José Mendoza, Megan Mitchell, and Tommie Shelby) for conversations about race over many years.

Bibliography

Anderson, Carol. 2019. *One Person, No Vote: How Voter Suppression is Destroying Our Democracy*. London: Bloomsbury Publishing.

Blum, Lawrence. 2023. "Race and Class Together." *American Philosophical Quarterly* 60 (4): 381–95.

Bradbury, Bruce, Miles Corak, Jane Waldfogel, and Elizabeth Washbrook. 2015. *Too Many Children Left Behind: The U.S. Achievement Gap in Comparative Perspective*. New York: Russell Sage Foundation.

Darby, Derrick. 2019. "Charles Mills's Liberal Redemption Song." *Ethics* 129 (2): 370–97.

Dawson, Michael. 2019. Interview with Charles Mills. New Dawn, (Re-released Sept 28, 2021): https://podcasts.apple.com/us/podcast/celebrating-charles-w-mills-1951-2021-retheorizing/id1213696020?i=1000452907879

Fraser, Nancy, and Axel Honneth. 2003. *Redistribution or Recognition? A Political-Philosophical Exchange*. Brooklyn: Verso.

Haney-Lopez, Ian. 2019. *Merge Left: Fusing Race and Class, Winning Elections, and Saving America*. New York: New Press.

Hooks, Bell. 2000. *Where We Stand: Class Matters*. New York: Routledge.

Jones, Richard A. 2022. "Smadditizin' with Charles W. Mills." *Radical Philosophy Review* 25 (2): 237–52.

McGhee, Heather. 2021. *The Sum of Us: How Racism Costs Everyone and How We Can Prosper Together*. New York: One World.

Mills, Charles. 1998. *Blackness Visible: Essays on Philosophy and Race*. Ithaca: Cornell University Press.

Mills, Charles. 2003. *From Class to Race: Essays in White Marxism and Black Radicalism*. Lanham: Rowman & Littlefield.

Mills, Charles. 2010. *Radical Theory, Caribbean Reality*. Kingston: University of West Indies Press.

Mills, Charles. 2012. "Reply to Nancy Holmstrom and Richard Schmitt." *Radical Philosophy Review* 15 (2): 337–43.

Mills, Charles. 2013. "Retrieving Rawls for Racial Justice? A Critique of Tommie Shelby." *Critical Philosophy of Race* 1 (1): 1–27

Mills, Charles. 2017a. *Black Rights/White Wrongs: The Critique of Racial Liberalism*. New York: Oxford University Press.

Mills, Charles. 2017b. "Intersectional Meditations: A Reply to Kathryn Gines and Shannon Sullivan." *Critical Philosophy of Race* 5 (1): 29–50.

Mills, Charles. 2017c. "Interview." In *On Race: 34 Conversations in a Time of Crisis*. Edited by George Yancy. New York: Oxford University Press.

Mills, Charles. 2018. "Black Radical Kantianism." *Res Philosophica* 95 (1): 1–33

Mills, Charles. 2019. "Race and Global Justice." In *Empire, Race, and Global Justice*. Edited by Duncan Bell. New York: Cambridge University Press.

Mills, Charles, and Carole Pateman. 2007. *Contract and Domination*. Malden: Polity Press.

Mills, Charles, and Katrin Flikschuh. 2018. "Racial Justice." *Aristotelian Society: Aristotelian Society Supplementary Volume* 98: 69–89.

Montiel, Jorge. 2022. "Charles Mills's Radicalism." *Radical Philosophy Review* 25 (2): 265–75.

Neukam, Stephen 2023. "These 10 states have not expanded Medicaid." The Hill, March 23, 2023. https://thehill.com/homenews/state-watch/3914916-these-10-states-have-not-expanded-medicaid/#:~:text=Wyoming%2C%20Kansas%2C%20Texas%2C%20Wisconsin,but%20cannot%20access%20it%20because

Rawls, John. 2001. *Justice as Fairness: A Restatement*. Cambridge: Harvard University Press.

Rodney, Walter. 2018. *How Europe Underdeveloped Africa*. Brooklyn: Verso.

Sandel, Michael. 2021. *The Tyranny of Merit: Can We Find the Common Good*. London: Picador.

Sayer, Andrew. 2005. *The Moral Significance of Class*. London: Cambridge University Press.

Scanlon, Thomas P. 2018. *Why Does Inequality Matter?* New York: Oxford University Press.

Sears, David O, John J. Hetts, James Sidanius, and Lawrence Bobo. 2000. "Race in American Politics: Framing the Debates." In *Racialized Politics: The Debate About Racism in America*. Edited by David Sears, James Sidanius, and Lawrence Bobo. Chicago: University of Chicago Press.

Sennett, Richard, and Jonathan Cobb. 1973. *The Hidden Injuries of Class*. New York: Vintage Press.

Tanchuk, Nicolas, Tomas Rocha, and Marc Kruse. 2021. "Is Complicity in Oppression a Privilege? Toward Social Justice Education as Mutual Aid." *Harvard Education Review* 91 (3): 341–61.

6

MILLS, CONTRACTS, AND THE LIMITS OF LIBERALISM

Clevis Headley

Ill-Conceived Involvement

There is no exaggeration in claiming that, upon publication, Charles W. Mills's *The Racial Contract* (1997) quickly became an object of intense scholarly interest and curiosity and, ultimately, an impetus for exuberant political advocacy. This reaction results partly from Mills's goal to initiate a global paradigm shift in academic circles and beyond. Indeed, Mills's writings at times display the passion and intensity of a new religious or political convert. This impression is further reinforced when premised on the assumption that Mills's disillusionment with dogmatic Marxism led him to identify race, rather than class, as the primary explanatory phenomenon of modern society. Hence, after a waiting time that felt long and unfruitful, the academic equivalent of manna from heaven had finally arrived—of the paucity of texts written by Black philosophers, a unique text written by an unapologetic Black philosopher that was fashioned into a narrative duly informed by the horrible realities of anti-Black racism. Mills achieved this objective by textually weaving, in the most conceivably dramatic way, the heterogenous discourses of history, philosophy, psychology, and economics.

Mills's text served, and continues to serve, as an indisputable example of politically committed and unqualified interdisciplinary engagement. Not to be denied or discouraged, Mills strategically deployed *The Racial Contract* to advocate for a radical paradigm change in philosophy and to challenge, in the most direct and unapologetic way, the alleged purity and apriorism of mainstream philosophy. This confrontation, as intended by Mills, exposes the "false/fake universality" of mainstream philosophy. And to the extent that Mills employed a distinct methodological strategy, it is not the kind of analytic method characteristic of analytic philosophy. His project best makes sense as the execution of a hermeneutics of suspicion in the tradition of Friedrich Nietzsche, Karl Marx, and Sigmund Freud—Mills is unmaking the normative claims of social contract theory and mainstream philosophy to expose the truth about modern society. He seeks to unearth the hidden truth that "white supremacy is the unnamed political system that has made the modern world what it is today" (1997, 1).

DOI: 10.4324/9781003349983-7

This chapter makes the case that Mills's involvement with liberalism is ill-conceived and that he grossly underestimates the extent to which liberalism is inconsistent with efforts to center race, racism, and racial injustice in mainstream political philosophy. Various theoretical and structural issues undermine Mills's project to render liberalism philosophically palatable within the perspective of a critical philosophy of race. So, while I do not fault Mills for correctly condemning the brutal history of racial subordination, his castigating of social contract theorists as de facto co-conspirators in developing and sustaining white supremacy is not altogether justifiable. While Mills acknowledges that there are differences among social contract theorists, he insists that the social contract tradition has advocated formal, normative, and philosophical practices that have rendered the actual nature of modern society opaque. One such feature is the racialization of being, an ontological event whose role in racial subordination has not yet been fully acknowledged or appreciated. But the urgency of attending to race and racism and to the extraordinary role of race in shaping modern existence are precisely the reasons for which we should critically engage with Mills.

Mills's interpretative momentum ironically undermines his attempt to place race and racism at the core of philosophy, given that Mills utilized race primarily as an analytical filter to propel his analysis of the issues and problems in modern and mainstream philosophy. The explicit absence of race from philosophy is, for Mills, an indication of the implicit presence of race in philosophy. Mills precludes the possibility of critically engaging the social contract tradition to expose its internal contradictions and limitations without invoking race. He fails to acknowledge that, from a strictly canonical perspective, while not denying the modern history of racism, slavery, and colonialism, the concept of race in its more familiar use is simply "noise." To the extent that Mills engages with social contract theory, a more apt critical strategy would have been for him to engage in meta-philosophical activities. Probing the conception of philosophy operative in the social contract tradition would have better positioned Mills to investigate the absence of race in this tradition. At least such an approach would have revealed the disciplinary and methodological barriers that have led to race's explicit absence from philosophy. Additionally, even if it were the case that the normative methodology of contractarians has not accommodated critical engagement with race, it would not follow that these philosophers set out intentionally to exclude race as we currently understand it from philosophy. It would be a fallacy of false cause for Mills to claim that it was social contract theorists' interest in excluding race and in promoting white supremacy that led them to pursue their normative philosophical activities.

Finally, Mills's treatment of race and racism is of a piece with the mythology of doctrines against which Quentin Skinner warns in efforts to understand and interpret texts (1969). Most recently, Vanita Seth has used Skinner's critique of the history of ideas to detail some of the pitfalls associated with efforts to trace race and racism prior to modernity. Seth maintains that one such pitfall is the danger of "imposing [arguments,] thoughts, concerns, and practices on [past philosophers] that [they] may not in fact have shared or even conceived of such thoughts, concerns, or practices" (2020, 347).

The structure of this chapter is as follows: the first section deals with Mills's *The Racial Contract* and its relation to socio-political philosophy. The second section focuses on Mills's perspective on the notion of contract and the contract device. The third section critically examines liberalism and Mills's relationship to liberalism. The fourth section focuses on Mills's critical engagement with John Rawls and his critique of the latter's distinction between ideal and non-ideal theory.

The Racial Contract on Traditional Socio-Political Philosophy

Philosophically, *The Racial Contract* interprets the fundamental methodological device of modern social and political philosophy as being complicitous in creating and sustaining white supremacy—modern racial oppression and subordination. Contractarians have historically used the contract device to model the equality of individuals as well as to normatively investigate the nature of political authority. Instead, for Mills, the contract device was a tool invented by white philosophers to engage in socio-political malfeasance. He is confident that his Racial Contract thesis is explanatorily superior to the traditional social contract because it provides a more accurate description and explanation of actual society. As Mills states,

> [T]he notion of a Racial Contract might be more revealing of the real character of the world we are living in, and the corresponding historical deficiencies of its normative theories and practices [social contract theory and Rawls's theory of justice], than the raceless notions currently dominant in political theory.
>
> *(1997, 7)*

But for Mills, the gravest mythology of social contract theory is its appeal to various fictions such as the state of nature and pre-social individuals:

> There is never a "state of nature," but always human beings in social groups of greater or lesser complexity. Correspondingly, the idea of a contract is misleadingly asocial, predicated on a methodological starting-point of "pre-social" individuals whose putatively innate (but actually socially created) characteristics are taken to generate patterns of human interrelation which are then, reversing things, read back into the natural.
>
> *(2000, 441)*

However, one would be sorely mistaken in assuming that *The Racial Contract* restricts its critical focus only to formal philosophical concerns. As we recall, *The Racial Contract* proudly proclaims its political indebtedness to at least three overarching structural insights: (1) white supremacy is an existing global reality; (2) white supremacy is not an epiphenomenon but a materially robust political system; and (3) the system of white supremacy is the historical product of a contract between white people.

Mills's effort to educate white philosophers is not an exclusive exercise in logic but also an exorcism. Mainstream philosophers, according to Mills, have been the victims of a philosophical myth. For Mills, and as Marx had previously noted regarding German philosophers, contractarians are guilty of inverting reality. Mills urges philosophers to reject pale self-subsistent concepts in favor of investigating the human activities and forms of social and political existence that encourage the creation of abstract categories. Hence, philosophers should begin with human activities, forms of social and political life, and derive categories from them. Instead of producing "phases about phases" and chasing after conceptual phantoms of the minds, Mills calls for mainstream philosophers to take seriously Marx's admonition to German idealist philosophers:

> [We] do not set out from what men say, imagine, conceive, nor from men as narrated, thought of, imagined, conceived in order to arrive at men in the flesh. We set out from real, active men, and on the basis of their real life-process we demonstrate the development of the ideological reflexes and echoes of this life-process. The phantoms formed in the human brain are also, necessarily, sublimates of their material life-process, which is empirically verifiable and bound to material premises. [...] Life is not determined by consciousness, but consciousness by life.
>
> *(1947, 47)*

While Marx faulted German philosophers for their blindness to the realities of class, Mills faults white philosophers (particularly Rawls and his penchant for ideal theory) for their blindness to race. White philosophers complacently become infatuated with the abstract categories and concepts of normative philosophy while at the same time remaining clueless about the structural and material realities of race.

Although Mills is critical of the social contract tradition, he nevertheless receives much inspiration from the contract device. Following Carole Pateman's use of the contract device in *The Sexual Contract*, Mills's objective is also to utilize this device to accomplish the same theoretical prominence for race that Pateman secures for gender/sex.

Mills and Contracts: Metaphor or Reality

In his use of the contract device, Mills boldly allies himself with Pateman's *The Sexual Contract* (1988). Although Mills acknowledges that his use of the contract metaphor is different from that of Pateman's, he fails to appreciate the ways in which Pateman's work represents a radical deconstruction or structural undermining of the contract device and of social contract theory. Mills writes,

> Carole Pateman's provocative feminist work [...], *The Sexual Contract*, is a good example of this approach [descriptive analysis grounded in history] (and the inspiration for my own book, though my use is somewhat different), which demonstrates how much descriptive/explanatory life there still is in the contract. Pateman uses it naturalistically, as a way of modeling the internal dynamic of the non-ideal male-dominated societies that actually exist today. So this is [...] a reversion to the original "anthropological" approach [where] the contract *is* intended to be historically explanatory. But the twist is [...] that her purpose is now subversive: to excavate the hidden, unjust male covenant upon which the ostensibly gender-neutral social contract rests.
>
> *(1997, 6)*

Mills does not intend for his exploitation of the contract device to constitute a textual metaphorical appropriation of the trope of "contract." He unabashedly claims that the racial contract is a "historical actuality" (19–31). While he confidently proclaims his recognition of a real racial contract, Mills ironically also contrasts his Racial Contract thesis with the contract of traditional social contract theorists that, he claims, "is not conceived of as an actual historical event" (10). Mills insists that his racial contract "is intended to be historically explanatory," while also enjoying a "descriptive/explanatory life" (6). Seemingly in opposition to normative philosophical practice, Mills states emphatically, "I use [the 'Racial Contract'] not merely normatively, to generate judgments about social justice and injustice, but descriptively, to *explain* the actual genesis of the society and the state, the way society is structured, the way the government functions, and people's moral psychology" (5). However, since its publication, Mills at times seems to be distancing himself from certain views expressed in *The Racial Contract*. Yet he also claims that his later thinking is both a continuation and a bold restating of *The Racial Contract*.

Mills both wants to remain faithful to *The Racial Contract*, while also moving beyond it. For example, he claims that his project was always reconstructive, though he did not communicate this goal in *The Racial Contract*. This reconstructive project involves remaining within the social contract tradition while revising the contractual framework. He states that he wishes to

> facilitate—within a contractual framework—the discussion of matters of non-ideal rectificatory theory. I did not actually draw out the implications of this revisionist approach in *The Racial Contract*, but I am trying to do so here. Given that I did not in the book provide an example of the positive reconstructive use I had in mind, [my] hope is that the present book will correct this mistaken impression.
>
> *(Pateman and Mills, 2007, 237)*

Indeed, five years after the publication of *The Racial Contract,* Mills writes, "The Racial Contract was *not* intended by me to be taken literally; I am not offering a *social-scientific* explanation of anything; and to the extent that I am offering an explanation of, or a way of thinking about something, it is *white supremacy*" (2002, 76). Within a decade, Mills completely retreats from his position in *The Racial Contract* and, in *Contract & Domination* (co-authored with Pateman), states that he "did not intend the 'descriptive/explanatory' claims to be thought of as attempted social science explanation, in terms of an actual literal agreement, but rather as located on the more abstract level distinctive of classic social contract theory, as updated and glossed by Jean Hampton" (2007, 236). Despite Mills's effort to recruit Hampton into the discussion, there remains a glaring contradiction between his earlier and later takes on whether his use of "contract" is metaphorical or literal. Even his new fondness for the notion of contract conceived at a higher level of abstraction directly conflicts with his admonition against the abstractness and normativity of traditional social contract theory, that is, the inverted conception of things characteristic of the social contract tradition that he vehemently opposed.

It is critically important to address Mills's refusal to provide a robust explanation of the relationship between social contract theory and race. Yet, to remain consistent, Mills must acknowledge that he must indeed provide an explanatory hypothesis. An explanation is a statement of the necessary and sufficient conditions for something being the case. Of the multiple types of explanations available, Mills must provide a theoretical explanation of the relationship between social contract theory and race, that is, his explanation must take the form of a theoretical hypothesis, and such a hypothesis will require justification, either in the form of reasons or empirical evidence.

Moreover, despite the fact that Mills is inspired by Pateman's *The Sexual Contract*, he nevertheless fails to appreciate her deconstruction of the notion of contract. As Pateman explains in *Contract & Domination*, "the way in which my argument in *The Sexual Contract* was developed was greatly influenced by the new techniques of theoretical analysis that were being used by deconstructionists and postmodernists in the 1980s" (2007, 219). Contrary to the traditional conception of contract as being consistent with freedom, rights, and property, Pateman states that "One thing that runs right through [my] book is the fact that contract, in my argument is central, as in practice it is the way in which an important form of subordination occurs" (2018, 94). Here, the device of contract is not a reliable prophylactic against exploitation and oppression. Ironically, in fact, a contract can serve as a basis for generating relations of domination. Elizabeth S. Anderson has produced a succinct and provocative framing of Pateman's argument:

> By equating goods in the person with external property, contractarian theory slips in, under a social form which is supposed to preserve the freedom of individuals, a justification for the sustained domination of one person by another. [Social Contracts] all involve the exchange of obedience for protection or subsistence. Contract establishes a sustained relation of domination, in which the party providing protection has the right to determine what the other person must do to fulfill her side of the contract.
>
> *(1990, 1802)*

Unlike Pateman, Mills does not champion the deconstruction of the concept of contract and, thus, his project differs from hers. He writes, "Though it may appear to be such, the 'Racial Contract' is not a 'deconstruction' of the social contract. [...] It criticizes the social contract from a normative base that does not see the ideals of contractarianism themselves as necessarily problematic but shows how they have been betrayed by white contractarians" (1997, 129).

Contracts do not miraculously remedy situations of inequality when the parties involved are not appreciably equally situated. In fact, contracts can mask, and even aggravate, situations of inequality. Pateman's deconstructive analysis of the contract device is lost upon Mills, who, despite his protests to the contrary, embraces an "idealized reconstructed contract," something that he had previously faulted traditional social contract theorists for employing. He writes,

> So from the fact that the actual contract was a bogus contract, it does not follow that an idealized reconstructed contract is not possible. And this is the move I would endorse myself. The point of mapping out the domination contract is then to elucidate both the mechanisms of injustice [...] and to expose the justificatory ideological belief-systems, factual and moral, that have obfuscated and rationalized that injustice.
>
> *(2000, 454)*

Another reason for which Mills's position is not fully consistent with Pateman's project is that he oversimplifies what is in fact an extremely complex position. Pateman's critique of the contract device in relation to (white) women reveals many asymmetries between the situation of such women and that of Black people. The structural dynamics between white men and white women are completely different from the structural dynamics between white people and Black people. For even if white women have been unwilling and unfortunate participants within a sexual contract, Black people were altogether absent from the racial contract. My purpose here is not to cast any disparagement or blame upon white women. Rather, I wish simply to underscore the cluster of asymmetries between these two cases, asymmetries that Mills completely obscures. To her credit, Pateman is aware of the formal differences between Mills's project and her own. She states, in response to Mills,

> We have some important differences about contract theory. [...] At the very broad level that you raise now, it is not so much your assumptions that I take issue with [...] but the notion of "contract" itself. The question I am asking is why, say, social justice has to be discussed or adjudicated using the metaphor of contract. [...] To see the whole of social and political life as no more than a series of contracts, to see individuals as packages of alienable property and to insist that "contract" is the metaphor for a free society is a very narrow view of humans and what they create. [...] Can "contract" be washed clean of the history of justification of subjection?
>
> *(2007, 14–15)*

The significance of underscoring Pateman's perspective on the contract device is to emphasize that, without an analytically valid notion of contract, liberalism is itself severely weakened. As indicated by both Pateman and Mills, the notion of an original social contract does indeed accommodate both a sexual and a racial contract. Moreover, the use of contract involving property-bearing individuals cannot reliably protect people against subjugation. But it is this critical assault on the structural integrity of liberalism that Mills fails to adequately acknowledge.

In light of the critiques raised after the publication of *The Racial Contract*, Mills does attempt to diversify his conception of social contract theory. In "Race and the Social Contract Tradition," he discusses his attempt to "make more explicit than I did in my book *The Racial Contract* [...] the strategic and theoretical value of a retention and development of the contract idea" (2000, 442). There Mills distinguishes between three ways in which "contract" can be thought of descriptively: "(i) the literal, historical contract; (ii) the hypothetical, idealized reconstruction contract; and (iii) the useful model contract" (443). Unfortunately, his updated conception of contract is not particularly persuasive, precisely because he tries to fuse the descriptive and normative accounts. The traditional hypothetical conception of contract has been employed for primarily normative ends, and it is absolutely not prohibited to use descriptive information to bolster normative pursuits. But there are other and more serious considerations that weaken Mills's descriptive and normative claims, particularly when we consider his own proclivity to degrade normativity. It is true that the standards of correctness for an accurate description of the world pertain to how things actually are, rather than to how they ought to be. However, the criterion of correctness in a normative account pertains to how things ought to be, not to how they are. Thus, while descriptive accounts must correspond to the world in order to be correct, the validity of normative accounts does not require correspondence to the world. The standard of correctness of a normative account is assessed at a metalevel.

Mills's use of the contract device is also weakened by his notion of the Racial Contract. First, his transition from a philosophical discussion of social contract theory to a causal history of modern racism is overly casual. It is an incredible leap that warrants robust justification, which is never provided. Establishing a causal link between textual analysis and material and institutional transformations is an extremely problematic undertaking. This exercise is challenging and potentially illegitimate due to the nagging problems that plague the concept of historical explanation. These problems include, but are not limited to, the structural problem of advancing a relation and determining the appropriate causal nexus between text and context. Second, although Mills explores several threads of analysis, these investigative activities do not terminate in any discernible pattern of connections. Instead, what emerges is an impressionistic collage of competing theories, culminating with Mills's conclusion that the only plausible common factor connecting these divergent streams of thought is either race itself or a racial contract. Thus, we can inquire about the reason for which a racial contract would be the best device for explaining modern society as opposed to, for example, a religious contract, a linguistic contract, a technological contract, a democratic contract, a capitalist contract, a political contract, a protestant contract, and so on.

Mills's take on the social contract is also plagued with incommensurability due to the conflicting perspectives that he seeks to balance. These perspectives range from an inverted white consciousness, a Black standpoint perspective, a social contract perspective, a philosophical perspective, and an historical perspective. These conflicting perspectives are expected to converge into a core thesis, but the ease with which Mills settles on the thesis of the racial contract is both enticing and credulous. To be clear, my purpose here is not to deny the persistence of racism, racial discrimination, or the brutal history of new world slavery and colonialism. Rather, though we must acknowledge historical practices such as white supremacy and racism, it is also imperative to locate these practices within the broader ontological context of the way in which human beings forge identities and structure societies. Racism is not simply a deviation from otherwise universal norms but, rather, it emerges from the ways in which self-interpreting human beings orient themselves on the plane of existence, that is, from the ways in which human beings generate meaning. Sylvia Wynter has alluded to this more complicated yet nuanced perspective:

> It was to be as a function of the West's institutionalization of itself in terms of its then epochally new self-conception or sociogenic code as Absolute Being [...] that the majority of the darker-skinned peoples of the earth [...] would come to be seen, known, and classified, as we also come to see, know, and classify ourselves, not as *other* human beings but, instead, as "Native," "Negro," "Blackfellas," and, ultimately, "Nigger" Others to the True Human Self of the West's Man.
>
> *(2006, 146)*

Unlike Mills, Wynter underscores the extent to which the relationship of the West relative to the non-Europeans, especially African and African-descended peoples, centered on issues of identity and meaning (worldmaking). In particular, the Western episteme was constructed with, among other things, the goal of establishing the human, which is to say a normative (ontological) conception of the human—the quintessential human as white. The fact that contractarians contributed to the construction of a distinctively Western mode of worldmaking and identity formation is undeniable. However, this concession need not entail that social contract thinkers were the principal architects of these human-specific generative projects.

Mills on Liberalism(s)

Mills's ambiguous relation to liberalism itself must now be examined in detail, since his desire to "occupy liberalism" signals some degree of cognitive dissonance. This dissonance becomes obvious when his attraction to liberalism is pitted against his stern condemnation of social contract theory and of mainstream political philosophy as forms of white philosophy that are blind to the historical realities of racial subordination and oppression. In his recent collection of essays, *Black Rights/White Wrongs: The Critique of Racial Liberalism* (2017), Mills transitions from a discussion of social contract theory to a direct confrontation with liberalism. His new goal is to retrieve liberalism, and he writes that he is "going to argue for the heretical thesis that liberalism should not be contemptuously rejected by radicals but retrieved for a radical agenda" (2017, 10). He also declares, "So I think we need to try to justify a radical agenda with the normative resources *of* liberalism rather than writing off liberalism" (14). Previously to writing *Black Rights/White Wrongs*, Mills had stated that "I want to endorse liberalism [...] a hybrid liberalism, detached from what are sometimes taken to be its necessary theoretical presuppositions" (2000, 455). To sustain this goal of "hybrid liberalism," he posits the existence of a plurality of liberalisms:

> Once we pluralize liberalism into *liberalisms* [...,] we should be able to see how many claims about liberalism's putatively problematic ontology and alleged incapacity to recognize and/or theorize social oppression really depend on the contingent features of its historically dominant [...] incantations. An emancipatory liberalism can, I contend, be reconstructed that is not theoretically constrained in these unfortunate ways.
>
> *(xvi–xvii)*

Indeed, Mills identifies an abstract philosophical liberalism and a racial liberalism:

> Abstract Platonized liberalism erases actual liberalism's racist history, a blinding white Form that, in pretending a colorlessness that it did not and does not achieve, obfuscate more than it illuminates. The problem is not abstraction as such, but a problematic mode of idealizing abstraction that abstracts away from social oppression, and in that way both conceals its extent and inhibits the development of the conceptual tools necessary for understanding and dealing with its workings.
>
> *(xv)*

Mills declares that liberalism can most successfully deracialize itself "by recognizing the centrality of a social ontology of race to the modern world and the acknowledgement of a corresponding history of racial exploitation that needs to be registered in liberal categories and addressed as a matter of liberal social justice" (xvii). So, his objective is to infuse liberalism with a historically informed awareness and consciousness of race that will enable it to better confront the social reality of race.

Mills identifies liberalism as consisting of three major components: (1) a set of value commitments that include individual's freedom, self-realization, and rights protection, among other things; (2) a social ontology of atomic individualism; and (3) a metanarrative of history as being progressive and linear (2000, 455). However, the third of these commitments, the idea that it is committed to "a metanarrative, history as progressive and linear," is quite odd. Philosophical liberalism is not necessarily, or even remotely, concerned with providing a metanarrative about history. Although Mills stipulates that there is no logical entailment between these three elements of liberalism, this claim seems to rely on his self-serving inclusion of the third component as a core feature of liberalism. This inclusion then allows him to conveniently declare that the core features of liberalism are neither logically coherent nor consistent.

Another puzzling aspect of Mills's description of liberalism is his reference to a racial liberalism that is distinct from a pure liberalism. This move contradicts Mills's own denial of the existence of any stable or idealized liberalism. Things are further complicated by Mills assumption that there is an identifiable residual liberalism that remains once traditional liberalism has been deracialized: the fact that existing liberalism has largely been racial, in its avoidance and denial of the reality of racial domination, or the actual accommodation to it, does not mean that a reconstructed non-racial liberalism is impossible:

> The liberalism I want to endorse [...] is the normative component. [...] I want to link this normative component with an alternative social ontology and an alternative account of recent global history, as summarized in the racial contract, to produce a liberalism informed by the racial facts. The fact that existing liberalism has largely been racial, in its avoidance and denial of the reality of racial domination, or the actual accommodation to it, does not mean that a reconstructed non-racial liberalism is impossible.
>
> *(2000, 455)*

Here, Mills's recognition of an abstract or model liberalism is undeniable. Yet he also claims that this idealized or abstract liberalism has been distorted. For him, the polluted version of liberalism is racial liberalism, and he presents a series of detailed descriptions to underscore its infectious nature. His preliminary strategy is to explain the way in which race, meaning white supremacy, has contaminated the core elements of liberalism. According to him,

> [The] overarching themes of epistemology, personhood, and property, all central to the liberal project, [are] all [...] shaped by race. [...] But racial domination interferes with objective cognition, denies equal personhood, and generates rationalizations of unjust white acquisition. [T]hey are all negatively transformed by the dynamic of racial liberalism (2017, xvi). [...] Racial liberalism [...] is a liberalism in which key terms have been written by race and the discursive logic shaped accordingly. This position expresses my commitment to what has been called the "symbiotic" view of racism, which sees race as historically penetrating *into* liberalism's descriptive and normative apparatus so as to produce a more-or-less consistent racialized ideology, albeit one that evolves over time, rather than seeing race as being externally and "anomalously" related to it.
>
> *(xv)*

Again, Mills remains hopeful regarding the prospects of decontaminating liberalism. But this presupposes the existence of an ideal and pure liberalism that will result from such decontamination. Indeed, he insists that liberalism's unfortunate involvement with race is a reversible historical contingency that does not permanently invalidate liberalism itself.

Believing that he can immunize liberalism against racial contamination, Mills craves the emergence of a deracialized liberalism. Accordingly, on his view, it is possible both to articulate and to construct a truly anti-racist liberalism. He explains, "Hence the hope of redeeming liberalism by self-consciously taking this history into account: recognizing the historic racialization of liberalism *so as better to deracialize it*—thereby producing a color-conscious, racially reflexive, anti-racist liberalism on the alert for its own inherited racial distortions" (2017, xv). Mills dismisses traditional philosophical efforts to clarify and understand the structural or internal logic of liberalism as being a Platonized liberalism that is blind to the actual history of liberalism. He does not accept that there is "an immanent conceptual/normative logic to liberalism" (13). Mills faults mainstream white philosophers for ignoring the history of liberalism and dismisses their interest in pure philosophical analysis. Yet, he also rejects the post-structuralist and post-colonialist recognition of a distinctive logic to liberalism, a logic that renders it structurally complicit with, among other things, the racist history of modernity. However, although Mills insists that liberalism should be grounded in history rather than some essence removed from history, his insistence that liberalism can be deracialized reveals a tacit assumption that there is some Platonic essence to liberalism that can be salvaged after decontamination. He, thus, seems guilty of the very same Platonizing tendencies of which he accuses traditional philosophical liberalism.

This discussion of Mills's position confirms the glaring tensions in his effort to add theoretical depth to his earlier articulation of *The Racial Contract* and its relation to liberalism. The crux of my criticism of Mills's references to plural versions of liberalism, his desire to deracialize liberalism, and his advocacy of a radicalized liberalism is that he is caught in the horns of a dilemma. Either he affirms the possibility of a pure, abstract Platonic liberalism or he affirms only the possibility of a racialized liberalism. It is my contention that Mills cannot coherently and consistently adopt either of these two options. First, if he stipulates that a historically uncontaminated, abstract, and Platonic liberalism is not possible, then it follows that there is only a racialized liberalism. This racialized liberalism is a liberalism that, to be consistent with Mills's own position, is entirely reducible to its history and is the kind of liberalism that sustains white supremacy. Thus, if abstract, pure liberalism is not an option, the only viable liberalism must be racialized. However, for the decontamination of a historicized and racialized liberalism to be a viable project, a pure and abstract liberalism must be possible. Thus, for Mills's own project to succeed, he must posit the possibility of a pure and abstract liberalism. But the dilemma arises because Mills rejects both the possibility of a pure and abstract liberalism while also affirming the possibility of de-racializing liberalism. To be fair, since he recognizes this dilemma, he offers the option of a hybrid liberalism but finds it difficult to clarify what such a liberalism would be. Because Mills does not clearly delineate his proposal for a liberalism that is both abstract and also non-ideal and historically informed, the option of a hybrid liberalism remains disconcertingly vague.

Because Mills has glossed over difficult theoretical matters, it is incumbent upon me at this point to provide a detailed discussion of liberalism. The purpose is not to deny the contestability of liberalism but rather to stabilize some of its core concepts, all the while acknowledging that these concepts meet with varied interpretations within the liberal tradition. I initiate this process by invoking Martha Nussbaum's insightful perspective on liberalism:

> Liberalism holds that the flourishing of human beings taken one by one is both analytically and normatively prior to the flourishing of the state or the nation or the religious group; analytically, because such unities do not really efface the separate reality of individual lives; normatively because the recognition of that separateness is held to be a fundamental fact of ethics, which should recognize each separate entity as an end and not as a means to the ends of others.
>
> *(1999, 62)*

Thus, a core feature of liberalism is the ontological primacy of the individual or the presupposition of the structural priority of the individual in the order of things. At its most basic level, then, liberalism commits to a social ontology of atomistic individualism, according to which the most fundamental and basic constituents of political reality are individuals. Within liberalism, atomistic individualism takes at least two distinctive forms of articulation. One is analytic, and the other is normative.

Within the analytical articulation, the individual is ontologically prior to the group or whole. Here, the whole or collective has no ontological priority over the individual and is entirely reducible to its parts. The individual always retains a non-negotiable ontological singularity. Within the normative articulation, the individual enjoys a certain ethical singularity, so that there is no ethical overriding of the separateness or distinctiveness of the individual. The individual claims intrinsic moral worth and should not be used to achieve or fulfill the ends of others, particularly the ends of the collective as represented by the group, the state, or society. Accordingly, individuals are ends and not merely means for the ends of others. Thus, ethics must prioritize the separateness of the individual and consider the distinction of persons as inviolable. From this perspective, the minimum conception of liberalism is the sovereignty of the individual.

Following the careful efforts of Nussbaum and Robert Talisse, liberalism can be said to possess an inner logic and formal structure that, if altered, produce a mutation dissimilar from the original. Talisse identifies, at a minimum, four core commitments that constitute liberalism: individualism, moral equality, rationality, and autonomy (2016, 22–24). What is distinctive about liberalism are not only the values that it endorses but the ontology that sustains the notions of individuality, equality, rationality, and autonomy. Its social ontology reveals that which liberalism recognizes as the ultimate or basic constituents of political reality. What is most real for liberalism is not the state or any other collective. Rather, what is most real is the ontological singularity or distinction of the individual.

Despite Mills's pronouncements to the contrary, it is his alliance with liberalism that creates structural barriers against the viability of his position. Once efforts are made to establish the purpose of a political theory, it becomes clear that liberalism confronts Mills with certain nagging problems. First, just as there is no immaculate perception of the natural world, there is also no immaculate perception of the socio-cultural world. The socio-cultural world need not be confronted as already being determinately structured, in complete independence of human beings. There are no social kinds that facilitate any objective structuring of the socio-political world, absent human consciousness. What, then, is the task of a political theory, such as liberalism, for example? Following David Johnson's take on the purpose of political theory, one can reasonably assert that, since there is no perspectiveless seeing, political theory facilitates a way of seeing the socio-political world. It provides a particular perspectival lens through which it is possible to interpret the socio-cultural world (1994, 5).

As a political theory, liberalism can be understood as a way of seeing the world. Using the analogy of a painting allows us to obtain a clear picture of how liberalism structures the world. First, liberalism foregrounds or centers the individual, in that the individual occupies the sovereign space of the socio-political world. Thus, liberalism holds that political arrangements must be justified by or answerable to the individuals viewed as bearers of rights. Second, liberalism sets aside or in the background groups, collectives, and aggregates that are seen as not being ontologically primary. Third, it is reasonable to claim that liberalism marginalizes the state in its picture of the socio-political world. State neutrality is one of liberalism's basic tenets. Individuals have autonomy, so that they are the focal point in framing and conceiving our conceptions of the good life, and the state is obligated to remain neutral regarding such matters. Hence, as a neutral part, the state should play no substantive role in defining conceptions of the good. Finally, liberalism requires that we leave certain things out of our interpretations of the socio-political world or, returning to the painting metaphor, there are certain things that are not represented. This kind of normative seeing is also a certain kind of "not seeing." As regulated by liberalism, it entails that we "not see" such things as gender, culture, class, or race. These types of contingencies are, in the words of Rawls, morally irrelevant, as he makes clear in his description of the original position:

> The original position is framed to eliminate prejudice and self-interest, and this is one reason for not letting people know certain facts about themselves—for example, their sex and race. [...] We want to abstract from certain social and natural contingencies. Our social position and class, our sex and race should not influence deliberations made from a moral point of view; and on this ground, these facts should be bracketed.
>
> *(1975, 268)*

In addition to structuring ways of seeing, a theory, Johnson explains, also functions to direct how we process and weigh information, how we determine what is significant and, finally, how we should manage perceptions (1994, 5–6). To the extent that liberalism facilitates the arranging of perceptions and the filtering of information, it directs us to look closely at information concerning the ability of individuals to frame and pursue their conception of the good life freely and autonomously. Information that is worth collecting is information about how well individual rights are being protected and respected. With a working understanding of liberalism in place, we can critically probe Mills's unfortunate choice to embrace liberalism.

In this probe, several critical questions emerge: can Mills successfully reclaim liberalism, or is his attempt to do this riddled with massive confusions, inconsistencies, and contradictions? Can Mills "decontaminate" liberalism and implement his proposed hybrid liberalism in ways that are consistent with the individualistic core of traditional liberalism? He writes,

> Contra the exponents of color-blindness [...] I argue that this project can only be accomplished through a color-conscious investigative genealogy and reconstruction. Thus I urge a self-conscious deracializing of liberalism that would begin by recognizing the

> centrality of a social ontology of race to the modern world and the acknowledgment of a corresponding history of racial exploitation that needs to be registered in liberal categories and addressed as a matter of liberal justice.
>
> *(2017, xvii)*

Here, Mills pays rhetorical homage to a variety of positions. For example, he mentions the idea of inserting a social ontology of race into liberalism, but he does not explain how such a social ontology would structurally alter the inner logic of liberalism. Nevertheless, it would be important for him to give such an explanation, since the inner structural and foundational logic of liberalism is grounded on a social ontology of individualism. To alter liberalism by replacing its social ontology of individuals with a social ontology of race would represent a radical change. It is radical because it moves away from considering isolated individuals as ontologically primary and considers groups or collectives as ontologically primary.

We should note here that it would be important to focus on understanding the dynamics of the ontology of collectives prior to invoking a social ontology of race. To treat a race as a singular collective with its own rights and privileges leads us back to an identity logic. Indeed, structurally speaking, this way of conceptualizing the racial collective presupposes the utilization of the formal logic of liberalism. Here, each race becomes a collective of one and, as a single collective of individuals, each collective counts only as one collective self. As a collective self, each collective has intrinsic rights. It does not seem that this move would be helpful at all, especially if races are treated like individuals that are formally equivalent and enjoy formal ontological parity.

The point here is not to deny the need for a social ontology of race or the ills of slavery, colonialism, and other forms of racial oppression. Rather, my reservations pertain to whether a social ontology of race can be effectively inserted within the core of individualistic liberalism. Surprisingly, and in response to Mills's ambivalent relationship to liberalism, a discussion of Rawls's view on such matters convincingly establishes that Mills's understanding of liberalism and of Rawls is misleading, and that his project is philosophically defective.

Mills against Rawls: Liberalism, the Ideal, and the Non-Ideal

Although Mills offers a comprehensive critique of social contract theory and mainstream white philosophy, Rawls becomes a central character in his confrontation with liberalism. Mills maintains that "the ignoring of race in Rawls's work is structural and symptomatic of white political philosophy in general" (2009, 169). Mills castigates Rawls for engaging in ideal theory while unadvisedly neglecting the actual conditions of society that require non-ideal theory. Although Mills attempted to graft ideal and non-ideal theory, he did not significantly modify his earlier critique of Rawls as having been too invested in ideal theory. Mills's basic objection to Rawls is that ideal theory becomes ideology when it leaves behind actual conditions of injustice and focuses on ideal circumstances. According to Mills, "Ideal theory [...] is really an *ideology*, a distortional complex of ideas, values, norms, and beliefs that reflects the nonrepresentative interests and experiences of a small minority of the national population" (2005, 172). Mills also contends that once we accept the conviction "that the ultimate point of ethics is to guide our actions and make ourselves better people and the world a better place, then [ideal theory] will not only be unhelpful, but will in certain respects be deeply *antithetical* to the proper goal of theoretical ethics as an enterprise" (172).

Mills seems not to have acknowledged the performative contradiction that entraps him. To maintain that deliberation about principles of justice should begin with actual conditions of injustice presupposes a theory of justice. So long as one claims that actual injustices are immoral, one is already appealing to norms about what is and is not morally acceptable. Hence, what Mills is implying is that one must invoke a conception of justice in order to deliberate about principles of justice, which is to engage in unproductive circular reasoning. From a different perspective, one can argue that the reason why it is appropriate to initiate deliberation regarding principles of justice with normative considerations is because a conception of justice will presuppose a moral theory, and the moral theory will in turn presuppose a philosophical anthropology—a philosophical conception about what it means to be human. This conception of the human will consist of an ontology of the human. This ontology of the human will enable us to draw conclusions about how people should be treated, what they are owed, why they are deserving of respect, and so on. This kind of normative activity is indispensable when addressing actual and historical conditions of injustice.

Mills claims that the absence of race in Rawls's writings indicates the extent to which Rawls completely ignores the injustice of racism. Furthermore, Mills maintains that the absence of race and racism as legitimate objects of philosophical engagement further substantiates the extent to which Rawls's position (and that of mainstream philosophy) is saturated with whiteness and is racist, even if unwittingly so. According to Mills, this neglect condemns Rawls's commitment to ideal theory. He writes, "[B]y analyzing the underpinnings of Rawlsian ideal theory, I try to make the stronger case not merely that Rawls and Rawlsians *have not* addressed the issue of racism, but that the apparatus itself hinders them from doing so adequately, not merely contingently but also structurally" (2017, xix–xx). In another context, Mills is even more blunt and unapologetic in his castigation of Rawls:

> Indeed, so far as I can tell from an illuminating textual search [...] even the *phrase* "racial justice" never appears in Rawls's writing. If he was so concerned about racial problems, this was an odd way of showing it. What was preventing him from addressing them? Fear of not getting tenure? Hope of landing a job at an institution more prestigious than the obscure liberal arts college in the boondocks at which, frustrated and unrecognized, he was forced to labor for so many unrewarding decades? Irony aside, to me, as earlier indicated, it's almost the exact opposite: that the theory was constructed to *evade* these problems.
>
> *(Pateman and Mills, 2007, 258)*

At times, however, Mills's critique strains credulity by suggesting that Rawls's lack of engagement with race and racism is due to his arbitrarily having judged them as unworthy of serious philosophical consideration. Mills does not even consider the possibility that Rawls did not center race and racism precisely because of his commitment to liberalism, which structurally disqualified race and racism as being philosophically or morally relevant. Thus, they are disregarded as relevant only because they conflict with the moral commitments of liberalism.

Given Mills's rather caricaturish portrayal of Rawls, it behooves us at this time to carefully consider Rawls's position. The irony that emerges here is that Rawls's own philosophical relation to race and racism is governed by liberalism, and it is precisely his commitment to liberalism that explains his philosophical attitude concerning race and racism within his theory of justice. This irony is doubly compounded when we consider Mills's own efforts to salvage liberalism by rendering it philosophically compatible with race in order to deploy it as a weapon against racism and racial subordination.

Rawls situates his work within the social contract tradition and directly defends a version of deontological liberalism. But, unlike classical contractarians, Rawls's use of the social contract device is not dependent upon a commitment to a pre-political existence. Rawls introduces the "original position" as a structural substitute for the "state of nature," but he does not intend for the original position to serve as an anthropological or historical account of the origins of political society or as the justification of political authority. The device of the "original position" functions as a framework for the way in which we are to think—if we are to think correctly about justice. The original position provides a style of thinking about justice. On Rawls's view, the original position accommodates a way of conceiving a hypothetical contract. Rawls refers to the original position as an "expository device" (1971, 21). As a thought experiment, the original position is, in the words of Talisse, "an exercise in which one places certain artificial or hypothetical constraint upon one's thinking in an effort to identify, clarify, and systematize one's own common-sense judgments" (2001, 32).

In response to Mills's strong denunciation of Rawls's involvement with ideal theory, it is critical to underscore something about Rawls's original position. Talisse claims that Rawls "is not offering an historical, anthropological, or psychological explanation of how conceptions of justice arise; rather, [he gives us] a theoretical framework within which to think about justice and a perspective from which to evaluate different conceptions of justice" (2001, 35). On the Rawlsian view, even if we were to restrict ourselves to actual conditions of injustice and pursue non-ideal theory, we would still have to evaluate different conceptions of justice in order not to unfairly privilege any conception of justice that may be morally tainted. For Rawls, the best way to evaluate different conceptions of justice is to engage in the kind of ideal theorizing that is facilitated by the device of the original position. The original position does not invite us to ignore circumstances of injustice but, rather, represents how we should think in order not to allow morally irrelevant factors to distort our thinking about justice. Furthermore, the original position works in conjunction with the veil of ignorance by allowing us to think about principles of justice that are not undermined by the morally irrelevant contingencies of nature and society. As Rawls explains,

> The description of the original position interprets the point of view of noumenal selves, of what it means to be a free and equal rational being. Our nature as such beings is displayed when we act from principles we would choose when this nature is reflected in the conditions determining the choice. Thus men exhibit their freedom, their independence from the contingencies of nature and society, by acting in ways they would acknowledge in the original position.
>
> *(1971, 255–56)*

Here, the original position sustains a style of thinking in which one brackets and sets aside "those aspects of the social world that seem arbitrary from a moral point of view" (15).

Hence, to think correctly about justice, one need not restrict deliberations only to non-ideal factors.

Rawls stipulates that in the original position, one adopts a veil of ignorance for the goal of securing a certain "blind egalitarianism." In adopting this perspective, Rawls specifies that "no one knows his place in society, his class position or social status, nor does any one know his fortune in the distribution of mental assets and abilities, his intelligence, strength, and the like" (1971, 12). Again, the original position is not a location. It is a theoretical construction. It is also obviously not "the view from nowhere" or a "God's eye" perspective. Therefore, although Rawls admits that, with regard to justice, "[w]e need a conception that enables us to envision our objective from afar" (22), he qualifies this point by writing, "not a perspective from a certain place beyond the world, nor the point of view of a transcendent being; rather it is a certain form of thought and feeling that rational persons can adopt within the world" (587). In short, the device of the original position formally prohibits the acceptance of principles of justice that are based upon race. Rawls states,

> From the standpoint of persons similarly situated in an initial situation which is fair, the principles of explicit racist doctrines are not only unjust. They are irrational. For this reason we could say that they are not moral conceptions at all, but simply means of suppression. They have no place on a reasonable list of traditional conceptions of justice.
>
> *(149–50)*

Again, on several occasions, Rawls emphasizes that his approach to justice does not negate empirical considerations, but this does not entail that there are no restrictions on the empirical matters that can be taken into account. In order to guarantee that the conception of justice emerging from the original position is "the result of a fair agreement," Rawls stresses the negation or neutralization of "the effects of specific contingencies which put men at adds and tempt them to exploit social and natural circumstances to their own advantage" (136). In *Justice as Fairness,* Rawls restated the concept of fairness as follows:

> It is natural to ask: Why are distinctions of race and gender not explicitly included among the three contingencies noted earlier? [...] The answer is that we are mainly concerned with ideal theory: the account of the well-ordered society of justice as fairness. Within that account we need to distinguish two questions: first, what contingencies tend to generate troubling inequalities even in a well-ordered society and thus prompt us, along with other considerations, to take the basic structure as the primary subject of justice; and second, how within ideal should the least advantaged be specified?
>
> *(2001, 64–65)*

Rawls acknowledges the strategic and instrumental distinction between ideal and non-ideal theory. Non-ideal theory addresses the specifics of the way in which individuals should respond to or rectify injustice. As Rawls explains, "Non-ideal theory [...] is worked out after an ideal conception of justice has been chosen; only then do the parties ask which principles to adopt under less happy conditions" (1971, 245–46). On the other hand, for Rawls, ideal theory "assumes strict compliance and works out the principles that characterize a well-ordered society under favorable circumstances" (245). In a critical sense, ideal theory serves not only as a measure for determining the moral gulf that separates non-ideal conditions of injustice from the ideal of justice, but it also provides a regulative road map for guiding efforts at rectification. While acknowledging the importance of addressing problems of injustice, Rawls writes that "the reason for beginning with ideal theory is that it provides, I believe, the only basis for the systematic grasp of these more pressing problems" (9). Rawls's point is not that actual injustices are unimportant but that, in order to adequately address them, it is best to work with a conception of justice that is unbiased and uncontaminated and that is neutral across the board. Rawls's theory of justice is principally a conception of justice that pertains to the basic structure of society. He states that "the basic structure is the background social framework within which the activities of associations and individuals take place. A just basic structure secures what we may call background justice" (2001, 10).

The purpose of this discussion of Rawls is not to offer an indirect defense of his position. Rather, the purpose is to clarify his position in light of Mills's misleading disparagement of Rawls for having ignored actual society and history. It is my contention that Rawls should not be faulted for not explicitly mentioning race or for invoking ideal theory. Instead, we must acknowledge that the absence of race from his consideration is an unfortunate outcome of taking liberal individualism as his starting point, which is a core hallmark of deontological liberalism. If it is true that what is morally significant about individuals is the fact that they are free and autonomous, then we are structurally required to bracket or ignore morally irrelevant characteristics of individuals when thinking about justice.

Since justice concerns only what is morally relevant, if race is considered a morally irrelevant characteristic of individuals, then it follows that race should be excluded from deliberations about principles of justice. According to liberalism, since we are obligated to safeguard our higher-order interests when making choices and framing our conception of the good life, we need not consider the physical, social, and cultural contingencies of individuals as morally relevant when we deliberate about the principles of justice. Consistent with (Rawlsian-Kantian) deontological liberalism, because the right is prior to the good, protecting and respecting the rights of individuals *qua* individuals is non-negotiable. Furthermore, because individuals are, on Rawls's view, moral personalities, contingencies of race, sex, gender, class, or natural abilities should be excluded from deliberation concerning principles of justice. It is precisely Rawls's liberal phenomenology that Mills fails to adequately consider.

Since, for Rawls, race is irrelevant, he states that "we view a democratic society as a political society that excludes a confessional or an aristocratic state, not to mention a caste, slave, or a racist one. This exclusion is a consequence of taking the moral powers as the basis of political equality" (2001, 21). For Rawls, once we morally erase artificial distinctions such as class, gender, race, or religion, we can embrace the principle of interchangeability. Thus, the liberal view stipulates that individuals qua individuals are interchangeable. The British historian of the United States, J. R. Pole, writes in his cutting-edge study of how the commitment to equality affected core aspects of American history: "The individualist principle dissociates people from the context of family, religion, class, or race and when linked with the idea of equality [...] it assumes the coordinate principle of interchangeability" (1978, 293). In his *Political Liberalism*, Rawls confesses that "among our most basic problems are those of race, ethnicity, and gender. These may seem of an altogether different character calling for different principles of justice, which *Theory* does not discuss" (2005, xxviii). Although Mills intimates to the contrary, Rawls was forthright enough to admit to the omission of race in *A Theory of Justice* when he stated, "This is indeed an omission in *Theory*; but an omission is not as such a fault, either in the work's agenda or in its conception of justice" (2001, 6). Thus, Rawls admits to the omission but intimates that the omission was justified. Perhaps Rawls should have also added that the ontological profile of these problems is beyond the analytical scope of liberalism.

Rawls explicitly admits that his conception of justice is unabashedly individualistic. Interestingly, however, he also acknowledges that, even if we accept the community as being important, its importance must be explained in terms of the individualistic conception of justice. As a matter of ontological privilege, the individual is primary and the community is secondary; the community, for Rawls, can never be ontologically prior to the individual. According to him,

> The essential idea is that we want to account for the social values, for the intrinsic good of institutional, community, associative activities, by a conception of justice that in its theoretical basis is individualistic. [...] We do not want to rely on an undefined concept of community, or to suppose that society is an organic whole with a life of its own distinct from and superior to that of all its members in their relations with one another. Thus the contractual conception of the original position is worked out first. [...] From this conception, however individualistic it might seem, we must eventually explain the value of community.
>
> *(1971, 264–65)*

Rawls's aversion to any ontological conception community is obvious. Clearly, for the deontological liberal, there is no need to mention race or even take race into active consideration once we appreciate that individuals are free and autonomous subjects. If we accept that individuals have the right to freely and autonomously choose, then a just society is not one that is structured along the lines of race or any other contingency. Rather, as the communitarian Michael Sandel succinctly explains, the liberal view holds that "Society is best arranged when it is governed by principles that do not presuppose any particular conception of the good, for any other arrangement would fail to respect persons as beings capable of choice; it would treat them as objects rather than subjects, as means rather than ends in themselves" (1982, 9).

Another communitarian critic of Rawls, Alasdair MacIntyre, underscores the ontological dominance of a social ontology of individualism in Rawls's conception of society. MacIntyre insightfully states that for Rawls, "a society is composed of individuals, each with his or her own interest, who then have to come together and formulate common rules of life. [...] Individuals are thus [...] primary and society secondary, and the identification of individual interests is prior to, and independent of, the construction of any moral or social bonds between them" (1981, 232–33).

To attribute to Rawls a social ontology of individualism is not a neutral insight. Rather, the charge is that the liberal ontology of individualism is modeled on an atomistic and mechanistic worldview according to which society is an aggregate of individuals and collectives are not considered as ontologically real. Although society is not treated as possessing any distinctive ontological status, predictions about the behavior of individuals are framed in a linear manner so that society operates without the kinds of friction that would derail or stifle the actions of individuals. But this traditional atomistic and linear conception of reality conflicts with developments in complex systems theory, which suggest that the intense interactions between individuals can generate emergent features that can causally and qualitatively alter the properties and ontological status of the system. Instead of the state of the system being dependent on the actions of atomic individuals, the system can experience autocatalytic phase changes. Within a socio-political context, the actions of individuals and the intense interactions between them can generate transformations over time that are both more consistent with collective action but are restrictive of the actions of individuals. Accordingly, even a society determinately committed to a social ontology of individualism can, over time, acquire the features of a socio-political system whose transformations are the outcomes of collectives rather than of isolated individuals. Rawls's conception of society, being linear and atomistic, cannot faithfully register the ontologically nonlinear dynamics of collectives.

Nevertheless, the impression might very well persist, in some circles, that Mills's critique of Rawls is so strong and definitive that Rawls's use of ideal theory renders his position alien to the actual injustices of society. However, to the extent that much of Mills's work is vested in denouncing Rawls's use of ideal theory and normativity, it is fair to consider Mills's own project as compromised once it is clear that his critique of Rawls is off target. Although Rawls utilizes the original position, its use was not to ground his theory or conception of justice on robust metaphysical grounds. Unlike Immanuel Kant, Rawls was sensitive to the need for cultivating principles of justice that are appropriate for actual human existence. Rawls avoided trafficking with the esoteric notions of Kantian metaphysics, which include ideal kingdoms of ends and transcendental selves. Accordingly, Rawls availed himself of the conceptual resources of a hypothetical situation called the original position, which was suitably qualified for deriving principles of justice that are consistent with and applicable to the circumstances of actual human beings. Put differently, for Rawls, justice must address imperfect human circumstances, not the circumstances of angels. As a matter of fact, although his claim that society is a "cooperative venture for mutual advantage" might lead one to interpret him as suggesting that the ideal society is one of angels, this is not the case. Rather, Rawls wanted to underscore the extent to which life is arbitrary with regard to the circumstances of life. Hence, from the moral point of view, when deliberating about principles of justice, no one person's interests should be considered more important than those of others. After all, for Rawls, justice is about fairness; it is not allowing what he considered arbitrary factors to erase the moral equality of persons. This approach does not need to imply that justice requires that human beings are angels.

As Rawls himself so insistently explains, while eschewing comprehensive metaphysical, religious, and political doctrines, the utilization of a method of reflective equilibrium was designed to develop an overlapping consensus that can serve as a thin conception of the good grounded in the dominant but basic beliefs of liberal societies. It is this approach that enables Rawls to characterize his conception of justice as "freestanding," as connected to core beliefs of a certain kind of society, not as reflective or representative of any comprehensive conception of the good. In fact, this is an instance of Rawls engaging in limited non-ideal theory. Ironically, it is Rawls, rather than Mills, who creatively exploits a hybrid method, although he never declares this as his intention. His creative strategy partly explains why Mills at times resorts to caricaturing Rawls's thinking. However, the fact that Rawls supports a deontological conception of justice does not necessarily lead him to engage in the radical pursuit of the transcendental excursions found in Kant.

Contrary to Mills, it does not follow that it is easy to jettison normativity or to castigate ideal theory as ideology, especially regarding principles of justice. Even in a world populated only by Black people who share a common culture and history, investigations of justice would also have to be pursued normatively. And the fact that one takes empirical evidence into consideration need not nullify involvement with normative activities. For Rawls, circumstances of justice require normative engagement:

> The circumstances of justice obtain whenever mutually disinterested persons put forward conflicting claims to the division of social advantages under conditions of moderate scarcity. Unless these circumstances existed there would be no occasion for the virtue of justice, just as in the absence of threats of injury to life and limb there would be no occasion for physical courage.
>
> *(1971, 128)*

The real challenge for social and political philosophy is to probe the analytical and theoretical limitations of liberalism. More specifically, we must probe critically the extent to which efforts to extend the scope of liberalism's social ontology to race are philosophically unviable. If it is indeed correct that the social ontology of individualism renders race an irrelevant feature of persons, then the problem with liberalism is that its historical silence on race is not the manifestation of any necessary racist intent. Rather, the silence on race is simply the result of the internal logic of liberalism itself. Thus, the problem with liberalism is a matter of its theoretical and analytical survival. Liberalism has always been confronted with the fact that accepting race as a real category, with its own basic insights and claims, would entail abandoning individualistic social ontology and the core principles that it supports.

Liberalism has historically been committed to both epistemic and ontological conservatism. Contra Mills, the liberal tradition's dismissal of race was not always motivated by racist beliefs or commitments but, rather, was designed to render liberalism philosophically consistent. Liberalism indirectly compounded its theoretical inability to accommodate race when it operated in ways that lent support to racist policies and outcomes within the nonpolitical sphere. This is particularly true with regard to liberalism's historical promotion of the gospel of color-blindness. Liberalism has treated race as an ontological fiction, invoking race's lack of biological legitimacy as justification for impeding the formulation of any viable conception of race. In short, the morality of liberalism entails an obligation for it to be blind to race simply because to see race is not to be color-blind. Color-blindness is the norm of liberalism, but of course, the problem is that theoretical color-blindness does not entail cultural and existential color-blindness.

This creates a problem for Mills since he favors a social ontology of races. Although the development of a social ontology of races is of major philosophical significance, Mills assumes that all that is needed for its achievement is that we recognize a purified and "deracialized" liberalism, one in which a social ontology of race would replace the social ontology of individualism. But this is not possible because the structural presuppositions of liberalism are, undeniably, the logics of sameness and symmetrical equivalence that do not accommodate thinking in terms of ontological difference. Thus, since these logics of identity are incapable of thinking of ontological difference, particularly racial difference, they are epistemically blind to history. Consequently, they are incapable of registering the historical complexity of the ontological structures of Blackness.

This inability directly impacts efforts to think through race and racism, to think beyond White supremacy, as well as the political and philosophical logic of modernity that undergirds liberalism. Mills wants to deracialize liberalism, and thus, it would be accurate to describe his project as an attempt to liberalize race. To succeed, Mills must explain how an ontology of race is consistent and palatable within the traditional grammar of liberalism, a grammar constructed on an ontology of individualism and on notions of individual self-ownership and self-determination. However, to the extent that Mills fails to recognize the impossibility of liberalism embracing ontologies of difference, his project of "reconceptualizing" and "deracializing" liberalism is bound to fail. Liberalism is constitutively incapable of registering the ontological reality of race in its various manifestations. Thus, regardless of how much he invests in rehabilitating and deracializing liberalism, Mills cannot overcome the structural limitations of liberalism that are bound to incapacitate his project.

Conclusion

This chapter establishes that, despite Mills's critique of mainstream political philosophy for being too white, Mills nevertheless remains a staunch supporter of a racially-challenged liberalism. Indeed, he favors a deracialization of liberation, arguing that liberalism, in itself, is highly relevant to addressing race and racism. Obviously, then, Mills remains within the liberal paradigm in political philosophy. While outside the scope of the present chapter, I would suggest that a more substantive option for him would have been to make the case for an ontology of race using the rich resources of existential phenomenology and escape the philosophical imaginary (the white mythology) of liberalism. For example, existential phenomenology, among other things, provides a basis for pursuing a sociogenesis of the ways in which everyday existence is structured and mediated through categories such as race. On this view, race claims its reality partly because of the existential role it performs in sustaining historical processes of self-formation as well as identity formation. Contra liberalism, race is neither an abstraction detached from the lifeworld nor an irrelevant, arbitrary construction. What Mills's example teaches us is to have the courage to place liberalism under erasure.

Bibliography

Anderson, Elizabeth S. 1990. "Women and Contracts: No New Deal Women." *Michigan Law Review* 88 (6): 1782–1810.

Johnson, David. 1994. *The Idea of a Liberal Theory: A Critique and Reconstruction*. Princeton: Princeton University Press.

MacIntyre, Alasdair. 1981. *After Virtue: A Study in Moral Theory*. Notre Dame: University of Notre Dame Press.

Marx, Karl, and Frederick Engles. 1947. *The German Ideology*. Edited by C. J. Arthur. New York: International Publishers.

Mills, Charles. 1997. *The Racial Contract*. Ithaca, New York: Cornell University Press.

Mills, Charles. 2000. "Race and the Social Contract Tradition." *Social Identities* 6 (4): 441–462.

Mills, Charles. 2002. "The Racial Contract as Methodology (Not Hypothesis)." *Philosophia Africana* 5 (2): 75–99.

Mills, Charles. 2005. "'Ideal Theory' as Ideology." *Hypatia* 20 (3): 165–184.

Mills, Charles. 2009. "Rawls on Race/Race in Rawls." *Southern Journal of Philosophy* XLVII: 161–84.
Mills, Charles. 2017. *Blacks Rights/White Wrongs: The Critique of Racial Liberalism*. New York: Oxford University Press.
Nussbaum, Martha. 1999. *Sex and Social Justice*. New York: Oxford University Press.
Pateman, Carole. 1988. *The Sexual Contract*. Cambridge: Polity Press.
Pateman, Carole, and Charles Mills. 2007. *Contract & Domination*. Malden: Polity Press.
Pole, J. R. 1978. *The Pursuit of Equality in American History*. Berkeley: University of California Press.
Rawls, John. 1971. *A Theory of Justice*. Cambridge: Harvard University Press.
Rawls, John. 1975. "Fairness to Goodness." In *John Rawls: Collected Papers*. Edited by S. Freeman, 267–85. Cambridge: Harvard University Press.
Rawls, John. 2001. *Justice as Fairness: A Restatement*. Cambridge: Harvard University Press.
Rawls, John. 2005. *Political Liberalism*. New York: Columbia University Press.
Sandel, Michael. 1982. *Liberalism and the Limits of Justice*. Cambridge: Cambridge University Press.
Seth, Vanita. 2020. "The Origins of Racism: A Critique of the History of Ideas." *History and Theory* 59 (3): 343–68.
Skinner, Quentin. 1969. "Meaning and Understanding in the History of Ideas." *History and Theory* 8 (1): 3–53.
Talisse, Robert. 2001. *On Rawls: A Theory of Justice and Justification*. Belmont: Wadsworth.
Talisse, Robert. 2016. *Engaging Political Philosophy: An Introduction*. New York: Routledge.
Taylor, Charles. 1985. *Philosophy and the Human sciences: Philosophical Papers, Volume 2*. Cambridge: Cambridge University Press.
Taylor, Charles. 1989. *Sources of the Self: The Making of Modern Identity*. Cambridge: Harvard University Press.
Thompson, Sharon, Hayes, Lydia, Newman, Daniel, Pateman, Carole. 2018. "The Sexual Contract 30 Years on: A Conversation with Carole Pateman." *Feminist Legal Studies* 26: 93–104.
Wynter, Sylvia. 2006. "On How We Mistook the Map for the Territory, and Re-Imprisoned Ourselves in Our Unbearable Wrongness of Being, of Désêtre: Black Studies Toward the Human Project." In *Not Only the Master's Tools: African-American Studies in Theory and Practice*. Edited by Lewis Gordon and Jane Anna Gordon, 107–72. Boulder: Paradigm Publishers.

7

A PAGE OF HISTORY

Mills's Black Radical Kantianism and American Legal (Racial) Realism

Timothy J. Golden

Overcoming Abstraction with History in Jurisprudence

Charles W. Mills, in his important essay, "Black Radical Kantianism," articulates a reformulation of Immanuel Kant's moral principles in the interest of racial justice (Mills, 2018). Tantamount to what I believe is a "Copernican Revolution" in social and political thought—I unpack this later in the chapter—Mills argues that racial justice cannot be attained through a mere application of Kant's abstract moral principles to concrete moral situations. Rather than taking such an ahistorical approach to racial justice, Mills contends that, prior to an application of Kant's moral principles, there must be a recognition of the historical reality of racial oppression; a history in which otherwise equal persons have been and continue to be distorted through racist social and political practices that organize them into an artificial division of what Mills calls "the privileged and the oppressed in a system of racial domination" (Mills, 2018, 11). Mills thus demands that philosophy reckon with history to attain racial justice, consistent with what he has termed "non-ideal theory" throughout his work, beginning with *The Racial Contract*. My aim in this chapter is to explore what I believe are the continuities between Mills's notion of "Black Radical Kantianism" (BRK) in Critical Philosophy of Race (CPR) and American Legal Realism (ALR) as the point of departure for Derrick Bell's notion of Racial Realism (RR) in Critical Race Theory (CRT). I am especially interested in the historical sensitivity of Mills's BRK and its resemblance to certain features of ALR—a theory of adjudication that, along with Bell's RR, figures prominently in CRT's keen interest in American constitutional law.

I argue in this chapter that Mills's BRK has philosophical implications for the United States Supreme Court's Fourteenth Amendment Equal Protection jurisprudence. My thesis is both descriptive and prescriptive. It is descriptive insofar as I argue that BRK has features that are already present in a species of constitutional adjudication most recently demonstrated in Justice Ketanji Brown Jackson's dissenting opinion in *Students for Fair Admissions v. President and Fellows of Harvard College* (2023). And it is a prescriptive thesis in that I contend that BRK's rejection of liberalism's notion of abstract persons, in favor of a starting point for political theorizing that takes historical injustices and

DOI: 10.4324/9781003349983-8

oppression into account *before* applying the categorical imperative, is not only an essential part of what Mills refers to as the "Afro-modern political tradition" but also *ought to be* applied in American constitutional law. To make this case, in section two, I discuss the salient features of Mills's BRK, emphasizing BRK as a sort of what Mills has called "non-ideal" theory.

Section three is a discussion of an analog to the differences between BRK and abstract Kantian moral principles: the differences between ALR and Legal Formalism. Section three concludes by pointing out that there is a continuity between ideal theory, Legal Formalism, and the *Rechtsstaat* on the one hand and non-ideal theory, ALR, and the *Rassenstaat* on the other hand. A corollary of this continuity is that CPR and CRT work together in my interpretation of Mills with Bell: both CPR and CRT not only eschew abstraction but also deepen the moral significance of the need to resist oppression—a moral significance reflected in Justice Ketanji Brown Jackson's dissenting opinion in *Students for Fair Admissions*, which demonstrates certain features of Mills's BRK and Bell's RR.

In section four, I present Justice Ketanji Brown Jackson's dissenting opinion in *Students for Fair Admissions* as an example of what BRK looks like in American constitutional jurisprudence. Justice Jackson's analysis unfolds in such close proximity to the non-ideal historical conditions of anti-Black racism in America that it represents, along with the progressive efforts of the United States Congress during Reconstruction, a legal iteration of what Mills has called a "corrective," which is integral to the "Afro-modern" political tradition. Justice Jackson's dissenting opinion also resonates strongly with RR's appropriation of ALR and its use of narrative intertwined with actual historical events. Also in section four, I discuss how Congress's efforts during Reconstruction were, by BRK and RR standards, an attempt at a *Rassenstaat*, and how the Supreme Court frustrated those efforts, essentially ending Reconstruction with its restrictive interpretations of the Civil War Amendments from the *Slaughterhouse Cases* through *Plessy v. Ferguson*, ensuring the legacy of *Dred Scott* deep into the twentieth century, and I offer a brief commentary on originalism and racism.

I conclude in section five that BRK, as understood through RR's appropriation of ALR, both *is and ought to be* an act of resistance that attempts to move from a *Rechtsstaat* to a *Rassenstaat*. Thus it is that CPR and CRT, though distinct, work together to reject a race-avoidant jurisprudential abstraction that maintains a status quo of oppression and to support a race-conscious, historically and socioeconomically attuned engagement that moves toward racial justice.

Black Radical Kantianism

Mills develops his notion of BRK through a Copernican Revolution in political philosophy, beginning with his landmark text *The Racial Contract*. Published in 1997, *The Racial Contract* presented a critique of the abstractions of classical political philosophy in the vein of John Locke and John Rawls. Mills argues throughout *The Racial Contract* that the articulation of social and political theories on the basis of principles derived from abstractions about a state of nature assumes a social and political equality that, historically and practically speaking, has never been a reality. Mills interprets Jean-Jacques Rousseau, often paired with Thomas Hobbes and Locke in synoptic histories of political philosophy, as providing a more accurate portrait of a state of nature than Locke because of Rousseau's acknowledgment of inequality as the basis for private property ownership, social policy, and political rule-making.

Even as Kant aimed to reform metaphysics and epistemology by asking the radical question of whether all our experience conformed to knowledge rather than our knowledge conforming to experience, and demanding in his transcendental idealism that spatiotemporal conditions be imposed on experience, Mills attempts a reform of political philosophy by asking the radical question of whether our starting point for political theory ought to be the actual historical conditions of oppression rather than the abstractions of ideal theory that fail to take such historical conditions into account, and thus altogether fail to address—or even perpetuate—their attendant injustices. Demanding the condition of historical considerations akin to how Kant demands the restrictions of space, time, and the categories of pure reason, Mills furthers his Copernican Revolution in political philosophy in his essay, "Black Radical Kantianism" by first situating his work within what Robert Gooding-Williams has called the "Afro-modern political tradition" (Gooding-Williams, 2009). The Afro-modern political tradition, according to Mills, "develops, as its name declares, in modernity, necessitated by resistance to the oppressive institutions of Atlantic slavery and European colonialism" (2). It is, then, against this historical backdrop of white supremacy that the form and function of the Afro-modern political tradition take shape, becoming, according to both Mills and Gooding-Williams, a political theory that "seeks to overcome the 'regimes of white supremacy' in their protean and ever-evolving guises" (2). Recognizing the myriad political views of the Afro-modern political tradition, Mills understands BRK as an important component of a synthesis of Afro-modern political theory, including a "Black radical liberalism" that draws from "Black Marxism, Black nationalism, and Black feminism" (2). For Mills, then, BRK is thus understood as "demonstrating how classic themes in this literature can illuminatingly be translated into a Kantian discourse reshaped by the realities of racial subordination" (2).

Mills then points out the reasons for Kant as his point of departure, which are two-fold. First, Mills argues that Kant is important because his work remains the most influential and is thus, strategically speaking, well-suited to a direct engagement between the Afro-modern and European political traditions (Mills, 2018, 3). Second, Mills believes that Kant's moral principles (dignity, respect of individuals, and rights), "once deracialized," are amenable to the establishment of the *Rechtsstaat*, a political order based on principles of human dignity and individual rights. In making this point, Mills writes: "The problem, in my opinion, has been less Kant's own racism (since it is simply bracketed by most contemporary Kantians) than the failure to rethink these principles and ideals in the light of a modernity structured by racial domination," which brings Mills to his third point:

> In contrast with, say, a dialogue between European and Asian political traditions, which at least for long periods of time developed largely separately from one another, the Euro modern and the Afro-modern traditions are intimately and dialectically linked. As emphasized at the start, the latter develops in specific contestation of the former, involving both resistance to and rejection of its crucial tenets insofar as they rationalize and justify Euro-domination, while nonetheless sometimes seeking to appropriate and modify others for emancipatory ends. So developing a "Black radical Kantianism" as a self-conscious enterprise should be not merely instrumentally and intrinsically valuable, but illuminative of a counter-hegemonic normative system already present in Afro modern

thought, if not self-denominatedly "Kantian," formed in opposition to white domination predicated on the denial of equal personhood to Blacks.

(3)

Mills's use of Kant is, then, strategic insofar as he does not want to reinvent the wheel—he wants to transform it. The theoretical framework for BRK is already in place insofar as the Afro-modern political tradition has been inevitably engaged with extensive social and political critique in ways that are consistent with his non-ideal theory.

Mills's BRK is an extension of his work that he began in *The Racial Contract* and that he continued in his 2009 essay, "Rawls on Race/Race in Rawls." There, Mills recapitulates his basic argument from *The Racial Contract* that classical political philosophy, in the vein of Hobbes and Locke, for example, which abstractly—and for Mills, quite incorrectly—identifies the foundations of social and political life in thought experiments, prevents one from taking into account the historical realities of injustice in the modern West. Such ideal thought experiments, Mills argues in *The Racial Contract*, are better understood as an agreement among whites to create oppressive social and political arrangements for their benefit rather than creating an egalitarian society based on spurious notions of colorblindness. Exacerbating this problem for Mills is John Rawls's admission in *A Theory of Justice* that he wants to take classical political thought to an even higher level of abstraction and generality, for arguing for a "veil of ignorance" in a hypothetical "original position" in which abstract "persons" select abstract principles of "equality" does nothing to ameliorate historical injustices, which are not considered in Rawls's notion of justice. Mills argues that such abstractions and generalities represent the worst of what he has termed ideal theory: social and political theorizing that is fundamentally ahistorical and thus impotent to redress the historical wrongs of racial oppression. From this, Mills concludes in "Rawls on Race/Race in Rawls" that Rousseau's work is preferable for an emancipatory politics because it is "non-ideal" in that it accounts for the historical inequities related to the ownership of private property (Mills, 2009, 181–82).

From *The Racial Contract* through "Rawls on Race/Race in Rawls" and concluding with "Black Radical Kantianism," Mills has consistently and forcibly argued against abstraction in political theory because its ahistorical thought experiments not only fail to address injustices but even perpetuate them. Mills's notion of BRK aims for a deployment of Kantian moral principles that he believes, with historical injustices taken into consideration, are helpful principles of an emancipatory resistance in the Afro-modern political tradition. Mills presents BRK as a theory that reformulates Kantian moral principles by informing them with the historical realities of white racial domination in the modern West before such principles are applied. Such is Mills's Copernican Revolution in political theory: rather than applying Kantian moral principles in the abstract, BRK only applies such principles after imposing the condition—in a Kantian sense—that white supremacy's historical wrongs are taken into account. So, BRK enables one to speak of "equality," but no longer in abstract, ahistorical terms. To speak of equality according to BRK is not merely to speak of a concern with a polity characterized by "rights" (a *Rechtsstaat*), in which the concept of equality is invoked to create a socially desensitized, artificial "starting point" that ignores history. Instead, equality, according to BRK, presupposes a polity that is historically conscious of racial oppression (a *Rassenstaat*) and takes the necessary steps to ameliorate its devastating legacy of institutional and systemic injustice.

So, for Mills, it is the imposition of conditions that establishes his Copernican Revolution in social and political thought. Rather than blindly applying abstract Kantian moral and political principles, Mills demands that such principles only be applied after reformulating them to account for modernity's history of racial oppression. Whereas Kant's transcendental idealism imposed conditions on the possibility of experience in the interest of metaphysics and epistemology, Mills imposes conditions on the possibility of politics in the interest of justice. Further, Mills's uses language in the above passage that resonates strongly with equal protection jurisprudence—he uses the phrase "equal personhood," referring to Black people, consistent with both the history and judicial language of the Equal Protection Clause of the Fourteenth Amendment. Such "equal personhood" has tragically been an ever-elusive reality for Black people in American constitutional history. The central moves of BRK having been discussed, I now turn to what I believe are the similarities between BRK, ALR, and ALR as appropriated by Bell's RR.

Mills and Non-Ideal Theories of Adjudication

There is a conceptual relationship between BRK, ALR, and the *Rassenstaat* that can be analogically stated: BRK is to Kantian moral principles what ALR is to Legal Formalism, and what the *Rassenstaat* is to the *Rechtssaat*. That is, BRK, ALR, and the *Rassenstaat* are all historically-informed, socially attuned theories—non-ideal theories in the sense that Mills discusses non-ideal theory throughout his corpus—which reject the abstractions of their theoretical counterparts (Kantian moral principles, Legal Formalism, and the *Rechtssaat*, respectively) as incapable of bringing about racial justice. Each of these non-ideal, historically-informed, socially attuned theories shares at least two central features that make them amenable to the pursuit of racial justice.

First, BRK, ALR, and the *Rassenstaat* are all anti-metaphysical in nature. Over-committing to rigorous, metaphysical views about the nature of ideal polities, ideal moral behaviors, and about the ideal nature of law in the abstract, for each of these views, is a nonstarter because such commitments preclude, *ab initio*, any consideration of white supremacy and its attendant racial oppression in the modern West. We see this in BRK's critique of abstract political theory as Mills discusses it throughout his corpus, in ALR's suspicion of being overly concerned with Legal Formalism's demand for rules, as seen in the jurisprudence of Oliver Wendell Holmes Jr., who claimed in *The Common Law* that "The life of the law has not been logic, but experience" (Holmes, 1991, 1),[1] and in the *Rassenstaat's* uniquely American race-conscious policies, such as the Civil War Amendments and the Freedmen's Bureau, which were themselves the first attempts at affirmative action, and that take precedence over the *Rechtsstaat's* concern for abstract rights that is so predominant in liberal political theory. And second, the rejection of metaphysics leads to each having an abiding concern with *how things actually work in the world*. Pragmatism's overtones can be seen in this point.[2]

Each of the non-ideal theories I am discussing here are concerned less with the correctness of things at a theoretical level and are instead concerned with their practical implications; for example, BRK rejects pure, abstract, Kantian social, political, and moral theory in favor of how such a theory works in the world for oppressed people, ALR has little interest in accurate, syllogistic form of a priori legal rules, instead favoring a data-driven, descriptive account of how judges decide actual cases affecting the lives of concrete persons, and lastly, a *Rassenstaat* understands that the vindication of liberalism's "rights" almost certainly means the maintenance of a racially unjust status quo. It is, then, a sort of pragmatism, hostile to metaphysics in the abstract, which creates a kind of family resemblance between BRK, ALR, and the *Rassenstaat*. I use this term, "family resemblance" intentionally here, as Ludwig Wittgenstein uses it in *Philosophical Investigations* to describe the destabilizing—perhaps even liberating—force of what he calls "language games" (Wittgenstein, 1958, 30–35). Even as Wittgenstein attempts a destabilization of language in the interest of showing its contingent rather than absolute character, I use the notion of "family resemblance" here to show that the language of abstraction, so prevalent in liberalism's political theories of "rights," is a sort of game that demands opposition from a culture arising from the denizens of the underside of racial oppression in the modern West. My aim on this point is not to show that the forms of resistance (BRK, ALR, and the *Rassenstaat*) are weakened—although on Wittgenstein's account they may still be considered "language games"—but rather to show that the a priori nature of law and abstractions about rights and individuals are weakened. So, rather than claiming what certain terms or concepts have in common, I am arguing here that BRK, ALR, and the *Rassenstaat* all share certain overlapping features in that all of them are not concerned with reforming Kantian moral principles, as is BRK. All are not concerned with theories of adjudication, as is ALR, and all are not aiming for a corrective, race-conscious polity, as is the *Rassenstaat*. And yet BRK's interest in reforming Kantian moral principles overlaps with ALR's rejection of abstract legal principles, and the *Rassenstaat* overlaps with and even follows from BRK's transformation from liberalism's abstract concentration on "rights" to a pragmatic, corrective focus on race. Hence, the notion of a family resemblance.

What follows in the remainder of this section is a discussion of each theory and its counterpart, beginning with BRK and Kantian moral principles, followed by ALR and Legal Formalism, and the *Rassenstaat* and the *Rechtssaat*. The discussion of the *Rassenstaat* and the *Rechtssaat* introduces another legal and moral theory, derived from ALR but distinct from it, in Bell's RR, which I discuss more in the next section as elements of it appear in Justice Jackson's dissenting opinion in *Students for Fair Admissions*.

Black Radical Kantianism and Abstract Kantian Moral Principles

Mills, in his essay, "Black Radical Kantianism," points out that the real problem with Kant's philosophy is not so much Kant's racism as it is "the failure to rethink these [Kant's] principles *in the light of* a modernity structured by racial domination" (2018, 3). Throughout his discussion of the role of race in Kant's philosophical system, Mills concedes that race is an organizing principle in Kant's critical philosophy. For Mills, Kant's racism is not peripheral but rather central to his work. Mills thus raises the following question: "How then do I propose to develop a Black radical Kantianism?" (Mills, 2018, 10). He answers that he will not simply "bracket off the racism and then assimilate Blacks and other people of color to the white population, which would only obfuscate the real difference that race makes" (10). Instead, Mills writes that he wants to "transform the significance of 'race.' We would still be working with a 'Kantianism' in which race is central, but now rethought from a critical philosophy of race perspective" (10). Race, then, in BRK is not, as it is in Kant, a biological hierarchy with whites at the top, but rather a "location of equals in a social hierarchy of the privileged and the oppressed in a system of racial domination" (11). For Mills, race retains a structuring role in what he calls "a corrective, anti-racist way," rather than an oppressive one. Mills writes of this transformed Kantianism that "So 'race' in this revisionist Kantianism would now be tracking something different, and the 'empirical content' that must guide our application of the abstract Kantian principles is to be derived from investigation of the historic and current reality of an unjust and racially structured world" (12). Mills assigns historically-conscious labels of "R1s" to represent those historically thought of as racially superior persons in a socially privileged position and "R2s" to represent those historically thought of as racially inferior persons in a subordinate position.

With the R1s and R2s thus assigned their respective positions in a historically-conscious social hierarchy, as opposed to an abstract, racially idealized—indeed, a racist—Kantian "human nature," CPR, in Mills's view, is now concerned with "exploring how issues of moral psychology, the necessary education of the virtues, and individual and social cognition are likewise affected by race" (12). With the historically-informed R1s and R2s in mind, Mills points to the work of Miranda Fricker as an example of how recognizing social relationships structured on domination exposes both testimonial and hermeneutic forms of epistemic injustice. Mills contends that such developments in social epistemology also ought to occur within the realm of moral cognition. Mills suggests that Kant's notion of enlightenment, then, has moral and not merely political consequences, as enlightenment, on the reconstructed account of Kantianism that is BRK, would be one's emergence from the moral immaturity of societally-generated racialized, cognitive impediments by rejecting racial dogmas and stereotypes characteristic of racially oppressive societies, such as those of the modern West. Even as Fricker's social epistemology resists the abstractions of, say, for example, the Gettier problem and its attendant counterexamples, Mills is calling for a socially and historically-conscious brand of moral cognition, in which people, aware of the defects in moral cognition because of their consideration of historical oppression and its legacy in contemporary social and political arrangements, overcome those oppressive dogmas in favor of applying moral principles in ways that will resist abstraction.[3] Mills's BRK, then, differs from the abstractions of Kant's moral philosophy because it takes the historical circumstance of oppression into account in a way that the straightforward application of Kant's moral principles does not. It is this difference, this radical reformulation of Kant's moral principles with a historical consciousness, that both connects BRK to the Afro-modern tradition and shows its anti-metaphysical, pragmatic nature, as I have discussed above. For Mills, the Afro-modern political tradition resists what happened when "liberalism sanitized its racial past and transformed this hierarchical essentialist metaphysics into an ontology of morally equal and symmetrically positioned atomic individuals. [...] In other words, the Afro-modern tradition is insistent that modernity is established on and structured by a social ontology of race" (14).

The difference, then, between BRK and Kant's moral principles is made evident: the former is historically and socially attuned, furthering CPR in its quest toward racial justice, while the latter is ahistorical, furthering oppression in its commitment to abstraction. A similar dialectic of historical-ahistorical and liberation-oppression occurs in the context of jurisprudence, specifically, adjudication—a judicial function which has played a significant role in the oppression of Black people in the modern West, and in particular, the United States. I take this up in the next section to show how BRK's emphasis on historical injustices and prevailing social conditions is compatible with ALR, and how this emphasis occurs in the Supreme Court's Equal Protection Jurisprudence.

American Legal Realism and Formalism

The general drift of non-ideal theory (and BRK, as discussed thus far) as anti-metaphysical and pragmatist-oriented is also recognizable in the differences between jurisprudential theories of adjudication such as ALR and Legal Formalism, specifically in ALR's indeterminacy thesis. The principal concern for ALR is not how judges decide cases through the application of strict legal rules to attain predictable outcomes (i.e., Legal Formalism) but rather how judges decide cases in real courtrooms involving real litigants. Generally speaking, the central thesis of ALR—what Brian Leiter calls its "core claim"—is that "judges respond primarily to the stimulus of facts" (Leiter, 2007, 21). Opposing this view is the view of Legal Formalism, which is the view that judges, in deciding cases, are responding to legal reasons, rather than non-legal reasons in their decision-making. For ALR, judges do not decide cases based on any abstract notion of "law." There are simply too many legal rules that enable judges to decide cases on whichever basis they choose so that judicial opinions may "write," that is, find justification in rationales independent of factual stimuli presented to the judge. Simply put, for ALR, there are no singularly correct legal principles that can be formulaically applied to cases to reach predictable outcomes.

The Realists tried to show, then, that with respect to cases that were pending on appeal, the law was fundamentally indeterminate. This is known as the indeterminacy thesis of ALR. According to Leiter, it was Critical Legal Studies (CLS) that extended the indeterminacy thesis from solely cases that were pending on appeal to an overall thesis about the nature of law in general (Leiter, 2007, 219).[4] Leiter includes CRT within the group of CLS. For CLS, legal indeterminacy, in its most radical sense, asserts that what we think is law is merely politics. The courtroom, then, becomes a venue for competing political ideologies, and power is the currency in such courtroom battles. Echoes of Thrasymachus in book I of Plato's *Republic* can be heard here, as one can argue that there is a sort of "justice is in the interest of the stronger" theory at work in CLS and CRT.

Legal Formalists, on the other hand, have argued that a notion of law that is fixed and independent of factual considerations that an individual judge finds appealing is a bulwark against the raw power of the courts in a constitutional democracy. Such a fixed, strong, metaphysical notion of law is a critical element in judicial restraint, essential in many contemporary Western constitutional democracies, to maintain the legislative and executive branches of government as coequal branches of the government with the judiciary, especially in America. Even as BRK destabilizes the abstractions of political and moral theory in favor of real-world considerations as to how such theories affect oppressed persons, ALR's legal indeterminacy thesis fundamentally destabilizes the notion of law in favor of real-world considerations as to how judges decide cases based on factual stimuli. But for Leiter, the indeterminacy thesis leads to a more scientific, naturalistic, empirical way of understanding law; it does not lead to law's complete destabilization, as with the postmodern jurisprudence of CLS and CRT.

Having discussed the foundational differences between ALR and Legal Formalism, I would argue that beyond being a theory of adjudication, ALR can, on its own terms, be engaged with issues of racial justice—despite the fact that many of the Realists ignored issues of race in the 1930s.[5] I turn to two examples in support of this claim, which show both ALR's incidental but significant engagement with race and the glaring contrast between ALR and Legal Formalism as theories of adjudication.

The first case is *Coppage v. Kansas* (1915), in which the Supreme Court invalidated a Kansas state law prohibiting so-called "yellow-dog contracts," which were employment contracts that contained clauses that prevented their employees from joining a labor union. A Kansas employer, Coppage, had such clauses in his contracts and fired an employee who refused to sign the contract. He was convicted of violating the Kansas statute. He appealed. The Supreme Court overturned his conviction, reasoning that the Kansas statute prohibiting yellow-dog contracts was unconstitutional, as it violated the freedom to contract, implied in the Due Process Clause of the Fourteenth Amendment. The majority opinion is an exercise in formalist jurisprudence, for the Court merely applied "liberty" and "freedom to contract" in the abstract, without regard to any of the attendant social and economic conditions of the parties. *Coppage* was decided in the same vein as *Lochner v. New York* (1905), the second example of a case (second here for explanatory purposes, but first chronologically) in which the Court invalidated a state law that infringed the freedom of contract. In *Lochner*, a New York statute regulated the working hours of bakers, and the Court ruled that the statute infringed on the freedom to contract of both the employer and the employee. Reasoning in this abstract manner, both *Coppage* and *Lochner* can theoretically be celebrated as decisions that affirm the "freedom to contract," recognizing that on one hand, both parties are "free," while failing to recognize on the other hand that the so-called "freedom" of workers, socioeconomically speaking, is non-existent, as workers, some of whom were Black, have little to no bargaining power at all.

Formalism ignores such socioeconomic realities in favor of abstract, vacuous notions of "freedom," but ALR does not. Indeed, in the *Coppage* decision, calling for *Lochner* to be overruled, Justice Holmes dissented, pointing out that "In present conditions, a workman not unnaturally may believe that only by belonging to a union can he secure a contract that shall be fair to him. [...] If that belief, whether right or wrong, may be held by a reasonable man, it seems to me that it may be enforced by law in order to establish the equality of position between the parties in which liberty of contract begins" (1915, 26–27). Justice Holmes' dissent is significant in that although race is not explicitly mentioned, Holmes refers to "present conditions." In making this reference in 1915, Holmes indicates an awareness of poor labor conditions and bargaining inequities for workers at that time in American history. Even assuming that such inequities in contractual bargaining power affect more whites than Blacks, it is highly likely that Blacks, living in an era of rampant lynching in the South and struggling to find work in the North, are also affected. To consider "present conditions," then, as Justice Holmes did, is to consider race, albeit indirectly. Moreover, the majority in the *Coppage* decision implies a right of contract into the Fourteenth Amendment's Due Process Clause in a way that will further reduce the already compromised bargaining power of potential Black workers—a tragic irony considering that the Fourteenth Amendment was explicitly concerned with protecting the rights of newly-freed slaves from white racial violence in the states, the places where Black workers were most likely required to sign yellow-dog contracts. This is especially so in the early years of the great migration, when many Black people were coming from the South to northern, western, and mid-western states looking for work, and statutes prohibiting yellow-dog contracts such as the Kansas statute had been passed in California, Colorado, Connecticut, Indiana, Massachusetts, Minnesota, New Hampshire, New Jersey, New York, Oklahoma, Oregon, Pennsylvania, Puerto Rico, and Wisconsin, all of which the *Coppage* decision declared unconstitutional in the name of a vacuous, borderline sinister notion of "freedom to contract." The realism of Justice

Holmes recognized this problem, but a formalist approach ignored it. So, even as BRK is socially attuned to unjust conditions in the explicit interest of justice for Black people, ALR is likewise historically and socially attuned to unjust conditions in a way that implicitly concerns racial injustice. The implicit engagement of ALR with race becomes explicit in Bell's notion of RR, which I turn to next.

Racial Realism and the Rassenstaat

Mills, in his transformation of Kantian moral principles, makes an abstract moral theory amenable to an emancipatory politics for CPR in the Afro-modern political tradition. Bell does something similar in his development of RR in CRT, but with a twist. Unlike Kantian moral principles, ALR is already concerned with the dangers of abstraction, as I have previously argued with reference to the *Lochner* era of the Supreme Court and the so-called "freedom to contract." Like Mills, Bell is operating within the Afro-modern political tradition, his influences being Black thinkers such as Ralph Bunche and Martin Delany. Unlike Mills, however, Bell takes an already concrete theory in ALR and appropriates it, making it specific to the plight of Black people in America. As a civil rights lawyer who litigated cases with the National Association for the Advancement of Colored People turned law professor, Bell had a specific and keen interest in American law that Mills did not, though both Mills and Bell are profoundly interested in developing an emancipatory politics for Black people. Bell thus finds inspiration in ALR, which he explores in detail in his seminal law review article "Racial Realism" in the *Connecticut Law Review* in 1992.

Bell opens his remarks in "Racial Realism" by pointing to the frustrations of Black Americans in their ongoing struggle for racial equality. The struggle for racial equality is so difficult that Bell concludes that "Racial equality is, in fact, not a realistic goal. By constantly aiming for a status that is unobtainable in a perilously racist America, Black Americans face frustration and despair" (Bell, 1992, 363). He then argues for a reformation of Black civil rights strategies, referencing ALR as a means of how this can be done:

> Black people need reform of our civil rights strategies as badly as those in the law needed a new way to consider American jurisprudence prior to the advent of the Legal Realists. By viewing the law—and by extension, the courts—as instruments for preserving the status quo and only periodically and unpredictably serving as a refuge of oppressed people, Blacks can refine the work of the Realists. Rather than challenging the entire jurisprudential system, as the Realists did, Blacks' focus must be much narrower—a challenge to the principle of racial equality. This new movement is appropriately called Racial Realism, and it is a legal and social mechanism on which Blacks can rely to have their voice and outrage heard.
>
> *(363–64)*

Bell goes on to describe ALR and ultimately concludes that RR "is to race relations what legal realism is to jurisprudential thought" (364). For Bell, RR both takes its point of departure from and expands upon ALR's claim of legal indeterminacy, extending it from empirical data that will show a multiplicity of rules to justify decisions in cases on appeal to cases involving race relations,[6] ultimately trying to show how American law bolsters rather than eradicates racism. Throughout "Racial Realism," Bell argues, from Supreme Court precedent, how he believes this to be the case. Bell writes of *Regents of the University of*

California v. Bakke (1978) that it "serves as an example of how formalists may use abstract concepts such as equality, to mask policy choices and value judgments. Abstraction in the place of flexible reasoning, removes a heavy burden from a judge's task" (369). This assertion about *Bakke* is based on Bell's argument about what the Court, in *Bakke*, was actually doing. Bell writes:

> Relying heavily on the formalistic language of the Fourteenth Amendment, and utterly ignoring social questions about which race in fact has power and advantages and which race has been denied entry for centuries into academia, the Court held that an affirmative policy may not unseat white candidates on the basis of their race. By introducing an artificial and inappropriate parity in its reasoning, the Court effectively made a choice to ignore historical patterns, to ignore contemporary statistics, and to ignore flexible reasoning.
>
> *(369)*

Bell continues his critique of legal formalism later in the essay when he writes that "a judge may advocate the importance of racial equality while arriving at a decision detrimental to Black Americans. [...] The message the formalist model conveys is that existing power relations in the real world are by definition legitimate and must go unchallenged" (376). For Bell, "Precedent, rights theory, and objectivity merely are formal rules that serve a covert purpose. Even in the context of equality theory, they will never vindicate the legal rights of Black Americans" (376). In contrast to the formalism of the Court in *Bakke*, Bell indicates what the *Bakke* decision would have looked like on a Realist account of adjudication:

> Following a Realist approach, the Court would have observed the social landscape and noticed the skewed representation of minority medical school students. It would have reflected on the possible reasons for these demographics, including inadequate public school systems in urban ghettos, lack of minority professionals to serve as role models, and the use of standardized tests evaluated by "white" standards. Taking these factors into consideration, the Court very well may have decided Bakke differently.
>
> *(369)*

Bell points out that despite this vastly different, and in his view, more just portrait of how *Bakke* should have been decided, "the basic formalist model of law survives," and "by reasoning that race-conscious policies derogate the meaning of racial equality, a judge can manipulate the law and arrive at an outcome based upon her worldview" to the detriment of Black people (376).

It seems, then, that even ALR's increased socioeconomic attunement is insufficient to stem the tide of abstraction. In response, Bell argues that "the Racial Realism concept would enable" Black people to "understand and respond to recurring aspects of" their "subordinate status. It would free them to think and plan within a context of reality rather than idealism" (377). For Bell, the harsh reality is that Black people suffer from societal ills such as poverty and lack of health care more than other ethnic populations in America, and the ideal is that racial equality in law will rescue Black people from this condition. Black people in America must move toward the real because of its empirical and historical force and abandon the ideal because of its illusory legal victories that formalist adjudication promptly transforms into defeats through the power of abstraction. Moving toward the real does not, however, signal defeat but instead represents a sort of victory in the struggle itself. Bell concludes that "We must realize, as our slave forbears, that the struggle for freedom is, at bottom, a manifestation of our humanity that survives and grows stronger through resistance to oppression, even if that oppression is never overcome" (378). Bell's RR thus at once demands allegiance to two theses: the realist thesis that racism is permanent and the resistance thesis that, despite the permanence of racism, resistance against it remains essential. Bell's RR is then, an advance on ALR in that it takes up race directly in a way that ALR did only indirectly. And in doing so, RR, like BRK, operates in the Afro-modern political tradition as an act of resistance in defiance of racial oppression in American law. The *Rassenstaat* that Bell's RR envisions is a perpetual battleground against racism. For Bell, we live in a race-conscious state that, on one hand, will always be racist but, on the other hand, will always be in need of tools to fight against it. And although racial equality, for Bell, does not come through the courts, a socioeconomically and historically attuned BRK can help fight some of the battles. Mills's BRK in CPR provides a valuable weapon in RR's endless battles against racism. Mills and Bell both oppose abstraction; they both, through radical commitments to history, demand a transformation of existing theoretical constructs that they both believe maintain white dominance, and they both pursue more just polities: Mills does so through a *Rassenstaat* that is corrective in nature, and Bell through a *Rassenstaat* that, though permanently racist, demands the corrective capacities of historically and socioeconomically attuned theories like BRK to help fight the battles in the never-ending war; a war the parameters of which Bell's RR defines and for which Mills's BRK is ammunition for those perpetually engaged in battle.

Thus far, I have argued that BRK, ALR, and RR are historically-informed and socioeconomically attuned theories engaged with concerns of racial justice; BRK through its Afro-modern orientation in CPR, ALR through its socioeconomic sensibilities, and RR through its African-American orientation in Bell's RR in CRT. As Mills understands it in the Afro-modern tradition, then, CPR's BRK can be read with Bell's resistance thesis of racial realism to produce an Africana-informed mode of resistance in the interest of racial justice. Bell and Mills work well together in this regard. I now turn to the next section of the chapter, in which I argue that BRK and its resulting *Rassensstaat* are present in the Supreme Court's Equal Protection Jurisprudence, specifically in Justice Ketanji Brown Jackson's dissenting opinion in the Court's recent affirmative action decision, which also displays features of Bell's RR in her use of fictional narrative. Mills's BRK still figures prominently here, in that Justice Jackson's dissenting opinion is discussed to show that BRK has a presence in Supreme Court jurisprudence that is both descriptive—it is "there," so to speak—and normative, in that I contend that such historically-sensitive adjudication ought to be how Fourteenth Amendment cases implicating the racial history of African Americans are decided.

Mills, Bell, and Fourteenth Amendment Originalism

Justice Ketanji Brown Jackson's dissenting opinion in *Students for Fair Admissions* contains elements of BRK's and ALR's historical and socioeconomic sensibilities, and elements of RR in her dissent's use of fictional narrative. My aim in this penultimate section of the chapter is to discuss each of these elements of Justice Jackson's dissent and conclude, based on the presence of these elements in her dissent, that her dissent itself is a normative act of resistance in both CPR and CRT; a normative resistance that must be maintained to withstand the relentless pressures of racism. At bottom, Justice Jackson's dissent articulates America's attempts to be a *Rassenstaat* and it embodies the vision that such a *Rassenstaat*, though not a reality, is nevertheless something worth our moral striving. I also want to comment briefly on how Justice Jackson's opinion is decidedly originalist in tone, despite being out-of-step with the conservative majority, who are all supposedly originalist adherents. On this point, one wonders about the doctrinal and hermeneutic legitimacy of originalism. I address this problem at the end of this section.

As for ALR, Justice Jackson's dissenting opinion begins with an observation of Justice Holmes that "a page of history is worth a volume of logic" (*New York Trust Company v. Eisner* 1921, 349). She thus sets the realist tone of her dissent. What Justice Holmes means by this statement is that a formalist understanding of law provides little insight as compared with an approach to law that takes history into account. Justice Holmes' point had been made long before when Frederick Douglass, in his 1845 autobiographical narrative, wrote that the slave's songs of sorrows did more to depict the horrors of American chattel slavery than "volumes of philosophy" could ever do. For Douglass, this means that a priori, idealized, conceptually clear philosophical arguments against slavery did little to impress upon one the moral wrongness of slavery as compared with the deep pathos of the slave songs. For Douglass, aesthetic expression born of tragedy trumps reason. And for Justice Holmes, history trumps reason because a page of history has far more explanatory force than a volume of logic. History is, then, for Holmes, not peripheral but integral to an understanding of law itself. Holmes writes in *The Common Law* that "The law embodies the story of a nation's development through many centuries, and it cannot be dealt with as if it contained only the axioms and corollaries of a book of mathematics. In order to know what it is, we must know what it has been, and what it tends to become" (Holmes, 1991, 1). Attempts to understand the law through the voluminous amount of legal principles are far more difficult than understanding the law as influenced by historical and social conditions. Law becomes frustrating, and indeed, even unjust when one is attempting to understand it apart from the human lives that it affects. That Justice Jackson cites Holmes is important for her reasoning in her dissenting opinion because she is essentially taking a realist stance on the Fourteenth Amendment Equal Protection case before the Court. In the spirit of Justice Holmes, Justice Jackson begins her analysis with history.

In being this attentive to history—a history of racial oppression in the United States, Justice Jackson makes a move with Equal Protection jurisprudence similar to the move that Mills makes with BRK against abstract Kantian moral principles: she is reformulating the abstractions of Equal Protection jurisprudence into historically-informed principles of equal protection that take race into account for corrective rather than oppressive reasons. Justice Jackson is, of course, not the first Justice to think in these terms. Justice Thurgood Marshall certainly did, as did many other government officials throughout American history. Indeed, it can be persuasively argued that Justice Jackson is actually attempting to return the Equal Protection Clause to its roots in American Reconstruction, when Congress attempted to establish a *Rassenstaat* through comprehensive legislative efforts, the Freedmen's Bureau, and the Fourteenth Amendment itself, which were arguably the first forms of affirmative action. Sadly, however, the Court on which Justice Jackson now sits, through its post-Reconstruction jurisprudence, ensured that the *Rassenstaat* would become a *Rechtsstaaat* of abstract rights.

From the *Slaughterhouse Cases* through *Plessy v. Ferguson*, the Court, practically speaking, returned Black Americans to the tragic legal status of the *Dred Scott* decision, despite Congress's herculean efforts to overrule *Dred Scott* with both landmark civil rights legislation and the Civil War Amendments, by striking down as unenforceable all of Congress's efforts. So it is that although the Fifteenth Amendment was ratified in 1870, Black Americans did not secure the right to vote in federal law until 95 years later with the Voting Rights Act of 1965. And although the Reconstruction Congress outlawed Jim Crow with its Civil Rights Acts of the 1870s, Jim Crow would not officially end until some 90 years later with the Civil Rights Act of 1964. The Court legitimized racial oppression—a *Dred Scott* state of affairs—for nearly a 100 years.

Fictional narrative plays an important role in CRT and in Bell's work, which is reflected in Justice Jackson's dissent. The use of narrative helps one to establish voices from other communities that are otherwise silenced through abstraction. There is a real danger that if one remains in the realm of abstraction, objectivity becomes inescapable and the voices of marginalized subjects sink into a black hole of oblivion in which the weight of abstraction is so strong that it exceeds the capacity to be heard. Even as light is trapped at the event horizon of a black hole because the escape velocity exceeds its speed, once absorbed into the portal of abstraction without narrative, marginalized voices lack the means of escape and remain muted beneath the oppressive weight of thought experiments. So, fictional narrative gives marginalized voices a means of resistance. Fiction serves another function, too, which is its ability to disabuse people of deceptions that hinder their moral progress; it is a sort of indirect communication in the Kierkegaardian sense in that it encourages subjective appropriation in ways that refocus the audience's attention on themselves and the moral problem (s) that confront them, motivating them to change their behavior. We see this in biblical narrative, as when Nathan confronted David with his moral shortcomings through a fictional narrative and David repented of his misdeeds. This is not to say that fictional narrative will always have the desired effect. At times it may not. But that is not the point. The point is that fictional narrative, successful at achieving the desired change or not, is a means of persuasion that appeals to subjectivity in a way that a sole reliance on objective abstractions cannot.

Justice Jackson's opinion in *Students for Fair Admissions v. President and Fellows of Harvard College* contains a story that serves both of these purposes. At the beginning of her dissent, she tells a story followed by the well-known dictum of Justice Holmes that has become the credo of ALR:

> Imagine two college applicants from North Carolina, John and James. Both trace their family's North Carolina roots to the year of UNC's founding in 1789. Both love their State and want great things for its people. Both want to honor their family's legacy by attending the State's flagship educational institution. John, however, would be the seventh generation to graduate from UNC. He is White. James would be the first; he is Black. Does the race of these applicants properly play a role in UNC's holistic merits based admissions process?
>
> To answer that question, "a page of history is worth a volume of logic."
>
> *(2023, 3)*

Justice Jackson begins her dissent with the word "imagine," which functions as an imperative to creativity that immediately gives a voice to James, a Black person whose voice would be unheard beneath the weight of abstraction. James is what literary theorists might call a "composite character," in that he represents the many oppressed Black persons who have been shut out of opportunities in higher education throughout American history. James, though fictional, has a place in the minds of the audience of one who has been marginalized that he otherwise would not have. Moreover, because James is styled as a citizen who wants "great things" for the people of his state and who wants to honor his "family's legacy by attending the State's flagship educational institution," he garners the sympathy of the audience because he, unlike his white counterpart, John, is a first-generation college student. Considering these two students, the question is whether race can constitutionally play a role in the admissions process at the University of North Carolina. In asking this question after setting the stage with such an endearing view of James, the legal question is almost offensive. In what sense is it proper to disrupt our sense of empathy for James with a question about constitutional interpretation? I think that Justice Jackson's opinion, then, has the potential effect of the audience being less inclined toward technical legal questions and more oriented toward James' self and personhood. James is thus effectively humanized in a way that he would not be if fictional narratives were not used in Justice Jackson's dissent. Like Bell's RR, then, Justice Jackson deploys fiction to engage historical truth.

In the final part of this section, I want to address the problem of originalism in *Students for Fair Admissions*. The nature of the problem is that, on one hand, originalism is a constitutional hermeneutic in which one must construe the constitutional provision consistent with the meaning of the provision at the time of its adoption. If this is the methodology, then it seems that Justice Jackson's reasoning ought to be the reasoning of the majority opinion, insofar as she is interpreting the meaning of the Equal Protection Clause based on what its meaning was at the time of its adoption, which was to provide equal protection of the laws to newly-freed slaves in a race-conscious way that would, going forward, help correct past injustices. In a word, the original understanding of the Fourteenth Amendment's Equal Protection Clause was the creation of, in Mills's terms, a *Rassenstaat*, or race-conscious state, as a corrective, which is what CPR wants to do through BRK. And yet, Justice Jackson is writing a dissent, when the majority of the justices, who are supposed to be originalist in their constitutional interpretation, are inattentive to the original, race-conscious meaning of the Equal Protection Clause, which seems to have overwhelming support in the historical record.

What are we to make of this problem? I propose that originalism, as an interpretive practice when deciding racial issues involving African Americans in the Supreme Court's Equal Protection jurisprudence, is an illegitimate doctrine not based on principle but rather on rank political ideology. I am, of course, aware of the genetic fallacy. My claim is not that originalism as such is phony because of its origins, but rather that there is a sort of phony originalism, as the current Supreme Court practices it, that lacks the starting point it purports to have, resulting in its unprincipled application. As practiced, then, originalism injects rank political ideology into constitutional interpretation.

Distinct from originalism "as practiced" is originalism as such, which has the virtue of a restraint on adjudication that protects democratic sensibilities in a constitutional republic such as the United States. Constrained by the original meaning of the Constitution, the policy-making function is reserved for Congress and the President—the branches of American government that are subject to the will of the people in electoral politics; the unelected federal judiciary must simply interpret the law. Many have argued this point, even viewing originalism as a corollary of natural law theory.[7] These sorts of arguments, while having some intuitive appeal, in my view, still fall short because of their overreliance on abstractions, which is precisely what Mills's BRK is trying to avoid.[8] This is too much to discuss here, so, in the spirit of BRK, ALR, RR, and indeed in the spirit of CPR and CRT, I make the following observations about the origins of the former originalism as practiced, and not the latter sort of originalism as such.

Originalism as practiced on the current Supreme Court derives from a November 1985 speech by President Reagan's Attorney General, Edwin Meese. President Reagan had just won the 1984 election by a landslide, winning 49 of 50 states. The entire electoral map from the 1984 election is red, except Minnesota, which was Walter Mondale's—Reagan's opponent's—home state. Embracing this electoral mandate, President Reagan's Attorney General, Edwin Meese, in his 1985 speech, called for federal judges who would look to the "original" meaning of the constitution. The speech begins with a naïve rendition of America's beginnings: "The young America of the 1780's and 90's was a vibrant place, alive with pamphlets, newspapers, and books chronicling and commenting upon the great issues of the day. We know how the Founding Fathers lived, and much of what they read, thought, and believed" (Meese, 1985, 2). Conspicuously absent from this idyllic account of America's beginnings is any mention of American chattel slavery and its systematic disenfranchisement of millions of Black slaves who were forbidden from reading. Undoubtedly, these slaves were unable to know what the "founding fathers" wrote and believed. From the beginning of Meese's remarks, then, one sees a devastating attempt at oversimplification in the interest of creating a clean, linear development of an America free from social, political, and moral dysfunction. What Meese is presenting instead is a sort of mythology much like the abstract mythologies of ideal theory in the political philosophies of Locke and Rawls that Mills condemns throughout his corpus, and especially in "Black Radical Kantianism." Meese's mythology continues later in the speech when he writes that "Still later, the Framers of the 14th Amendment were concerned not simply about the rights of Black citizens to personal security, but also about the equal protection of the law for all persons within the states" (3). This statement is mind-boggling, considering that the overwhelming weight of historical evidence is that the principal concern was not the rights of "all persons," but rather the rights of newly-freed slaves.

Meese's mythology continues in this speech when he claims that reading one's own values into constitutional interpretation produces various "lodestars" that, for him, have led to "questionable economics, governmental disorder, and racism—all in the guise of constitutional law" (11). Meese's reference to racism hearkens back to his earlier point that the passions and prejudices of the time ought not to be read into the Constitution. Meese points out that:

> In the 1850's, the Supreme Court under Chief Justice Roger B. Taney read Blacks out of the Constitution in order to invalidate Congress' attempt to limit the spread of slavery. The *Dred Scott* decision, famously described as a judicial "self-inflicted" wound, helped bring on the Civil War. There is a lesson in this history. There is danger in seeing the Constitution as an empty vessel into which each generation may pour its passion and prejudice.
>
> *(9)*

The myth that begins with America's idyllic depiction of a Lockean state of nature in which all persons are rational, free, and equal, and reading the writings of America's founders is furthered in the above passage by an appeal to racism as an anomaly. Consistent with Gunnar Myrdal's "anomaly thesis," which claimed that racial oppression in America is an aberrant occurrence in an otherwise linear, progressive trajectory of the nation towards justice, Meese suggests that the *Dred Scott* decision was the singular result of Justice Taney's passion and prejudice—as if chattel slavery had never existed, as if the entire social, political, and moral fabric of the country had not grown accustomed to seeing Black slaves as property rather than persons, and as if James Madison did not write of the dual nature of the slave in Federalist 54 as part person and part property in an attempt to justify the now-infamous, always-nefarious three-fifths compromise. Meese so badly mythologizes American history that he makes racism an aberration resulting from one individual Supreme Court justice when it had been the abiding norm resulting from a racist national consciousness for centuries at the time of his speech. It is this linear mythology that renders racism an aberrant nullity in the service of maintaining a racist status quo. Here, I am reminded of an old Christian adage that Lucifer's greatest achievement is to persuade people that he does not exist. This seems to be the case with Meese's mythology: if racism only exists in the minds of intemperate judges like Taney, then a mythological account of racism can be used to bolster actual racist practices to maintain the racist status quo. In short, the myth of racism not existing supports its continued existence. Such a metaphysical sleight of hand is frightening, especially coming from America's Attorney General.

It is an originalism of this sort, then that in my view is not a legitimate doctrinal and interpretive theory of constitutional law. It is actually an ideology shrouded in myth that deploys the idea of an aberrant racism to conceal American racism's much more abiding, darker character. And when Justice Antonin Scalia was confirmed to the Court a year after Meese's speech, he gave originalism a veneer of legitimacy through his opinions. This veneer, however, which masks this sort of phony originalism and causes the problems I highlight here, is unacceptable, as it is not a principled approach to constitutional interpretation, but rather is merely an ideological practice that is originalism in name only.

A final point on Justice Ketanji Brown Jackson's dissenting opinion is that she presents an accurate and compelling account of American history, enabling one to reclaim an accurate interpretation of Justice Harlan's dissent in *Plessy v. Ferguson* from the clutches of a perverse and misleading judicial rhetoric about the Fourteenth Amendment's Equal Protection Clause. An abject failure of *Students for Fair Admissions* is its ahistorical, naive invocation of Justice Harlan's dissent in *Plessy* in an attempt to create a "color-blind" jurisprudence, which, again, is inconsistent with the original meaning of the Equal Protection Clause. Judicial conservatives tirelessly invoke Justice Harlan's *Plessy* dissent to support a notion of colorblindness that Justice Harlan himself never supported. Such misleading views demand correction.

To get a sense of what Justice Harlan actually did support, one must turn to his dissent in *The Civil Rights Cases* in 1883—a dissent politically unpopular in conservative judicial circles. In that decision, the Court struck down vigorous attempts at enforcing the Reconstruction Amendments with the Civil Rights Act of 1875, which did what the Civil Rights Act of 1964 would ultimately do some 89 years later: end Jim Crow. Lamenting the majority's decision, Justice Harlan wrote in his dissent that "What the nation, through Congress, has sought to accomplish in reference to [Black people] is—what had already been done in every State of the Union for the white race—to secure and protect rights belonging to them as freemen and citizens; nothing more" (61). Justice Jackson's dissent cites Justice Harlan's dissent in *The Civil Rights Cases*, and, in so doing, encourages an interpretation of Justice Harlan's view of race that is historically and hermeneutically more accurate than what many judicial conservatives portray today, which is that when Justice Harlan wrote about colorblindness in his *Plessy* dissent, he did so to make the point that the Constitution was "colorblind" to prevent oppression from Jim Crow, not to facilitate oppression by ignoring race to the detriment of oppressed people.

The Civil Rights Cases were, as was the Fourteenth Amendment, color-conscious attempts at racial justice—attempts at a *Rassenstaat* as contemplated by BRK—as was the Freedmen's Bureau, the Thirteenth Amendment, and the Fifteenth Amendment. The Reconstruction era of U.S. Constitutional history can, by today's standards, rightly be called the Constitution's "affirmative action era." It thus seems that originalism, an interpretive theory to which the Justices writing in the majority opinion in *Students for Fair Admissions* would ascribe, would dictate the exact opposite result from the one the Court reached. But not so. Why not? Because, as I have argued above, originalism does not arise from any sound, transcendent legal or interpretive principles. Instead, originalism, as practiced by the current Supreme Court on Equal Protection Clause issues involving African Americans, has its genesis in the rank conservative political ideology of the Reagan administration; a political ideology in which a mythological account of racism, strangely enough, supports rather than eliminates American anti-Black racism.

Conclusion

The intellectual legacy of Charles Mills is a legacy of resistance to racism and white supremacy in the modern West. His work in CPR is extraordinary, as it takes a social ontology of race seriously and works within the liberal political paradigm to make space for those who have historically been excluded. Mills was, moreover, the consummate philosopher. Always rigorous and clear, he never avoided difficult arguments; he engaged them with superb arguments of his own. Over the last 35 years or so, the exposure of Kant's racist views may have deterred lesser minds from grappling with them. But not so for Mills. Indeed, not only did Mills grapple with such conceptual and moral difficulties, he also propounded new theories and doctrines of his own throughout his corpus. One such theory and doctrine is that of BRK, which I have written of in this chapter, trying to show both its presence and its preference: its presence in Equal Protection jurisprudence and a preference for it within Equal Protection jurisprudence over abstract notions of equality.

In trying to make this case, I have perhaps raised at least just as many questions as I have tried to answer—maybe more. Three of these questions are worthy of mentioning here, as they form the basis for my ongoing interest in CPR and its relationship with CRT, specifically with Bell's thesis of Racial Realism, which is the first question. What is the difference between CPR and CRT? I believe that, though distinct, there is something symbiotic about these two schools of social and political thought. I have gestured toward this symbiosis in this chapter, and this work will continue as I move forward in my philosophical research. The second question is, what do we make of originalism? If one ought to interpret the Constitution according to the meaning of its provisions at the time they were ratified, it seems that Justice Jackson's dissenting opinion in *Students for Fair Admissions* would have been the majority opinion. But it was not. So, what then, is originalism? Answering this question demands that a distinction be made between originalism as such and originalism as practiced by the current Supreme Court. The former is a principled theory. The latter is a racially problematic political ideology masquerading as a legitimate constitutional hermeneutic; it is not.

Lastly, the relative invisibility of Bell in mainstream jurisprudence is disturbing, especially as related to Whitman's omission of Bell's work that I discussed at note five. A way of conceptualizing Bell's invisibility is in existentialist terms. Consider the difference between Fyodor Dostoyevsky's "Underground Man" and Ralph Ellison's "Invisible Man." The former, a reflection of the white Russian author, retreats into a subterranean realm of hyper-reflective consciousness, while the latter, a reflection of the Black author, yearns to be seen. Bell's absence amidst mainstream jurisprudential academic discussion is disturbing and a poignant reminder that the yearning to be visible is as strong as ever for Black intellectuals—even those of Bell's and Mills's high caliber.

These ruminations aside, I have tried to extend a certain understanding of BRK into constitutional adjudication. Mills's work, so concerned with racial oppression, I believe, is already present in the work of ALR and CRT, especially Bell's thesis of RR. As we strive for more just social and political arrangements and resist oppression, may we recognize American law as a place where the moral, social, and political thesis of BRK is not only welcome but is preferred over formalistic, abstract notions of equality. May CPR and CRT exploit their similarities in the interest of a more just world, even as we appreciate their differences. May Mills's work forever inspire us to do better, and, above all else, may we continue to resist.

Notes

1 See Bell 1992, 365. For an extensive discussion of Bell's RR and its connection to ALR, see Golden 2022.

2 For a good discussion of the extent to which Justice Holmes may be labeled a "pragmatist," see Haack 2019.

3 One wonders, on this point, if Mills would gesture toward Aristotelian notions of virtue, as did Fricker. We sense the "what" in Mills—a reformed Kantian ethics—while one may ask "how" one orients oneself toward a historically and socially attuned consciousness. Perhaps some sort of Aristotelian notion of habituation, in the interest of developing a disposition (*hexis*) toward virtue, would be workable. Or, is it the case that a Kantian moral ethic would follow throughout the reformed Kantian moral principles? Kant is, I think, a better fit for Mills than Aristotle in this regard. Indeed, unlike Aristotle, Kant does not believe a virtuous disposition is attainable, certainly not in a finite period of time, which is why Kant argues for the postulate of an immortal soul in the *Critique of Practical Reason*. Thinking of the "how" for Mills, then, in Kantian terms, makes the anti-racist work of CPR amenable to the resistance thesis of Bell's RR: as it relates to conditioning oneself to resist racism and white supremacy, one is perpetually improving but racially speaking, ever unjust. We can thus be better but never good. The hard moral work of resisting racism and white supremacy is perpetual in Kantian terms more so than Aristotelian terms, and accordingly, a Kantian "how" is, in my view, a better fit for Mills than an Aristotelian "how."

4 See Leiter 2007, 9–12.

5 See Whitman 2018, 157. Whitman also points to what he believes are troubling links between Nazi and American forms of legal realism, indicating that some prominent American racists in the 1930s embraced ALR. Again, however, Whitman points out, most legal realists ignored America's race problem altogether (157).

Whitman's discussion on legal realism and Nazism appears on pages 146–61 of *Hitler's American Model* (2018). His exploration of the affinities and connections between ALR and its use or inspiration for a similar sort of adjudication in Nazi jurisprudence, while initially troubling, in my view, is ultimately incomplete and inaccurate. Consider that Whitman's claim is that racists embraced ALR, not that ALR embraced racist ideology (157). Racists can—and often have—misappropriated myriad doctrines, theories, and texts for their corrupt ends. But that does not make the doctrine, the theory, or the text corrupt. For example, sacred texts have been used to justify all manner of evil in the name of the text itself, as the Bible was used to justify American chattel slavery. But the same text used to justify slavery was cited in favor of its abolition. See Golden 2022b.

Similarly, racists may have embraced ALR, but so have Black scholars, such as Bell, for emancipatory rather than oppressive political purposes. Indeed, Bell explicitly appropriates ALR for the emancipatory ends of his RR, citing Justice Holmes in doing so. Bell writes:

> Black people need reform of our civil rights strategies as badly as those in the law needed a new way to consider American jurisprudence prior to the advent of the Legal Realists. By viewing the law—and by extension, the courts—as instruments for preserving the status quo and only periodically and unpredictably serving as a refuge for oppressed people, blacks can refine the work of the Realists. [...] The Realists took their cue from Oliver Wendell Holmes, who staged a 50 year battle against legalistic formalism.

"Racial Realism" (1992, 363–64, 365).

It is, I think, significant that Whitman, himself a law professor who writes at length about what he believes is such a troubling connection between ALR and the legal realism of Nazi Germany, makes no mention of Bell, also a law professor, in *Hitler's American Model*. The index is devoid of any reference to Bell, CRT, or Bell's notion of RR, which, again, Bell explicitly derives from ALR. For an extensive discussion of Bell's RR and its connection to ALR, see Golden 2022a. Bell's absence in Whitman's account of ALR in *Hitler's American Model*, is, t2hen, beyond conspicuous. It is astonishing.

6 Despite Bell's expansion of ALR's indeterminacy thesis, Bell retains a deep commitment to empiricism and is, in this sense, not a "postmodernist" in the classical sense of that term. Bell's commitment to empiricism puts him squarely within the tradition of ALR. Moreover, there is scholarship suggesting that abandoning Bell's empiricism or uncritical references to Bell as a "postmodernist" or a "racial idealist" is problematic because of the erasure of Black thought and its implications for Black men. See Curry 2011 and 2021.

7 See O'Neill 2005 and Arkes 2023.

8 For an account of the original meaning of the Constitution that takes anti-Black racism and oppression into account—as Mills would—see Higginbotham 1980 and 1998.

Bibliography

Arkes, Hadley. 2023. *Mere Natural Law: Originalism and the Anchoring Truths of the Constitution.* Washington, D.C.: Regnery Gateway.

Bell, Derrick. 1992. "Racial Realism." *Connecticut Law Review* 24 (2): 363–79.

Civil Rights Cases. 1883. 109 U.S. 3.

Coppage v. Kansas. 1915. 236 U.S. 1.

Curry, Tommy J. 2011. "Shut Your Mouth When You're Talking to Me: Silencing the Idealist School of Critical Race Theory through a Cultralogic Turn in Jurisprudence." *Georgetown Journal of Law and Critical Race Perspectives* 3 (1): 1–38.

Curry, Tommy J. 2021. "Decolonizing the Intersection: Black Male Studies as a Critique of Intersectionality's Indebtedness to Subculture of Violence Theory." In *Critical Psychology Praxis: Psychosocial Nonalignment to Modernity/Coloniality*. Edited by Robert K. Beshara. New York, NY: Routledge.

Golden, Timothy Joseph. 2022a. "From Psychology to Resistance: Racial Realism and American Legal Realism." In *Racism and Resistance: Essays on Derrick Bell's Racial Realism*. Edited by Timothy Joseph Golden. Albany: State University of New York Press.

Golden, Timothy, Joseph. 2022b. *Frederick Douglass and the Philosophy of Religion: An Interpretation of Narrative, Art, and the Political*. Lanham: Lexington Books.
Gooding-Williams, Robert. 2009. *In the Shadow of Du Bois: Afro-Modern Political Thought in America*. Cambridge: Harvard University Press.
Haack, Susan. 2019. "The Pragmatist." In *The Pragmatism and Prejudice of Oliver Wendell Holmes, Jr*. Edited by Seth Vannatta. Lanham: Lexington Books.
Higginbotham, A. Leon, Jr. 1980. *In the Matter of Color: Race and the American Legal Process, The Colonial Period*. New York: Oxford University Press.
Higginbotham, A. Leon, Jr. 1998. *Shades of Freedom: Racial Politics and the Presumptions of the American Legal Process*. New York: Oxford University Press.
Holmes, Oliver Wendell. 1991. *The Common Law*. New York: Dover Publications.
Leiter, Brian. 2007. *Naturalizing Jurisprudence: Essays on American Legal Realism and Naturalism in Legal Philosophy*. New York: Oxford University Press.
Lochner v. New York. 1905. 198 U.S. 45.
Meese, Edwin. 1985. "Address of the Honorable Edwin Meese III, Attorney General of the United States, Before the D.C. Chapter of the Federalist Society Lawyers Division." Friday, November 15.
Mills, Charles W. 2009. "Rawls on Race/Race in Rawls." *Southern Journal of Philosophy*. 47 (S1): 161–84.
Mills, Charles W. 2018. "Black Radical Kantianism." *Res Philosophica* 95 (1): 1–33.
New York Trust Company v. Eisner. 1921. 256 U.S. 345.
O'Neill, Johnathan. 2005. *Originalism in American Law and Politics: A Constitutional History*. Baltimore: Johns Hopkins University Press.
Regents of the University of California v. Bakke. 1978. 438 U.S. 265.
Students for Fair Admissions v. President and Fellows of Harvard College. 2023. 600 U.S. 181.
Whitman, James Q. 2018. *Hitler's American Model*. Princeton: Princeton University Press.
Wittgenstein, Ludwig. 1958. *Philosophical Investigations*. Translated by G.E.M. Anscombe. Oxford: Basil Blackwell.

8

BUILDING (CONCEPTUAL) BRIDGES

Mills's Non-Ideal Theory and Disciplinary Whitopias

Emmalon Davis

Non-Ideal Theory as a Conceptual Bridge

Charles W. Mills's *The Racial Contract* (1997) offers a dual indictment, both of white supremacy as a global political system of domination and of white dominant political philosophy that has rendered white supremacy and its study invisible through its privileging of ideal theory. Concerning the former, Mills offers a historically grounded account of white supremacy as a feature of the social contract—developing the "Racial Contract" as a conceptual tool to identify and delineate its expansive global influence. Concerning the latter, Mills's account articulates the need for, and advances a model of, non-ideal theory as an alternative methodology in moral and political philosophy. Non-ideal theory refuses to treat idealized abstractions as realities, recognizes racial injustice as a fact (indeed the *norm*) of political life and of political theorizing, and advances the study of unjust systems as the starting point of our normative inquiry. Mills's contribution thus operates on two levels simultaneously, as political critique and methodological critique.

At the same time, *The Racial Contract* also develops a sustained metaphilosophical critique, and this critique will be the focus of this chapter. As Mills observes, academic philosophy is both demographically and conceptually white. Yet these facts are not unrelated. Mills cites philosophy's historic demographic whiteness as a cause of its conceptual whiteness, and likewise, cites the conceptual whiteness of philosophy as a cause of its continued demographic whiteness. Mills characterizes philosophy's conceptual whiteness in terms of its "abstractness," which he says "typically elides, rather than genuinely includes, the experience of racial minorities" (1997, 2). As Mills notes, however, while the presence of more non-white philosophers may shift the profession's *demographics*, this does not necessarily shift philosophy's *conceptual* whiteness. Given the historical disciplinary dominance of ideal theorizing, Mills observes that many non-white practitioners in moral and political philosophy have tended to either produce work that is conceptually "indistinguishable from that of their white peers" or, alternatively, produce work that concerns what Mills calls "local [race] issues," where such work does not "aggressively engage the broader debate" (2).

DOI: 10.4324/9781003349983-9

Mills's admonition to "engage the broader debate" provides the context for *The Racial Contract* (the book), and it is in this spirit that Mills characterizes the "Racial Contract" (the theoretical apparatus) as a conceptual bridge.[1] If the "Racial Contract"—and a non-ideal methodology more broadly—is to be understood in terms of a conceptual bridge, we should first ask: *which domains does the bridge serve to connect?* Answering this question, Mills writes,

> The "Racial Contract," then, is intended as a conceptual bridge between two areas now largely segregated from each other: on the one hand, the world of mainstream (i.e., white) ethics and political philosophy, preoccupied with justice and rights in the abstract, on the other, the world of Native American, African American, and Third and Fourth World Political Thought, historically focused on issues of conquest, imperialism, [...] colonialism.
>
> *(1997, 4)*

On one side, Mills identifies a theoretical space he describes as naturalistic/fact-based/historical. It is largely engaged by non-white practitioners and presumes the centrality of issues of concern for members of those groups. The theoretical space occupying the other side is described as ahistorical/abstract/idealized. It is largely engaged by white practitioners, presumes a race-neutral society, and deploys idealized abstractions in ways that preclude engagement with the racially unjust features of our society. This separation into two distinct philosophical spheres is not inevitable, but rather, it is a matter of contingent fact—the result of a long history of methodological and demographic segregation in academic philosophy.

Mills's initial mapping of the theoretical and demographic landscape (and the role of non-ideal theory within it) thus diverges quite substantially from the debate as it has been subsequently articulated by mainstream political theorists. Summarizing this mainstream characterization, Ingrid Robeyns states,

> By its very nature, ideal theory is an enterprise that is different from non-ideal theory and justice-enhancing action design. Since ideal theory relies on assumptions that are not met in reality—idealizations—its resulting principles of justice cannot serve as principles for the non-ideal world. They need to be adapted or reinterpreted or further developed for the non-ideal world.
>
> *(2008, 355)*

For Robeyns, it is ideal theory and non-ideal theory that are understood to be "different enterprises." The challenge of moving from ideals to their adaptation in non-ideal society—typically referred to as the transition problem—is *by its nature* not part of ideal theory. Instead, it is a theoretical task for non-ideal theory to solve. Yet for Mills, the representation of ideal theory and non-ideal theory as "different enterprises" does not reflect any natural or neutral theoretical division; rather, it reflects a forced separation of ideal from reality, in a context in which white dominance in political philosophy enables such theoretical choices to *appear* natural and to assume an elite status, setting the agenda for the broader debate.

If separate enterprises are to be bridged here, it is not (as Robeyns suggests) ideal theory and non-ideal theory. For Mills, the *real* conceptual chasm is between the historical concerns of white thinkers and the historical concerns of non-white thinkers—the inability in analytic political philosophy for these concerns to be brought to bear upon each other. Thus, the primary question for Mills is not how to transition from the ideal to the non-ideal and vice versa, but rather, how to make ideal theorists acknowledge the unjust reality in their narrow conception of their normative task. As Mills claims,

> Though it may appear to be such, the "Racial Contract" is not a "deconstruction" of the social contract. [...] It criticizes the social contract from a normative base that does not see the ideals of contractarianism themselves as necessarily problematic but shows how they have been betrayed by white contractarians. So it assumes intertranslatability, the conceptual commensurability of degraded norm and critique, and brings them together in an epistemic union. [...] It is explicitly predicated on the *truth* of a particular metanarrative, the historical account of the European conquest of the world, which has made the world what it is today.
>
> *(1997, 129)*

Mills's "Racial Contract" thus rejects the distinction between ideal and non-ideal theory—rendered by analytic political philosophers as separate enterprises—as a false dichotomy. What is called for is a reform in the landscape of inquiry itself.

For Mills, it is the political thought of non-white thinkers—Native American, African American, and Third and Fourth World Political Thought—that constitutes an autonomous "enterprise" in its own right, and it is because of the professional dominance of white ideal theorists in mainstream political philosophy that these contributions have been segregated and obscured. It is *this* separation of domains that Mills aimed to connect, and it is non-ideal theory (modeled, in one instance, by the "Racial Contract") that Mills proposes as a methodological and conceptual bridge.

Re-Constructing the Bridge: Purpose, Function, and Orientation

With this understanding of the philosophical domains that Mills's bridge aims to connect, we might inquire further into the bridge's construction. *What is the function and orientation of the bridge, its materiality, and its structural support?* In this section, I identify three features of Mills's non-ideal theory as modeled by the "Racial Contract" and articulate a structural weakness inherent to each. First, Mills's non-ideal theory is "naturalized" in a way that renders it vulnerable to a (racialized) disciplinary hierarchy between normative and descriptive theorizing. Second, it is characterized as normatively significant only insofar as it is theoretically adjoined to ideal theory. Third, it is presented in the form of an appeal, thus preserving a conceptual whiteness in the orientation of its address.

Non-Ideal Theory Naturalized: Just the Facts?

As Mills makes clear, the role of the "Racial Contract" is in large part descriptive and explanatory; that is, it offers a "naturalized," factual account of the *actual* state of society (1997, 5). As Mills notes, "The 'Racial Contract' is simply realist—willing to look at the facts without flinching, to explain that if you start with this, then you will end up with that" (120). A theory that assumes responsibility for providing "the facts" is necessary, given the goals of moral theory more broadly:

> Insofar as the moral theory and political philosophy of present-day contractarianism are trying to prescribe ideals for a just society, which are presumably intended to help transform our present *non-ideal* society, it is obviously important to get clear what the facts are. [...] If the facts are radically different from those that are conventionally represented, the prescriptions are also likely to be radically different.
>
> *(121)*

If ideal theory engages abstractions that are idealized to the point of obscuring reality, it cannot, by itself, offer prescriptions that are appropriate to the conditions we find ourselves in. Thus, our ability to bring about the ideal state of affairs requires an understanding of how the actual, non-ideal world works—how far the reality is from the ideal, but also how facts about our actual world may prevent us from accurately conceptualizing and pursuing the ideals (or rectifying those injustices that have taken us far away from those ideals).

Yet Mills's characterization of non-ideal philosophy's descriptive and explanatory nature risks re-entrenching non-ideal theory within a hierarchical division of philosophical labor, in which non-ideal philosophy (coded "non-white") is responsible for supplying "the facts" while ideal philosophy (coded "white") is where the actual "normative theory" occurs. In this hierarchy, theorists of color are seen as capable of reporting facts, but nonetheless *not* capable of engaging in "rigorous" philosophical theorizing.

To illustrate the historical deployment of such a division of labor, consider Frederick Douglass's analysis of his early participation in the white-led arm of the abolition movement. In *My Bondage and My Freedom*, he writes:

> During the first three or four months, my speeches were almost exclusively made up of narrations of my own personal experience as a slave. "Let us have the facts," said the people. So also said Friend George Foster, who always wished to pin me down to a simple narrative. "Give us the facts," said Collins, "we will take care of the philosophy." Just here arose some embarrassment. It was impossible for me to repeat the same old story month after month and keep up my interest in it. [...] "Tell your story, Frederick," would whisper my revered friend, Mr. Garrison, as I stepped upon the platform. [...] I could not always curb my moral indignation for the perpetrators of slaveholding villainy, long enough for a circumstantial statement of the facts which I felt almost sure everybody must know. Besides, I was growing and needed room.
>
> *(2003, 266)*

Douglass explicitly resists the way in which his contributions and his personhood were strategically deployed by white abolitionists who indulged racist presumptions of Black intellectual inferiority. As Douglass emphasizes, the imperative to "give us the facts" left no room for him to express his moral indignation. What he desired was to contribute to, and more importantly, *to shape* the normative character of the abolitionist movement with his own voice and agency, a power he subsequently finds as he frees himself from the constraints of white-led abolitionist genres.

Philip Yaure analyzes this phenomenon, through which Douglass's standing to participate in public political discourse is initially curtailed: "Douglass's role is circumscribed to narrative. [...] This particular role compromises Douglass's capacity to participate in deliberative politics, insofar as his white interlocutors treat the categories of offering narrative and doing philosophy as mutually exclusive in this context" (2018, 24–25). Narrative and argument are not merely rendered by white abolitionists as exclusive discursive activities, but moreover, as *unequal* discursive activities. As Yaure observes, this categorization underscores a "broader hierarchical division of labor" in which "the white abolitionists, whose recognized standing in the community is secure, take on overarching organizational roles" (25). In the context of a racially stratified social and political movement, organizational hierarchies are thus maintained through a conceptual separation of "the facts" from "the philosophy."

In the disciplinary context of white dominant political philosophy in which Mills was writing, an implicitly racialized and hierarchical distinction between "normative theorizing" and "fact-telling" similarly undergirds a hierarchy of practitioner value. Like Douglass, who is repeatedly encouraged to "narrate wrongs," non-ideal theorists who are restricted to the domain of the purely naturalistic, narrative, and fact-based "need room to grow." Mills seemingly anticipated this concern. As we will see, Mills took great care in attending to this exact question: in what sense is the "Racial Contract," though anchored in a descriptive analysis of the actual world, *normative*?

But while Mills anticipated this worry, he may have underestimated the significance and resilience of its force. Reflecting on the success of this particular endeavor, Mills retrospectively comments:

> But the point is that we would then be able to discuss these matters in a non-ideal theory contract framework that made white racial domination central rather than marginal. However, there has been little engagement in the profession with the work in which I set out this agenda in greatest detail... Therefore, at this stage it is an open question whether this use of the "racial contract" will be found worthy of further exploration. It could be that *The Racial Contract* will continue to be adopted as a text that summarizes in a *straightforward and accessible narrative the history of white supremacy, namely the descriptive side of the contract, but that my attempts to develop it as a normative device of representation as well will not gain support.*
>
> *(2017, 73, my emphasis)*

As I will suggest, part of the reason for its under-appreciation as a "normative device of representation" is that the normative significance of non-ideal theory was, on Mills's own account, understated. In an effort to construct a bridge, Mills locates the normative value of non-ideal theory in its capacities as a moral corrective. Yet as a moral corrective, the value of non-ideal theory is largely derivative—its normative force derives from its relationship *to* ideal theory. Accordingly, the underlying logic which determines the disciplinary value assigned to each theoretical endeavor remains insufficiently challenged.

Non-Ideal Theory as Moral Corrective

Mills clearly emphasizes that non-ideal theory is intended to be both descriptive *and* normative. But in order to make sense of non-ideal theory's normative status, we must understand Mills's conception of its complementary relationship to ideal theory. Mills writes,

> The "Racial Contract" *recognizes the actuality of the world we live in*, relates the construction of ideals, and the *non*realization of these ideals, to the character of this world,

> to group interests and institutionalized structures, and points to what would be necessary for achieving them. Thus it unites description and prescription, fact and norm.
>
> *(1997, 130)*

Mills identifies non-ideal theory as "uniting" description and prescription by bringing fact to bear on fiction and illuminating (and amending) the fiction in cases where it purports to be something it is not. Thus, ideal theory and non-ideal theory are engaged in a kind of joint normative venture, as Mills notes that "it is obviously crucial to understand what the original and continuing 'contract' actually was and is, so that we can correct for it in constructing the ideal 'contract'" (7).

In *The Racial Contract*, the relationship between non-ideal theory and ideal theory thus emerges, perhaps somewhat surprisingly, as one of symbiosis:

> Whereas the ideal contract explains how a just society would be formed, ruled by a moral government, and regulated by a defensible moral code, this non-ideal/naturalized contract explains how an unjust, *exploitative* society, ruled by an *oppressive* government and regulated by an *immoral* code, comes into existence. If the ideal contract is to be endorsed and emulated, this non-ideal/naturalized contract is to be demystified and condemned.
>
> *(1997, 5)*

Importantly, then, for Mills, *both* ideal theory and non-ideal theory are explanatory *and* normative in their aims. The task for non-ideal theory is to demystify ideal theory's descriptive pretenses and to normatively correct for them. Ideal theorists should therefore accept and acknowledge ideal theory's dependence on the contributions of non-ideal theory to illuminate and supplement its descriptive shortcomings in non-ideal (i.e., actual) circumstances.

Indeed, the Mills of *The Racial Contract* did not (yet) espouse the view that ideal theory was a thoroughgoing failure—only (willfully) incomplete and in need of reform. Ideal theory is thus characterized as deficient in ways that necessitate non-ideal theory as a sort of critical moral intervention. In this vein, Mills refers to the "Racial Contract" as "part of the necessary foundation for contemporary political theory" (1997, 122), as a "counterimage" to "the powerful image of the idealized contract" (121), and as a "drastic theoretical correction" (125).

Accordingly, Mills was careful not to assert non-ideal theory as a "usurper" of ideal theory, despite his assessment of the "Racial Contract" as "superior" to the raceless contract of ideal theory as an actual model of the world. He explains that "the 'Racial Contract' as a naturalized account is theoretically superior to the raceless social contract as a model of the actual world and, correspondingly, of what needs to be done to reform it. I therefore advocate the *supplementation* of standard social contract discussions with an account of the 'Racial Contract'" (1997, 120, my emphasis). While non-ideal theory as "moral corrective" is permitted to move beyond "the facts" to prescribe various aspects of reform (e.g., to guard against factual misunderstandings, to offer critical reflections on prior modes of theorizing), Mills nonetheless cautiously positions non-ideal theory as a sort of theoretical under-laborer. As "corrective," as "necessary foundation," and as "counterimage," non-ideal theory lacks normative theoretical legitimacy independent of its relationship to ideal theory. Its descriptive offerings are normatively valuable only insofar as they can be conjoined, *via supplementation*, in service of the normative project of ideal theory.

There are certainly strategic reasons why Mills adopts this approach in *The Racial Contract*, and we will turn to explore these in the following section. But Mills also offers remarks that give reason to think that, at this point, he saw potential for non-ideal theory as a kind of "best of both" theoretical worlds. For example, Mills expressed concern about what he identified as a risk of a kind of parochialism and particularism in some Black political theory (as well as some feminist political theory), popular at the time of his earlier writing, that he thought made universal and objectivist challenges difficult. He likewise embraced the importance of some abstractions in theory, both those abstractions that could help make sense of the past and those more speculative "grand" abstractions, ideals of a hypothetical future marked by equality and justice. Yet Mills recognized that both our theoretical comprehension and practical realization of those ideals required that they not be obscured, as he later put it, "through a glass, whitely" (2018, 44). Indeed, he states,

> Unlike the social contract, which is necessarily embarrassed by the actual histories of the polities in which it is propagated, the "Racial Contract" *starts from* these uncomfortable realities. Thus it is not, like the social contract, continually forced to retreat into illusory idealizing abstraction, the never-never land of pure theory, but can move readily between the hypothetical and the actual, the subjunctive and the indicative, having no need to pretend things happened which did not, to evade and to elide and to skim over.
>
> *(1997, 130)*

The problem was not idealization, per se, but a "reliance on idealization *to the exclusion, or at least marginalization, of the actual*" (2005, 168, my emphasis).

Mills was at this point, I think it's safe to say, quite optimistic—one might even say *idealistic*—about the potential of a kind of political philosophy that could integrate (and explore the tensions between) the descriptive and normative, the particular and abstract, the objective and subjective, and that such an endeavor could be undertaken in a professional domain in which these approaches might no longer be hierarchically separated from one another. In this regard, Mills shares the dialectical vision that Angela Davis articulates when she writes, with respect to a political theory of freedom, that:

> The history of Black Literature provides, in my opinion, a much more illuminating account of the nature of freedom, its extent and limits, than all the philosophical discourses on this theme in the history of Western society. Why? For a number of reasons. First of all, because Black Literature in this country and throughout the world projects the consciousness of a people who have been denied entrance into the real world of freedom. Black people have exposed, by their very existence, the inadequacies not only of the practice of freedom, but of its very theoretical formulation. Because, if the theory of freedom remains isolated from the practice of freedom or rather is contradicted in reality, then this means that something must be wrong with the concept—that is, if we are thinking in a dialectical manner.
>
> *(1971, 4)*

In a similar fashion, Mills hoped to advance a dialectic in which Black political thought might be valued and studied for its ability to expose the deficiencies of a theory (i.e., ideal theory) contradicted in practice.

Indeed, it is from this place of theoretical and professional optimism that Mills writes that the "Racial Contract" "makes it possible for us to connect the two rather than, as at present, have them isolated in two ghettoized spaces, Black political theory's ghettoization from mainstream discussion, white mainstream theory's ghettoization from reality" (1997, 132). Here, however, Mills clearly espouses *two* philosophical goals. Of course, nearly anyone familiar with Mills is aware of his political project, throughout his career, to bring white mainstream political theory in touch with the reality of race. Derrick Darby refers to this "grand philosophical project" of "remaking liberalism" as Mills's "calling card over the years" (2019, 378). At the same time, however, Mills was also engaged in a second "grand philosophical project," namely, a professional and metaphilosophical one which takes the discipline *itself* as its subject.

As with Davis above, Mills observes that the separation and ghettoization of theoretical investigations not only track tradition and methodology but also race, history, and practitioner situatedness. At the heart of Mills's metaphilosophical project, then, was the creation of dialectical conditions under which Black thinkers and Black political thought could assume a more prominent position in the academic philosophical landscape. In what follows, however, I show that Mills's own methodological and dialectical strategy was, in some important respects, in tension with this broader aim.

Non-Ideal Theory as Appeal

In Mills's early estimation, the path to success for this "dialectical" project was twofold. First, it required that white philosophers—of which the mainstream was almost exclusively comprised—stop systematically ignoring and disvaluing the contributions of Black and other non-white thinkers, as they had effectively done for most of the field's historical existence. It also required, as indicated by Mills's repeated entreaty, that non-white thinkers "engage the mainstream discussion." For dialogue to occur, those in disparate discourses must make a mutual effort to engage each other. As Mills saw it, non-ideal theory could provide a "conceptual bridge" through which such engagement might be facilitated.

This broader disciplinary project explains why Mills adopts the framing tactic he does, in which he "uses the vocabulary and apparatus already developed for contractarianism to map this unacknowledged system" (1997, 3). Mills was well aware that if the contributions of non-white philosophers were to have any chance of becoming "equal" in mainstream analytical philosophy, *it would be because they looked like the stuff white philosophers typically took seriously*. He writes, "Both at the primary level of an alternative conceptualization of the facts and at the secondary (reflexive) level of a critical analysis of the orthodox theories themselves, the 'Racial Contract' *enables us to engage with mainstream Western political theory to bring in race*" (7, my emphasis). Thus, while the conceptual bridge of the "Racial Contract" purportedly "assumes intertranslatability" (129), the direction of transport was, in one major respect, uni-directional by design.

Mills uses the inclusive "us" and "our" throughout the book to refer to those who might benefit from the theoretical apparatus he has offered, but the real intended beneficiaries of these efforts are unveiled at the end of the book. In the final pages, Mills locates *The Racial*

Contract within the "honorable tradition of oppositional Black theory" and pays tribute to the Black activists and political thinkers who have "always recognized white dominance… as a political system of exclusion and differential privilege" (1997, 131). But if Black activists and Black political thinkers are "literally, the men and women who know too much" (132), who, then, have these attempts at translation and explanation been for? The answer is, of course, white contract theorists.

The Racial Contract thus assumes the form of an appeal. Indeed, Mills writes, "it does what Black critique has always had to do to be effective: it situates itself in the same space as its adversary and then shows what follows from 'writing "race" and [seeing] the difference it makes'" (1997, 132). But a conceptual bridge that "situates itself in the space as its adversary" raises several subsequent problems.

First, Mills's conceptual proposal leaves relatively unchanged an unfair distribution of philosophical labor, with non-ideal theorists left to pull double duty. Non-ideal theorists must become knowledgeable about the relevant histories, explanatory realities, and facts on the ground, but they must also be skilled and knowledgeable in the conceptual frameworks, lingos, and literatures of ideal theory. That is, they must know (and speak ably about) Rawls and other essential figures in the tradition, so as to ensure that their contributions appear relevantly normative and professionally authorized. Having gained entry to the bridge, they must still pay the toll to enter into the "main" land. No such dual requirements are placed on mainstream political theorists, however, who nonetheless retain the authority to determine which "goods" successfully cross over the bridge and through the port.

Second, as an appeal to white ideal theorists, *The Racial Contract* reproduces within itself the whiteness it aims to reject. Lewis Gordon raises this concern in an early symposium on *The Racial Contract,* noting that "it is clear that this work is designed specifically for white audiences. It is meant as a form of therapy for the powerful" (2010, 221). On this basis, Gordon asks: "What is the authoritative force of *The Racial Contract*? Does not a white focus group make *The Racial Contract* normatively white?" (221). As Gordon suggests, Mills's proposal reinscribes something like a white gaze—reinforcing a presumed omnipresence of white norms and standards—as a necessary feature of the construction of its address.

Toni Morrison outlines the function of the white gaze as a controlling perspectival force: "whose eye, whose language is controlling this?" Identifying its prevalence in early traditional African American literature, Morrison says,

> When I began to write, […] the publishing world vis-à-vis African Americans was leaning heavily toward […] the traditional African American novel where the oppressor is the white man or the white idea. […] That's who they were confronting—Ellison, Baldwin, Richard Wright. […] They were responding to, defending themselves, or aggressively attacking that idea of the white oppressor. And I thought, I can't do that. What is the world like if he's not there?
>
> *(2013)*

For Morrison, the white gaze operates in the form of an assumed (white) audience and an accompanying language and confrontation that thereby structures the nature of the author's address. The gaze of this assumed audience imposes restrictions on the author—the author must be responsive to *this* audience and *their* concerns. While such an orientation does not necessarily preclude others from engaging with its content, these others are not prioritized in the language of its address.

While Mills undoubtedly constructed *The Racial Contract* in a way that could be (and quite effectively has been!) understood and appreciated by a wide variety of audiences, this does not mean that the needs of all audiences were equally foregrounded. Rather, the conceptual and cognitive preferences of white contract theorists were prioritized, therein assuming the status of a universal language. At a distance of 20 years, Mills unambiguously identifies these objectives:

> I wrote *The Racial Contract* twenty years ago in an attempt to demonstrate that race and white racial domination should be taken seriously as legitimate topics of political philosophy. At that time, the top-ranked philosophy journals and university presses had very little interest in these issues. Seeking a respectable mainstream philosophy framework into which they could be "translated," I hit on social contract theory.
>
> *(2017, 65)*

In one respect, then, Mills's strategy makes eminent sense. Mills was clearly correct in his assessment that fairly extraordinary measures would be needed if such a dialogue were to become possible. But as Gordon asks, "why think that the ignoring of Black people's thought has been a matter of bad packaging?" (2006, 115). *The Racial Contract* offers a methodological solution—a shared conceptual framework—in response to a problem that is, at bottom, created and sustained by an unfair distribution of racialized power and attention in the field. Indeed, it was precisely because of *these* inequalities that a strategy such as the one Mills adopts was deemed necessary in the first place.

Summarizing the outcome of these efforts, Mills writes: "Depending on the criteria one chooses to invoke, the book is either a success or a failure" (2017, 73). Success, says Mills, consists in its status as an academic bestseller, its widespread multidisciplinary course adoption, and its broad engagement by scholars within progressive and radical research networks. In what sense, however, is it a "failure"? Mills writes, "It has had no impact at all on how mainstream 'white' political philosophy in general, or 'white' social contract theory and Rawlsianism in particular, are done. Therefore, multidisciplinary success has not translated into success in my home discipline, at least within these circles" (2017, 73). Such failure is perhaps all the more remarkable, given the centrality of this aim in the construction of the book. In the remainder of the paper, I examine in greater detail the disciplinary conditions in which such "failure" persists. Specifically, I turn to the following question, namely, *what is the relationship between once isolated domains after a bridge has been constructed?*

Testing the Bridge: Connecting Domains

One major challenge in the development of a conceptual bridge is that one opens oneself up to criticisms on either side. On the one hand, the Mills of *The Racial Contract*—most frequently engaged by scholars working on race—is often accused of making too many concessions to white political philosophy, ideal theory, liberalism, and so on. In the preceding sections, I have considered some of these worries. On the other hand, however, Mills's 2005 paper, "Ideal Theory as Ideology"—the piece of his most frequently cited by mainstream political philosophers, typically in the context of the ideal/non-ideal theory debate—is usually characterized as being *too critical* of ideal theory.

By 2005, Mills undeniably took a more critical stance toward ideal theory. But while defenders of ideal theory typically cite *this* Mills as "anti-ideal theory" or as a "critic" of ideal theory, they do so without situating this argument in the context of *The Racial Contract* (which, essentially, serves as its prolegomenon). The engagement of mainstream political philosophers with one but not the other is reflective of the continuing professional separation of two domains—mainstream political philosophy and philosophy of race—despite Mills own efforts to bridge them. *The Racial Contract* is as much about ideal theory (and is thus relevant for ideal theorists) as it is about race, and "Ideal Theory as Ideology" is as much about race as it is about ideal theory (though the racial dimensions are frequently overlooked by ideal theorists who have cited it). To treat these two pieces in isolation or to cherry pick their relevance is to willfully miss the disciplinary metanarrative and critical normative discourse that Mills develops across the two pieces.

Read together, however, a new characterization of his critique emerges. While the Mills of *The Racial Contract* wholeheartedly calls for minoritized philosophers to engage in the "mainstream debate," a more muted characterization of non-ideal theory as a "conceptual bridge" emerges in 2005 when he claims that "in certain respects it engages with mainstream ethics on what are nominally its own terms, thereby (at least in theory) making it somewhat harder to ignore and marginalize" (166). Mills is quite clear that non-ideal theory's engagement with mainstream ethics "on its own terms" is strategic, highlighting that this engagement is only partial ("in certain respects") and "nominal." Moreover, Mills likewise admits a bit of cynicism regarding the strategy's likelihood of success, noting that even the modest goal of being "somewhat harder to ignore," though *theoretically* plausible, had not necessarily been born out in practice.

In 2005, Mills characterized ideal theory as not merely *incomplete* (as he seemed to characterize it in *The Racial Contract*) but "ideological," where Mills is here careful to clarify that he means this in the "pejorative" sense. Mills writes that as an ideology, ideal theory is a "distortional complex of ideas, values, norms, and beliefs that reflects the non-representative interests and experiences of a small minority of the national population—middle-to-upper-class white males—who are hugely over-represented in the professional philosophical population" (172). As such, he concludes, it is "patently deficient, clearly counterfactual, and counterproductive" (172). Mills's later, more explicitly negative assessment of ideal theory derives in part from his observations concerning how his earlier work was taken up—or rather *not* taken up—in elite political philosophy spaces in which ideal theory was the norm. Read alongside *The Racial Contract,* Mills's 2005 critique is thus much more plausibly interpreted as a critique of the ongoing ideological role of ideal theory *in the profession,* as opposed to a critique of ideal theory in the abstract, as many defenders of ideal theory have taken him to mean (see, for example, Simmons 2010, Hamlin and Stemplowska 2012, Valentini 2012, Táíwò 2023).

Ideal Theory/Non-Ideal Theory: A Practical Problem?

Though central to Mills's work, it is worth considering how little attention this dimension of the problem—namely, the professional hegemony of ideal theory in analytic political philosophy—has received in the debate. Of the many scholars who acknowledge and respond to Mills's 2005 critique of ideal theory, no more than a handful explicitly mention the problem of professional hierarchies, and virtually none acknowledge the racial implications of them. Among those who do, very little time (if any) is spent beyond mere mention.

For example, Robeyns distinguishes the theoretical value of idealizing approaches from "the daily practice of theorizing about justice," and identifies several needed interventions concerning these approaches. These include, for example, more scholarly attention to the task of bridging ideal and non-ideal theory, clarifying what makes each approach good, and greater scrutiny concerning bad idealizing assumptions in theory (2008, 362). Robeyns attends to each consideration in some detail in the paper, and these topics have continued to enjoy substantial attention in the literature. By way of conclusion, however, Robeyns turns to examine "the current hierarchical status of ideal theory," writing:

> We have to ask whether the professional culture within political philosophy and the incentive structures in academic institutions, including the reputations of journals and implicit and explicit value judgments about different kinds of theory (i.e., more versus less abstract, "pure," formal, and so forth) steer us disproportionally into the direction of ideal theory. I contend that this is the case, but would be more than happy to be proven wrong.
>
> *(362)*

Though the possibility of this problem is admirably acknowledged, it is not substantially investigated, as the author only turns to it in the final sentences of the paper.

In a similar fashion, Eva Erman and Niklas Möller raise this concern, only to immediately set it aside. The bulk of the paper is dedicated to proving that "the philosophical cases against ideal theory [...] seem either to be based on a too narrow or elusive idea of what being 'informative' or 'useful' (or whatever property ideal theory is claimed to lack) amounts to" (2022, 539). The authors offer several arguments defending this proposal and conclude that their analysis "has aroused a suspicion [...] that there is little in the way of genuine philosophical problem involved in the debate on ideal and non-ideal theory" (539). Having taken themselves to have dispelled any "genuine philosophical problem," the authors nonetheless briefly conclude by acknowledging a "practical" critique. They write,

> There may of course be a practical critique that might be justified, stating that thinking about non-ideal circumstances is more useful in the real world than theorizing about ideals, and that we should therefore do more of the former and less of the latter (e.g., Farrelly 2007; Mills 2005). Although this critique seems to be based on a faulty analysis of the utility of ideal theory, it might still be true. Perhaps the ratio of non-ideal theorists to ideal theorists should be different; we take no stand on the issue.
>
> *(539)*

Like Robeyns, the authors gesture toward the possibility of a problem in their conclusion. But though tentatively acknowledged, it is nonetheless passed over in silence.

Erman and Möller's distinction between "genuine philosophical problems" and mere "practical problems" already calls to mind a troubling value hierarchy of normative concerns. More importantly, however, what the authors raise as the relevant "practical" critique—attributed to Colin Farrelly (2007) and Mills (2005)—is, in my view, more appropriately understood as *two* critiques. While Farrelly is primarily concerned with the "uselessness" of ideal theory—i.e., the inadequacy of a normative theory that fails to guide practical prescriptions—this is hardly Mills's only concern. Like Farrelly, Mills challenges the value of an ethical theory that cannot, at least not with substantial supplementation, guide our actions in the real world. But he is *also* challenging the conditions in which an ethical theory with these limitations could become the dominant and privileged mode of inquiry in a particular philosophical domain. Here, Mills target is not ideal theory in the abstract, but rather, "the so-called ideal theory more dominant in mainstream ethics" (2005, 166). Speaking specifically of *Rawlsian* ideal theory, Mills notes that its discipline-shaping methodological influence, despite its acknowledged limitations, "reflect[s] deeper structural biases in the profession" (169).

Insofar as Mills is concerned with the ratio of ideal and non-ideal theorists, it is not merely a "practical problem." Rather, it is a genuine philosophical problem—a matter of *professional ethics*. Thus, the attribution of a shared "practical critique" to Farrelly and Mills obscures an aspect of Mills's critique which is consistently elided by defenders of ideal theory. Mills's critique is not merely about ideal theory's practical usefulness (e.g., which types of theories matter and why), but about professional ethics (e.g., how professions are structured and which inquiries are incentivized).

A Professional Ethics Problem?

One scholar has, to my mind quite helpfully, proposed a reframing of the debate between ideal and non-ideal theorists—from "a meta-level debate *about* normative theory" to "a ground-level debate *within* normative theory" (Frazer 2016, 177, my emphasis). Michael Frazer locates this normative debate specifically within professional ethics, defined as "the field of applied moral philosophy concerned with the special responsibilities of each vocation in a modern society" (176). Though the subject of analysis is the profession itself, Frazer is clear that the inquiry is a *moral* one—it concerns the responsibilities that practitioners incur through their professional engagements. All vocations have ethical dimensions to their practice, and the relevant question here pertains to the moral demands on academics and the scholarship they produce.

On Frazer's account, the obligations of professionals are at least partially determined by normative relations between those in the profession and those outside of it. Indeed, Frazer writes, "Even political philosophers and theorists, ensconced comfortably in their armchairs, need to think about how their activity—and their claim on scarce social resources—is justified in terms of its place within the larger division of economic, civic, and moral labor" (2016, 177). While scholars can permissibly engage in a range of activities—including ideal theorizing—within the context of their vocational practice, what at least partially "justifies these activities is always the way they feed back, directly or indirectly, into common life" (179). Understood this way, certain aspects of the debate between ideal and non-ideal theorists can better come into view. Focusing on the utopic aspect of some ideal theorizing, Frazer argues,

> What is impermissible [...] is for everyone who thinks and writes on this subject to focus exclusively on building utopias. We must therefore be vigilant lest the system of incentives that structures our profession encourage only utopian theorizing, something that I will argue it is dangerously inclined to do.
>
> *(178)*

The worry, as Frazer sees it, is that our professional incentive structures can constrict our ability—as a discipline—to live up to the full range of our professional responsibilities. Put differently, a problem arises when "self-governing professional communities... develop norms that privilege the internal, intrinsic values of the profession over the external, instrumental values that provide public reasons for these professional practices" (188).

Though I personally share this more public-facing view of what justifies scholarly activities, academics undoubtedly disagree about exactly how much research must "feed back into common life." I do not wish to get hung up on this point. For our present purposes, the main virtue of Frazer's account is that it (1) situates disagreements between ideal and non-ideal theorists within the domain of professional ethics, such that we can (2) attend to the ways in which dominant disciplinary incentive structures often determine—but do not necessarily justify—our professional practices. Rather than treat this as a mere "practical problem," Frazer invites us to see it as a genuine philosophical problem.

While Frazer draws our attention to a normative relationship that exists between those in the profession and those outside of it, Mills repeatedly draws our attention to worrying hierarchies and normative relationships operating *within* the profession. Professional communities are not internally homogenous, and dominant norms often marginalize the value of nondominant practitioners (and their contributions) within the professional space. On Mills's account, the political thought of non-white thinkers constitutes an autonomous enterprise, but it is only because of the historical professional dominance of white political philosophers—who by and large do not engage in questions of this sort and who maintain incentive structures and cultures that reproduce the kind of work they enjoy reading—that these other political investigations have been obscured. Mills is in effect bringing these issues—of race, content, methodology, and practitioner bias—into one conversation to interrogate *what professionals owe to each other*. Situating this discourse within the context of professional ethics (as Frazer suggests) thus illuminates a genuine philosophical problem.

An Epistemic Problem?

Finally, while increasing attention has been paid to developing non-ideal theory as a legitimized theoretical apparatus, the contemporary debate has largely erased the "racial" aspect of Mills's critique. This ongoing elision demonstrates at least one way in which ideal theory is, as Mills came to charge, ideological. That is to say, the elite status of ideal theory plays *an ideological role in mainstream moral and political philosophy*. By 2018, Mills argued that ideal theory was not just ideological but epistemically unjust.

Indeed, toward the end of his career, Mills explicitly turned to examine the moral-epistemic dimensions of this problem, applying the concepts of epistemic injustice (Fricker 2007) and epistemic oppression (Dotson 2014) *to academic disciplines themselves*. What first looked like it might be attributable in part to Black and other minoritized philosophers' self-isolation—a failure to "engage the broader debate"—now most plausibly looked to be a willful case of intellectual white flight, resulting in the creation and maintenance of what Mills referred to as a "Whitopian" project. Here, Mills transports the concept of "Whitopia" (Benjamin 2009) from its application in suburban neighborhoods formed through geographic white flight to academic discourses where race-evasion is carried out through practices of "spatial retreat and [...] conceptual disavowal" (Mills 2018, 51).

A disciplinary stronghold in favor of a particular (idealized) style of philosophical investigation structurally restricts the development of more socially grounded political inquiry, rendering political philosophy less hospitable to theorists who pursue such inquiry. To illustrate the effects of these structural epistemic exclusions, consider three scenarios:

> During Grace's time in graduate school, exactly one contemporary political philosophy course is offered, the bulk of which is dedicated to reading Rawls' *Political Liberalism*. She sees no on-ramp to discuss more applied issues, and so she writes a final paper on Rawls' shifting conceptions of justice. Even though she is not interested in Rawls and is not intellectually served by his apparatus, she feels that if she wants to pursue political philosophy, her work must focus on Rawls, in part because he is the main political theorist she has been exposed to. After a year of struggling to find a suitable dissertation topic, she decides instead to write a dissertation in epistemology rather than political philosophy, as the former demonstrates more avenues for exploring the social and political dimensions of embodied human realities.
>
> Grace is a new assistant professor, tasked with building several upper-level courses. She decides to put together a social and political philosophy course of the sort she would have liked to take as a student. The course explores marginalized political thinkers—including Frederick Douglass, Martin Delany, Harriet Jacobs, Maria Stewart, and Sojourner Truth—via nontraditional philosophy texts, such as letters, pamphlets, speeches, and slave narratives. On the first day of class, after discussing the syllabus, she asks if there are any questions. A disgruntled white male student asks "How are you going to have a political philosophy class without Rawls?" Grace is slightly baffled by this student's question, since the title of the course he had enrolled in was "Nineteenth-Century Abolitionist and Suffragist Political Thought." She responds by saying that surely it was permissible to have just one political philosophy course without Rawls on the syllabus. The student continues to heckle her with the obvious intention of diminishing her credibility in front of the class.
>
> Grace is developing a research project on Black women's political thought, and she has received encouragement to submit her work to "top" moral and political philosophy journals. Despite this encouragement, she encounters increasing difficulty publishing in these venues. On one occasion, a reviewer reports that her Black feminist methodology is not "neutral" enough. On another occasion, a paper is rejected on the basis of one negative reviewer (despite several positive ones) who writes that "while I would like to see more Black feminism published in this journal, the Rawls was just not done rigorously enough."

In each instance, an exclusion occurs at the level of content, methodology, or contributor identity. These exclusions affect the philosophical resources available to Grace as a student, her authority to shape educational resources as a professor in her own classroom, and her ability to contribute to scholarly conversations as a peer. While I have initially described these examples in the third person—to create some distance for the reader in contemplating them—all three are derived from my personal experience. If one doubts the veracity or commonality of such experiences, one need only consult other philosophers of color working on issues of race and racism in the analytic tradition. Similar experiences abound.

As these fairly recent examples (all occurring within ten years of this writing) show, Mills's increasing pessimism was not unwarranted. The disciplinary dominance of a Rawlsian framework—in a domain in which scholars of color and scholars working on race are systematically devalued—exerts an epistemic influence over how political philosophy is conceived and practiced. In such a context, Mills writes:

> it may not be a matter of a few discrete gaps or problematic categories rendering incomplete or mildly tainting hermeneutical resources otherwise acceptable, requiring only sharply targeted epistemic surgical insertion or excision for a successful operation. Instead, a more complex intervention is likely to be required [...] challenging and rethinking an entire conceptual system, and instituting a new reconstructed cognitive regimen to correct its pervasive epistemic injustice.
>
> *(2021, 198)*

Here, Mills moves far from the strategy pursued in *The Racial Contract,* clearly acknowledging the insufficiency of a "conceptual bridge" aimed at the development of common epistemic resources. Echoing a similar sentiment elsewhere, Mills writes,

> The idea of common epistemic resources would in this case understate the adversarial dynamic and conflicting group interests involved, and obscure the fact that the subordinate Black worldview (proposing much more than a simple conceptual supplementation) cannot simply be brought additively into relation with the ideology of white domination, since it is in fundamental opposition to it.
>
> *(2017, 107)*

The distance between ideal theory and non-ideal theory, or between white dominant ideologies and Black counternarratives, cannot be bridged through mere conceptual addition, supplementation, or integration. Having identified an entire discursive landscape as tainted by epistemic injustice and epistemic oppression, Mills suggests that what is required is "challenging and rethinking an entire conceptual system."

Building Bridges to Whitopia?

Mills's characterization of mainstream political philosophy as a Whitopia is, I think, quite apt. Yet Mills's later reckoning naturally invites us to rethink his earlier conception of the "Racial Contract" as a conceptual bridge. Why build bridges to Whitopias? As Mills came to observe, no theory can undermine the whiteness of mainstream political discourse while conforming to the cognitive and conceptual limitations of those who are epistemically empowered (and motivated) to ignore such interventions. But, as I think Mills's larger corpus demonstrates, there is still significant normative value in critically documenting what happens when you try.

For Black philosophers—and especially for those in the analytic tradition—our minuscule numbers and the marginalization of our perspectives are often palpably felt. This has meant a paucity of Black teachers, mentors, and peers within our departments, scarce inclusion of Black thinkers or traditions in journal pages, course syllabi, and conference programs, and disinterested or hostile reactions from many students, teachers, and colleagues when we push back against the status quo. Too often, being Black in analytic philosophy is an exercise in chronic alienation. Not everyone in Whitopia is white, and not all of us are thriving. Some of us are trapped on the mainland; some are drowning in the waters just offshore.

Mills understood this anguish well. Throughout his work, Mills candidly traces his own sense of incongruence both as a student and as a professional. In one instance, Mills writes of the "frustration" and "utter disconnection [he] felt between Rawls' work and [his] interests" (2012, 54). He tells the story of himself as a graduate student who wanted to work on race, only to find that the tools available were antithetical to that endeavor. Writing frankly of his own intellectual trajectory, he states:

> Not finding any appropriate philosophical frameworks in a white field in an all-white department in a white Canadian university without even a Black studies program to assist me, I decided to do a dissertation on Marxism instead. So in a sense, my 1990s turn to race in my work was a *re*turn, a coming back to what I had originally wanted to do. Because by many conventional measures—publications, recognition, visibility—I have succeeded, it might be illuminating to reflect on what this "success" is worth, and the changes I have seen, as well as the changes I have not seen, in academic philosophy over this period, and what they say about the profession. My conclusions are, unfortunately, somewhat pessimistic.
>
> *(45)*

Mills's counter-narrative provides an alternative resource against which Black and other marginalized philosophers can evaluate their experiences. This written record establishes a sense of familiarity with those who read it and works to offset feelings of self-doubt and inadequacy that arise in profoundly alienating environments. If one can see that the problem is not that one is unsuited to perform the work, but rather that one is literally "unwelcomed," the feeling and experience of being out of place can itself be redefined.

Indeed, it is still not unusual for a Black student, who discovers philosophy for the first time at a PWI (predominately white institution), to never have been taught by a Black philosophy professor or to have discussed the work of Black philosophers in class. While this state of affairs is slowly changing, Mills's influence in this regard cannot be understated. Well before the publication of *The Racial Contract*, Mills expressed this concern in a teaching-focused journal, writing that "the shortage of suitable introductory material [on race and Black perspectives] means that one often has to rely on journal articles, which would be heavy going even for undergraduate majors, let alone those with no background at all" (1994, 236).

In writing *The Racial Contract*, Mills answered his own call, noting "the book was written to establish a kind of beachhead on this inhospitable terrain" (2010, 239). Mills landed on the shores of Whitopia and wrote S.O.S. in big letters on the sand. *The Racial Contract* has seemingly broken through as "the" text of a Black philosopher that could assume canonical status in philosophy courses in analytic departments at PWIs. This was, of course, no easy feat. To reach the student, as Mills came to discover, one must first appeal to the syllabus-builder(s). It is within the context of this pedagogical landscape that students now encounter Charles Mills's work, in the form of *The Racial Contract* (alongside numerous others of Mills's contributions). For some of these students, Mills's work is not so much a bridge as it is a lifeline.

The Racial Contract is an artifact of a particular moment. Yet Mills revisited *The Racial Contract* again and again—he wrote *about* writing it and about how it was received. Here, Mills's subject of analysis was the professional discourse in which he had been participating for over 20 years. As Mills wrote and rewrote this project, he developed a critical perspective on the discursive context in which the work was produced. In between the lines and main contours of his arguments, Mills's corpus thus provides a critical cartography of the discipline itself.

Through this ongoing, critical narration, Mills maps the contours of the space that he traversed and offers us an assessment of the discipline—where it needed intervention and the strategies he deemed necessary to make those interventions possible. He evaluates how those strategies have fared, where resistances have been encountered, and how this understanding engenders new conceptions of the problem. In this sense, Mills's research takes the discipline as a whole—its structures and practices—as its subject. This critical map is grounded in principles of mutual transparency and accountability. Leaving a map of these efforts, as Mills does, offers a vantage from which others may chart different trajectories. It is thus diagnostically valuable, normatively guiding, and methodologically flexible.

What, then, of non-ideal theory? As a methodology in contemporary analytic political philosophy, non-ideal theory is still in its infancy. We are still figuring out how to do it well. Importantly, non-ideal theory as Mills developed it in *The Racial Contract* is, as he initially stated, "*one* possible way" (1997, 3, my emphasis). What we inherit from Mills is the opportunity to allow the bridge of *The Racial Contract* to serve as a high point that enables us to discern—and bravely pursue—alternative paths, including those that do not always lead to familiar places. As Mills perhaps somewhat prophetically wrote in 1994: "The ultimate aim would be to transform the discipline" (238). Mills's tremendous legacy calls upon us to pursue this transformative work. The contours of the map must be continuously redrawn until, instead of Whitopia, we have a place that feels like home.

Note

1 *The Racial Contract* advances existential, conceptual, and methodological claims. This chapter is primarily concerned with the methodological and conceptual uses of the "Racial Contract," that is, the way it functions as a "rhetorical trope and theoretical method for understanding the inner logic of racial domination" (1997, 6). Following Mills, I utilize quotation marks—the "Racial Contract"—when referring to conceptual and methodological uses. I use the disquotational phrase—the Racial Contract—to pick out existential uses, or "the racist reality itself" (2016, 65). I use italics—*The Racial Contract*—when referring to the book. For discussion on the "Racial Contract" as methodology, see Mills 2002.

Bibliography

Benjamin, Rich. 2009. *Searching for Whitopia: An Improbable Journey to the Heart of White America*. New York: Hachette Books.

Darby, Derrick. 2019. "Charles Mills's Liberal Redemption Song." *Ethics* 129 (2): 370–97.

Davis, Angela Y. 1971. "Lectures on Liberation." New York Committee to Free Angela Davis.

Dotson, Kristie. 2014. "Conceptualizing Epistemic Oppression." *Social Epistemology* 28 (2): 115–38.

Douglass, Frederick. 2003. *My Bondage and My Freedom*. New York: Penguin Classics.

Erman, Eva, and Niklas Möller. 2022. "Is Ideal Theory Useless for Non-ideal Theory?" *The Journal of Politics* 84 (1): 525–40.

Farrelly, Colin. 2007. "Justice in Ideal Theory: A Refutation." *Political Studies* 55 (4): 844–64.
Frazer, Michael. 2016. "Utopophobia as a Vocation: The Professional Ethics of Ideal and Non-ideal Political Theory." *Social Philosophy and Policy* 33 (1-2): 175–92.
Fricker, Miranda. 2007. *Epistemic Injustice: Power and the Ethics of Knowing*. New York: Oxford University Press.
Gordon, Lewis R. 2006. *Disciplinary Decadence: Living Thought in Trying Times*. London: Routledge.
Gordon, Lewis R. 2010. "Symposium on the Racial Contract: Contracting White Normativity." In *Radical Theory, Caribbean Reality: Race, Class and Social Domination*. By Charles Mills. Kingston: The University of the West Indies Press.
Hamlin, Alan, and Zofia Stemplowska. 2012. "Theory, Ideal Theory and the Theory of Ideals." *Political Studies Review* 10 (1): 48–62.
Mills, Charles W. 1994. "Non-Cartesian Sums: Philosophy and the African-American Experience." *Teaching Philosophy* 17 (3): 223–243.
Mills, Charles W. 1997. *The Racial Contract*. Ithaca: Cornell University Press.
Mills, Charles W. 2002. "The Racial Contract as Methodology (Not Hypothesis)." *Philosophia Africana* 5 (1): 75–100.
Mills, Charles W. 2005. "'Ideal theory' as Ideology." *Hypatia* 20 (3): 165–183.
Mills, Charles W. 2010. *Radical Theory, Caribbean Reality: Race, Class, and Social Domination*. Kingston: The University of the West Indies Press.
Mills, Charles W. 2012. "Philosophy Raced, Philosophy Erased." In *Reframing the Practice of Philosophy: Bodies of Color, Bodies of Knowledge*. Edited by George Yancy. Albany: State University of New York Press.
Mills, Charles W. 2016. "Philosophy and the Racial Contract." In *The Oxford Handbook of Philosophy and Race*. Edited by Naomi Zack. New York: Oxford University Press.
Mills, Charles W. 2017. "Ideology." In *The Routledge Handbook of Epistemic Injustice Routledge*. Edited by Ian James Kidd, José Medina, Gaile Pohlhaus, Jr. London: Routledge.
Mills, Charles W. 2018. "Through a Glass, Whitely: Ideal Theory as Epistemic Injustice" Presidential Address. 115th Central Division Meeting of the American Philosophical Association.
Mills, Charles W. 2021. "The 'White' Problem: American Sociology and Epistemic Injustice." In *The Oxford Handbook of Applied Epistemology*. Edited by Jennifer Lackey. New York: Oxford University Press.
Morrison, Toni. 2013. "Reading the Writing: A Conversation Between Toni Morrison and Claudia Brodsky." Interview with Claudia Brosky. Cornell University, March 7. https://www.cornell.edu/video/toni-morrison-on-language-evil-and-the-white-gaze
Robeyns, Ingrid. 2008. "Ideal Theory in Theory and Practice." *Social Theory and Practice* 34 (3): 341–62.
Simmons, A. John. 2010. "Ideal and Non-ideal Theory." *Philosophy & Public affairs* 38 (1): 5–36.
Táíwò, Olúfẹ́mi O. 2023. "Uncommon Features: Defending Ideal Theory with Model-to-World Inference." In *Routledge Handbook of African Political Philosophy*. Edited by Uchenna Okeja. New York: Routledge.
Valentini, Laura. 2012. "Ideal vs. Non-ideal Theory: A Conceptual Map." *Philosophy Compass* 7 (9): 654–64.
Yaure, Philip. 2018. "Deliberation and Emancipation: Some Critical Remarks." *Ethics* 129 (1): 8–38.

LIST OF CONTRIBUTORS

Lawrence Blum, *Professor Emeritus of Philosophy, Distinguished Professor of Liberal Arts and Education, University of Massachusetts Boston, USA*

Emmalon Davis, *Assistant Professor of Philosophy, University of Michigan, USA*

Timothy J. Golden, *Visiting Professor of Philosophy, Whitman College, USA*

Clevis Headley, *Associate Professor of Philosophy, Florida Atlantic University, USA*

Corey Reed, *Assistant Professor of Philosophy, Butler University, USA*

Taylor Rogers, *Assistant Professor of Philosophy and Interdisciplinary Studies, Governors State University, USA*

Rafael Vizcaíno, *Assistant Professor of Philosophy and Director of Teaching Practicum, DePaul University, USA*

Mark William Westmoreland, *College Lecturer II, Ocean County College, USA*

George Yancy, *Samuel Candler Dobbs Professor of Philosophy, Emory University, USA*

INDEX

Printed in Dunstable, United Kingdom

68210687R00098